Murder in Room 117

Solving the Cold Case That Led To America's Longest War

Arthur Kent

Skywriter Inc.
Los Angeles

PUBLISHED BY SKYWRITER INC.

 Published in 2021 by Skywriter Communications, Inc., Los Angeles.

www.skyreporter.com

Library Of Congress Cataloging-in-Publication Data

Kent, Arthur

Murder in room 117: solving the cold case that led to America's longest war

LCCN 2020924380 (print)

ISBN 978-1-7361482-0-4

Printed in Canada

For all those who serve abroad in the interests of peace.

Contents

Introduction *7*

PART ONE

1. Pilgrims in Paradise *10*
2. Carter's New Man in Kabul *17*
3. Spike Goes to Work 23

PART TWO

4. Deciphering in the Dark *39*
5. By Persons Unknown *55*
6. The Dead End Gang *66*

PART THREE

7. Running Out of Time *81*
8. The KGB's Order to Fire *96*
9. Horror and Loss 112

PART FOUR

10. A Comedy of Liars *120*
11. A Tragic Homecoming *140*
12. The Show Goes On *145*
13. Spies, Guns and Money *159*

PART FIVE

14. From Russia With Clues *181*
15. Challenging the Colonel *192*
16. Under a 21st Century Microscope 202
17. Resolutions Then and Now 216

Epilogue 221
Afterword 225
Sources And References 226
Acknowledgments 233
Related Bibliography 235
Photo Credits 237
Index 239

Introduction

THE AMERICAN foreign service officers recognized the newcomers for who and what they were. If the KGB ran a store for dead-giveaway spy wear, these guys shopped there. Then again, this was their turf. The Union of Soviet Socialist Republics was just one border away.

All four Russians wore black. The stocky, stern looking character who seemed to be the leader wore a mid-length leather coat, belted at the waist. Long cloth overcoats cloaked the other three men. All four heads were crowned with black, narrow-brimmed hats, Soviet style; a kind of East Bloc fedora, tipped low over the eyes.

The youngest looking Russian was lugging a duffel bag of tan canvas. It looked heavy, and its sides bulged here and there with the secrets stuffed inside. But it was the group's leader the Americans were most concerned with.

"It's Bakhturin," one of them said. Gradually, the others realized this was true. The lead KGB officer was none other than Lt. Col. Sergei Bakhturin, an openly declared Russian spy, who doubled as the Soviet Embassy's security officer. What the hell was he doing there?

The Americans were posted far from home for the U.S. government's Department of State. Dare they hope the unexpected appearance of the KGB quartet might serve a helpful purpose? For instance, to bring some kind of order to the confusion and chaos all around them? If so, the Americans would be grateful. But just in case, the most senior officer walked over to Col. Bakhturin and told him straight and clear: no action should be taken that might threaten the life and well-being of President Jimmy Carter's personal representative, Ambassador Adolph "Spike" Dubs.

The Russian nodded politely. "I assure you," Bakhturin said in fluent English. "Nothing of the kind will happen. We are here as advisers. We are here to help."

Bakhturin's pledge somehow made the Americans even more uneasy. It was February 1979, a time chilled by the cruelest winds of the Cold War. Indeed, the Colonel's promise only underlined the Westerners' sense of helplessness.

Their boss, one of the most experienced and highly regarded statesmen in Washington's diplomatic corps, was being held by armed kidnappers in an upstairs room of a gloomy old hotel in one of the most remote places in Southwest Asia. The gang was breaking all the rules of Kidnapping 101. They had backed themselves into a building, and a room, that was swiftly surrounded by armed police and troops. The room had no telephone, and the kidnappers lacked two-way radios or any other means of communication. They were trapped, just like their distinguished hostage, and had put no ransom demands to the only party with anything to offer for the ambassador's release: the United States government.

And that was only where the Americans' troubles began. Their State Department bosses were on the other side of the world in Washington, DC. There, the entire administration was distracted by one geopolitical crisis heaped upon another. Chinese troops were poised to invade Vietnam. In Iran, an angry crowd was at that very moment preparing to overrun the U.S. embassy, a terrifying precursor of the hostage taking later in the year. The Soviet Union, meanwhile, was resisting President Carter's attempts to agree a second nuclear arms treaty. Against all of this, Carter's most senior aides, his Secretary of State and National Security Adviser, were constantly at odds.

Even as the Americans stood there, desperate to save their ambassador's life and facing off against Soviet spies and heavily armed Communist troops, President Carter was preparing to fly to Mexico to restore relations with America's closest southern neighbor.

And where had these U.S. foreign service officers landed themselves? In a diplomatic backwater. An impoverished, if charming, Third World basket case of a country few Americans had even seen on a map of the world. An ancient Asian crossroads called Afghanistan, where until then, Valentine's Day of 1979, the best minds of Washington's state security apparatus had identified the threat level to Americans to be zero; exactly nothing, no threat at all.

Yet here they were, analysts and political officers, a freshman consul, a doctor and a drug enforcement cop and an intelligence officer, none of them armed but standing their ground, and staring down a hotel corridor at a trio of Russian spies and as many jittery, befuddled, rifle-toting Afghan regime soldiers that could be packed into a space not much bigger than a public transit bus. Just yards apart, the two camps were separated by an empty space, a kind of no-man's-land, in front of a door bearing three numbers in tarnished brass: 117.

It was the Cold War in miniature, a superpower standoff with the life of one of the West's most gifted and capable Russia hands on the line. Could the Americans dare to hope about the contents of that canvas duffle, the one hanging heavily from the hand of the junior KGB officer? Had the Russians brought along a couple of two-way radios, or some other means of finding out what the kidnappers were after? Or was the clattering sound the bag made as it was finally placed on the floor exactly what it sounded like: gun metal.

PART ONE

Chapter 1

Pilgrims in Paradise

IT WAS A DIFFERENT TIME. A time when distant travels were more about the thrill of exploration, less about assessing risks. When people spun a globe on its spindle, or leafed through a weighty, printed atlas, page after page, to look at countries on the other side of the world. It was a time when those unfamiliar regions rendered in bright colors would stir thoughts of adventure, not terrorism; of discovery, not open warfare. True enough, the 1960s and '70s posed the menace of the Cold War—the risk of global annihilation by nuclear weapons. But the sheer immensity of that prospect, the specter of the earth reduced to a smouldering ember as it tumbled through space, made it somehow remote to most human minds. Distant lands still shone with enchantment, with the promise of escape from the humdrum familiarity of home.

So it was that in the late 1970s, Americans working in their country's foreign service viewed postings to Afghanistan as a journey of exploration, a way to travel not only to the other side of the world, but also back in time. Bernie Woerz was a State Department veteran looking for a turning point in his career. After five successive overseas posts from Africa to Tokyo, followed by several years back in Washington, Bernie craved something different. His State Department career counselor had just the ticket. Rio de Janeiro, she asked? No thanks, Bernie said; he had somewhere else in mind. His team of administrative officers had fielded request after request from State personnel posted to Kabul, Afghanistan. Grant me and my family an extension here, they pleaded. We're doing important work and we love the place. "I told my wife things must be super there, judging by all those requests. Plus, she'd likely be hired to teach at the American school there, and we could sock away a bit of a nest egg."

Doug Wankel got into policing to leave his Midwestern farming heritage behind. In 1970, he became a Special Agent at the Kansas City, Missouri office of the Bureau of Narcotics and Dangerous Drugs, a forerunner of the Drug Enforcement Administration. Transferred to Detroit, he honed his investigative skills and set his sights on a foreign posting. In January 1978, he got his wish. He was appointed assistant to the DEA's country attaché to Afghanistan. Promotion came quickly. After nine months, he took over as attaché. Doug was now the DEA's top agent in Kabul.

Titles aside, there was something that helped him keep his feet on the ground: the Afghans he met on the street and in the bazaaars. "I'm a blue collar guy, and that's how the Afghan people impressed me. What you see is what you get. They're much more straightforward than a lot of people." There was also a hypnotic spell of history in the air. "Nothing could prepare you for the country itself. You think about Tamerlane, Alexander the Great, Genghis Khan—it was fascinating all the empires that ruled Afghanistan."

Doug arrived a few months before the April 1978 coup that brought the Afghan Communist party to power. This was known as the Saur Revolution, so named for having occurred in the second month of the Persian calendar. After the People's Democratic Party of Afghanistan seized control, Russian diplomats and advisers became much more obvious. Doug recalls seeing them in the fabled Chicken Street bazaar, where shops selling carpets and brass pots sat side by side with dealers in antique guns and swords. "The shopkeepers would be almost spitting on them, saying the Soviets don't spend any money, they're no good for us. They'd say: 'We want you Americans here 'cause you guys spend money.'"

In time, word reached Kabul of armed unrest in the countryside. Homegrown guerrilla fighters had taken to defending their land and Islamic traditions against the radical reforms of their Communist countrymen, backed by the Russians. But in Kabul, rumors of war seemed distant. It was a matter for the embassy staffers' day jobs, not for their down time after work. "Often we would go to the Intercon, where a Sri Lankan band played disco tunes," Doug recalls. "Trouble was, the curfew was pressing. If you left getting home a little too late, it was always possible one of those jittery Afghan sentries might shoot at the approaching headlights."

Mike Malinowski was serving at the U.S. embassy in Mexico when a friend overseas began raving about his experiences visiting Afghanistan. It sounded like the most exotic and romantic place on earth. A quick look revealed an opening had just been posted for Kabul: the head of the consular section. Mike ran it by his wife, Karen. The pair had met as social workers in Chicago and married soon after. Now they had something else in common: a hunger to go to Afghanistan.

As the new American Consul in Kabul, Mike became pals with Doug Wankel. Over a beer one day, they had a brainstorm. The Afghan capital's diplomatic community was surprisingly large and vibrant, swelling with young families from around the globe. Why not set up a volleyball tournament? It would be great for socializing over drinks, with both men and women welcome to play. The other embassies wholeheartedly joined in.

Soon, however, the U.S. co-ed team, calling themselves "The Fighting Kachaloos" ("potatoes" in the Afghan Dari tongue), found themselves scrapping for survival in an alarmingly competitive, male dominated league. The Bulgarian team pigheadedly argued every point, especially against other Soviet Bloc squads. But it was the local team of Afghan hotshots who taught all their expat opponents a lesson in sporting prowess—and guile. Playing as the house squad of the new Kabul Intercontinental Hotel, the locals gradually subbed in players from Afghanistan's world-class national team.

Passions finally peaked at the championship match, the United Nations v. Intercon. As the wrangling over points reached half time, Mike and Doug looked at each other. "Let's get the hell out of here," they agreed. Not for the last time, competing international interests had taken things just a bit too far in the Afghan capital.

Jeannene Cramer's interest in working far from home was sparked by a lengthy Asian backpacking trip. A nurse with experience in family practice and emergency rooms, she joined the State Department in 1978. Kabul was her first tour, but she had a sense of the region, having spent two years living in Iran, Afghanistan's neighbor to the west. There, she'd learned a little Farsi or Persian, the mother tongue of Dari. "I arrived just after the Communist coup, so the place was already swarming with soldiers." Still, like nearly all of her compatriots in the U.S. mission, Jeannene drove herself about town. In her blue Volkswagen Beetle, she frequently motored from the dispensary on the USAID compound in Kabul's southwest, to the embassy in the center of the city. Or to Chicken Street, just a few minutes to the west of Embassy Kabul.

On one occasion, she was seconded for three months to the U.S. embassy in Islamabad, Pakistan. Since she wanted to have her trusty Beetle with her, Jeannene decided to drive. Jim Taylor, the embassy's senior political officer, volunteered to follow along with his wife Louise, convoy style. After all, it was a 300-mile trek, with the scenic, but sometimes perilous, Khyber Pass midway along. Jim and Louise had business in Peshawar, just beyond the pass, so Jeannene was glad to have them in her rear-view mirror.

This was a stroke of luck, as things turned out. The Beetle blew a tire after passing through Jalalabad. Jim Taylor took the lead in fixing the flat. Jeannene's snapshots speak to the generosity and hospitality shown by Afghans to foreigners, particularly Americans. A clutch of Afghan National Army troops gathered around the stricken Volkswagen. Fate and politics had rendered them soldiers of the Communist regime, but they were still Afghans. So they shouldered their Kalashnikovs and pitched in, holding up the rear end of the Volkswagen while Jim swapped in the spare.

In February 1979, Steve Rotz was a 15-year-old high school junior at the American International School in Kabul, or AISK. Each morning, he and his younger sister Christie would board a Blue Bird bus, shipped in from the States and decked out in standard yellow, for the ride across town to class. Their school had a lot going for it. Along with other Americans, there were kids from Turkey, India, Canada and Germany, and a global array of teachers, too. Classes were from kindergarten to 12th Grade, with only 10 to 14 students in each classroom. There were sports of all kinds, and the school's teams regularly travelled to U.S. embassies in Pakistan and India for basketball and baseball tournaments. The school canteen, "The Greasy Spoon," boasted hamburgers with Afghan seasonings. "They were pretty delicious," Steve recalls.

Steve and Christie arrived in Afghanistan just after New Year's '79 with their parents, Lloyd and Marlene. Lloyd was pursuing a new career with the State Department, replacing the outgoing Embassy Kabul physician. Along with Jeannene and her fellow nurses, Lloyd's practice was based at the dispensary in the sprawling walled compound of the U.S. Agency for International Development, USAID, just up the road from the kids' school.

Soon enough, the whole family was warming up to their new home. Steve fell in love with the place. "When my dad first told us about Afghanistan, my mom's first question was: "Is it safe?" At 13, Christie would have preferred staying home in Michigan with her friends. But within a few weeks, she was discovering the Afghan capital to be an exciting new home. "As a diplomatic family, we lived in kind of a golden ghetto," Steve says. "We had a comfortable two-story home, larger than we needed, with two servants." From the balcony upstairs, the Rotzes could look over their compound's high walls onto the homes of the well-off Kabulis who were their neighbors. "There were Russians in our neighborhood, too," Steve says, "but they were beginning to relocate into the big Soviet embassy compound. After the Communist coup, they weren't that popular with a lot of the locals."

Steve's father, Lloyd, found that caring for the embassy's staff and dependents generally kept him at a safe distance from Kabul's political intrigues. But that could change without warning. Like the afternoon one of the embassy's military attachés stumbled out of a taxi and into the dispensary. "I've been drugged," the officer gasped, collapsing into Lloyd's arms. The alcohol on the attaché's breath indicated a far more common affliction. As Lloyd helped him into the procedure room, his patient explained he had been at the Czechoslovak embassy, meeting one of his Communist Bloc counterparts. Czechoslovakia was a Soviet satellite state, boasting one of the KGB's most dreaded allies in espionage, the StB.

The American attaché told Lloyd his objective had been to "turn" one of the Czech officers, or at least coax some useful information out of him. Instead, the Czechs plied their guest with beer and cognac. Nothing more than he could handle, the attaché assured Lloyd; but then some real trouble strolled into the room. This was in the form of two women, heavily made up and dressed for a very different kind of liaison. Recognizing the honey trap, the American struggled to his feet and made good his escape.

Lloyd was skeptical. Back in Michigan, his diagnosis would be simple intoxication. The man was drunk. Nevertheless, he drew some blood and sent the sample to Washington. The test came back positive for chloral hydrate: the American attaché had indeed been slipped a Mickey Finn. Not for the last time, the Cold War cast its shadow over the humble USAID dispensary in Kabul. Soon, and in much graver circumstances, Lloyd would come to realize he was practicing medicine on the front lines of a deadly superpower conflict.

CHAPTER 2

CARTER'S NEW MAN IN KABUL

FAR FROM HOME in this strange, enchanting place, American foreign service officers and their families expected more from their leader than was the case at most overseas U.S. missions. Their ambassador needed to provide much more than instructions and orders. It was encouragement they needed most: the reassurance that a skilled, seasoned skipper was at the helm of the USS Kabul. Because for all its wonder, Afghanistan was in the grips of a revolution, and not a popular one.

In Adolph "Spike" Dubs, they found that kind of ambassador. Among both peers and superiors at the State Department, Spike was held to be one of the best officers in the service. Chicago-born and deeply spiritual, Dubs considered entering the ministry after high school. Instead, he chose to study political science at Beloit College in Wisconsin, a liberal arts school. With Hitler's Blitzkrieg savaging Europe, Dubs' classmates decided he was far too nice a guy to be known by the Fuhrer's given name. The nickname they bestowed on him stuck, not least after Spike graduated from Beloit in 1942 and joined the U.S. Navy.

The war in the Pacific had a profound impact on Spike's faith, convincing him that humanity's finest ambition was the pursuit of peace. Serving as a lieutenant on the destroyer USS Caldwell, Dubs and his shipmates fought in the Battle of

Leyte in the Philippines in December 1944. One morning at Ormoc Bay, the Caldwell's crew, still shaking off the previous day's combat with Japanese warplanes, struck up a chorus of *Oklahoma!* from the hit 1943 Broadway musical. The sailors barely finished the show tune before another wave of enemy aircraft attacked. A kamikaze pilot scored a direct hit on the Caldwell's bridge, killing 33 of Spike's crewmates and wounding another 40.

Spike's daughter Lindsay says the war recast her father's lingering thoughts of becoming a minister. "He didn't lose that sense of wanting to bring people together and see how the world could work better. But he came to understand the ministry wasn't the way for him, that he wanted to take those kinds of ideals into diplomacy. That's what motivated him to sign up for the foreign service."

After the war, Spike pursued his education with a vengeance, first at Georgetown University, then with foreign service studies at Harvard and Washington University in St. Louis. Hiring on to State, he started his ascent up the foreign service ladder, with posts at U.S. embassies in Germany, Liberia and Canada. Ottawa was where Lindsay's travels began with her dad and mother, Jane Wilson Dubs, Spike's college sweetheart. After a posting to Yugoslavia, the 7-year-old Lindsay found herself in an even stranger land, the Soviet Union. For her father, this was a homecoming of sorts. Although Spike was born in Chicago in 1920, his parents Alexander and Regina had been members of southeastern Russia's Volga German community. They emigrated to the United States before World War I.

One day in particular stands out in Lindsay's memories, a day in October of 1962. At her school in Moscow for children of foreign diplomats, some "very stern looking people" appeared in her classroom. The strangers ordered American children only to leave the building. They should board the bus waiting for them outside. Approaching at the U.S. embassy, the kids made their way past Soviet army tanks and through a growing throng of Russian onlookers. Finally, they reached the compound. American soldiers were busy boarding up the windows of the embassy's lower floors. Guards ushered the children inside and to their families, who were waiting on the upper floors of the building.

All of this, Lindsay's father explained, had to do with some missiles the Soviet Union sent to Cuba. It was his job to help monitor the cable traffic between President John F. Kennedy in Washington, DC and the Soviet leader, Nikita Khrushchev, in Moscow. Though Spike's Russian language skills were basic at that time, they were improving. With the "hot line" between DC and Moscow not yet established, translating and analyzing the cable traffic during the Cuban Missile Crisis was a vital service. And a revealing one, Spike realized. "He told me there was a certain point in reading these cables where he felt some sense of relief. He could tell from the language and way things were worded that Khrushchev was going to retreat from his position and things were going to calm down."

A decade later, in the mid-1970s, Spike returned to Moscow as deputy chief of mission. By now he was one of the State Department's top Kremlinologists and fluent in Russian. Soon he was named chargé d'affaires, in effect the interim ambassador. He had also reached the top of the surveillance protocols of a Soviet organization named the Komitet Gosudarstvennoy Bezopasnosti, or Committee for State Security—the KGB. Spike assumed he was under constant watch by Russia's spies. Indeed he was, as history would show.

This was no minor concern. The KGB had earned a reputation as the world's largest, most ruthless organ of state security. Its vast spy network was able to reach into any Soviet citizen's life, and far beyond Russia's borders into foreign lands. From its headquarters in the forbidding Lubyanka building, the KGB could snuff out internal dissent at home or project aggressive espionage operations anywhere on earth. The agency's culture of fear had been accrued through more than five decades of arbitrary imprisonment, extra-judicial executions and state-sanctioned murders, from its birth as the Cheka in 1917, through the NKVD era in the 1930s and '40s and reorganization as the KGB in 1954.

Spike Dubs and his colleagues came under the purview of the KGB's Second Chief Directorate. In Mother Russia, this branch was responsible for monitoring foreign embassy personnel. No fewer than six of the directorate's 12 departments were tasked with continuously keeping watch over officials of a U.S. chargé's seniority. Spike accepted this fact, but wasted little time looking over his shoulder. Instead, he switched his diplomatic lights to high beam. He gloried in meeting top Soviet officials on Moscow's ambassadorial circuit or at embassy receptions on his home turf.

As a rising star among Western diplomats posted to Moscow, Spike ensured his dealings with the Soviet leadership were not weighed down with doctrinaire condescension. Later in his career he wrote to Lindsay: "If we were a perfect society in every respect, I would be much less uneasy about pointing the finger... Before becoming indignant about situations in other countries, I would like to see us getting our point across by becoming a model other societies would consider worthy of emulation."

Thus Spike was viewed by his colleagues as "a positivist" in dealing with the Soviet leadership, even as he fully appreciated the dangers posed by the U.S.S.R.'s belligerent expansionism. An appetite for world domination had become the hallmark of the politburo during the lengthy tenure of Leonid Brezhnev. Succeeding Khrushchev in 1964, Brezhnev presided over an ever-more-assertive foreign policy that eventually took his name as its motif. The Brezhnev Doctrine held that a threat to any Soviet Bloc state was a threat to them all. As well, once a nation turned to Communist rule, it must not be allowed to turn back.

Once Soviet-backed Communists seized power in Kabul in April 1978, U.S. Secretary of State Cyrus Vance recognized there could be no better choice for America's new Ambassador to Afghanistan than Spike Dubs. Jimmy Carter agreed. By now back in Washington, DC, Spike leapt into his appointment by the president. He was formally nominated as Ambassador to Afghanistan on June 1, 1978. His Senate confirmation followed just three weeks later. Vance's special adviser on Soviet affairs, Marshall Shulman, said of Spike's enthusiasm for the Kabul job: "He was restless. He was eager to get into the field again. He knew it was a tough post."

Two years earlier, Spike and Jane divorced. He had remarried, to Mary Ann Parsons, an assistant editor at the Congressional Record. Although Mary Ann's job would keep her in DC, she planned to visit Kabul as often as she could, and wanted to know all about her husband's new posting. So she accompanied Spike to many of his briefings in Washington. One of their guides on this journey of discovery was a seasoned Afghan hand and scholar named Thomas Gouttierre. A baker's son from Maumee, Ohio, Gouttierre had first traveled to Afghanistan with the Peace Corps in 1965. He taught English, with his wife Marylu giving classes in office skills. So began a lifetime of service and education, all focused on the Afghan people.

Early in his Peace Corps tour, "Mr. Tom," as the Afghans called him, was invited to coach basketball. He astonished even himself by taking a group of undisciplined high school basketball players and turning them into a winning national team. No sooner had the Gouttierres said goodbye and headed home than they found themselves longing to go back. They did just that in 1969, when Tom was awarded a Fulbright fellowship to Kabul. Now the couple immersed themselves in the country and its people even more completely. By the time they returned home in 1974, Gouttierre was named Director of the Center for Afghan Studies at the University of Nebraska Omaha.

It only made sense, four years later, that State would summon Tom to Washington to help prepare Spike Dubs for his Afghan post. "He and Mary Ann listened attentively for two full days, plus a third morning. Spike thanked me afterward. He told me the sessions really helped him gain an appreciation for the Afghan people and their culture."

Joining Spike and Mary Ann at some of the DC briefings was a young foreign service officer named David Litt. He was also Kabul bound, to an economic officer's posting. He would be accompanied by his wife Beatrice, a former lawyer in her native Sicily. As a consular staffer in Palermo, Italy, Litt's interest in Afghanistan had been sparked by a visiting inspector from Washington. "He told me: it's beautiful, exotic, out of the way, and they love Americans. The people are wonderful. He also said it's of no strategic interest to the United States, so Washington doesn't bother you. So if you ever have a chance to go there, take it."

Litt did just that. He met Spike at the State Department's headquarters in Foggy Bottom in the early summer of 1978. "I got to meet him in a very personable way. He had such a wealth of knowledge. I just remember basking in this aura of this lovely man, he was such a pleasant person to be with."

Chapter 3

Spike Goes To Work

SPIKE DUBS ARRIVED in Kabul in mid-July 1978. He discovered a people and a culture even more intoxicating than his briefings had suggested. From his first encounters with the U.S. embassy's Afghan local hires, or Foreign Service Nationals, to the merchants in the city's many bazaars, he found the people of Kabul to be remarkably warm and hospitable, especially with Westerners.

Still, as the incoming U.S. ambassador, he couldn't allow his new post's beguiling attractions to distract from the dangers posed by the political machine seeking to consolidate its power over Afghanistan and its people. He didn't waver in that obligation; his professionalism wouldn't allow it. But there were limits to the ability of any outsider to fathom the dark and chaotic inner workings of the Communist regime, the People's Democratic Party of Afghanistan or PDPA. Beyond that, Spike had no inkling that his fate would become intertwined with two individuals with deep and troubled roots in this strange land.

One of them was the second most powerful Afghan minister in the regime, a hopelessly unstable egomaniac whose plodding, doctrinaire Marxism masked a ruthless ambition. The other was an accomplished Soviet espionage officer, a Russian spy with many successful black operations to his credit. Within months, Spike's efforts to maintain and nurture the

U.S.-Afghan relationship would put him on a collision course with Hafizullah Amin and Sergei Bakhturin.

First, however, came the formalities of diplomacy. He described the process in a letter to Lindsay on July 23, 1978. The letter marked the continuation of a Sunday ritual dating to Spike's second posting to Moscow. At that time, in the early '70s, Lindsay remained in college in New York. Now it was her life and work in Washington that was keeping them apart. So, with pen and paper each weekend, Spike composed a lengthy letter to his daughter:

> My dearest Lindsay,
> I'm happy to report that the presentation of my credentials went off smoothly. I have been cordially received by the Chairman of the Revolutionary Council (and Prime Minister) and other members of the Cabinet. I plan on calling on all twenty-one.
> There is no doubt that they want good relations with us, knowing that we can provide much-needed economic and technical assistance. This nation needs help from where it can get it. Where this government will eventually go is uncertain at this point.
> Internal problems abound and the Soviet presence is very pervasive. Nevertheless, we hope that our activities here will provide it with some room for maneuver so that it can avoid the all-encompassing embrace of the Soviets. We shall see!
> Mary Ann said she very much appreciated having you along for the drive home from the airport. She believes that you and I are very much alike in many ways. Being like you pleases me a lot.
> Much love and affection, Dad

The DEA's Doug Wankel remembers the impression Spike

made among his embassy team members. "He arrived with quite a lot of fanfare. People had heard a lot about him. He had great interpersonal skills, but he had another talent that you don't see very often, whether it's in business in government or whatever. He was Ambassador Dubs during the work day and during official functions, but in the off hours he was Spike. Easy to talk to, a good guy. People revered him."

Embassy Kabul had a staff of just over 160 Americans. With wives and children, it was a sizeable community–and an active one. Even after the Communist coup, the Americans delighted in driving themselves around Kabul and into the surrounding countryside. Even trips to distant provincial capitals like Kandahar were possible.

In the capital, the Americans operated cultural facilities that were hugely popular among Afghans living in and around Kabul. The U.S. Agency for International Development, known simply as AID among the Americans, had deep roots in Afghanistan's education system. Kabul University was founded by AID and had many American faculty members. Other nations had assistance programs, notably the Germans, French, Soviets and Chinese, as well as the U.N. But the crown jewel among them was arguably the American Cultural Center.

The Center had 1,500 Afghan students in its English language classes, and boasted a 15,000 volume library. This was reputed to be the largest "open stacks" library of English language books in Southwest Asia. It offered cool, relaxed escape for local people, particularly for Kabulis seeking relief from the heat of summer, and the chill cast by the Communist regime's secret police. At the time of Spike's arrival, Louise Taylor was serving as the Center's Director. "It was the happiest I think I was in my Foreign Service career. The atmosphere in Kabul was wide open. Afghans, third country nationals, just about everybody participated in everything." This included staging ambitious plays, even musicals. Penciled into the calendar for early 1979 was a production of *Oklahoma!* More than 60 members of Kabul's American and expatriate communities would be needed to fill out the cast and crew, including a 27-piece live orchestra.

By the late summer of 1978, however, the regime could no longer ignore this cultural oasis provided to the local population. Afghan Army soldiers began stalking the street near the Center's entrance. Embassy officers like Doug Wankel began getting the cold shoulder from their contacts in the government's ministries. "I worked very closely with the Afghan authorities at the Ministry of Interior as far as intelligence concerning cultivation of opium and hashish. I was often at the ministry compound. More Soviet advisers were coming in, and they started restricting access to that compound."

As well, the regime's secret police were stalking Embassy Kabul's Afghan staffers. One of Mike Malinowski's consular employees, Shuja Parwiz, was arrested by plainclothes officers from the interior ministry. The regime failed to respond to repeated diplomatic notes from the Americans, who later discovered Shuja was alive but imprisoned. Sohila Sherdil, a secretary, was taken in for questioning and pressed to become a regime informant. She refused and was eventually released. Sohila returned to the embassy and reported everything she had been subjected to, including threats that the permit allowing her to work for foreigners would be revoked if she didn't become a Communist agent. For Doug's DEA team, the regime's repressive tactics hit closer to home. His driver, a cheerful, savvy professional named Ewaz Ali, was arrested, questioned and beaten. For a full week, he resisted demands that he become an informant for the Interior police. Bruised but unbowed, he was finally released by his captors. He went straight to the embassy and told the whole story. Without hesitation, Doug put Ewaz back behind the wheel.

The chill felt by Spike's embassy team came up in his

correspondence with Lindsay:

> I enjoyed your comments about the power plays in Afghanistan and how the situation appears to you. Outwardly, the situation is rather calm here in Kabul, but the regime rants every day in the press about the "black reactionaries" and the "Muslim devils" who are using religion as a mask to conduct counter-revolutionary activities.
>
> Given the history of this country and people, I do not rule out a violent attempt to change things. The big question then would be: In what direction?
>
> In the meantime, I feel that our leverage here is marginal; so we will have to sit on the sidelines pretty much as observers rather than significant actors in events.

AMONG ALL the ministers of the faction-ridden PDPA regime, one individual in particular had been red-flagged by Spike's advisers as a potential intermediary. In other words, an Afghan Communist the Carter administration might be able to do business with. Hafizullah Amin was a senior figure in the PDPA's ruling Khalq or Masses faction. He also served as the regime's Foreign Minister and Vice-Premier. A 48-year-old former teacher, Amin had attended two universities in the United States. In the late 1950s, he took his MA in education at Columbia University. Returning in 1962, he was briefly at the University of Wisconsin before pursuing his doctorate at Columbia's Teachers College.

Despite these sojourns in America, Amin remained a country boy with several big chips on his shoulder. He was born in Paghman, the country retreat of Afghan royals just west of the capital. He grew to loathe what he viewed as the country's privileged urban class, especially King Zahir Shah and his court. He dedicated himself to delivering the Afghan masses from the country's royalist past. Once in Kabul, Amin immersed himself in political networking among other aggrieved leftists. He was charismatic and a notorious over-achiever, ruthlessly seizing every advantage to elevate himself above his peers within the nascent Afghan Communist party. Only when battling rival Communists, the PDPA's Parcham or "Flag" faction, did he bond closely with his Khalqi comrades.

Initially, Amin quenched his thirst for power by becoming a fawning disciple of Nur Mohammed Taraki, a former journalist who became the first general secretary of the PDPA and the regime's founding president. With Amin's keen assistance, Taraki fashioned a cult of personality for himself. Amin ordered the state press to refer to the newly-installed president as "The Great Leader" and "The Great Thinker" and "the learned teacher of the people." But behind the scenes, Amin was already angling for his boss's job. It was onto this roiling political landscape that Spike went to work in late July 1978.

After a brief initial encounter with Amin to present his credentials, Spike sought out a second meeting. Amin agreed, and over time he would receive Ambassador Dubs for face to face discussions on no fewer than 14 occasions. "Amin agreed to meet Spike regularly for two reasons," says Tom Gouttierre, who got to know Amin well a decade earlier. "First, he was arrogant and liked to show off, especially in front of people like Spike, a respected foreign official. Second, he craved the Soviets' respect. In his mind, meeting the American ambassador would show the Russians he was his own man."

For all his psychological flaws, Amin was adept at accruing power. "He could be quite charming," Gouttierre says, "and he had a good many girlfriends." These had included an American aid worker in Kabul. But Amin's most notable courtships were among commanders of the Afghan Army. In 1978, he persuaded the generals to side with his Khalqi PDPA cohorts against the republican president, Mohammed Daoud

Khan. Daoud had himself seized power in 1973 with the help of the PDPA and the Soviets, deposing his cousin, King Zahir Shah. Once in government, Daoud lost the Communists' support and alienated his Soviet allies by seeking to renew ties with the West. He paid dearly for underestimating Hafizullah Amin's influence within the military: Daoud was assassinated with most of his family in the Communist coup.

Amin wasted no time consolidating his position as the new regime's Foreign Minister and second in command. Instinctively, he did so by resorting to further violence and repression. His closest ally was a thuggish police commandant named Sayed Daoud Taroon, the Security Chief at the Ministry of Interior and a committed Khalqist. For Spike's team at the U.S. embassy, Commandant Taroon became one of their principal points of contact with the regime—and easily the most intimidating. On several occasions, Consul Mike Malinowski had to attend Taroon's office to plead the case of an American student or tourist arrested by the regime. "I had to deal with him professionally. He put me through some very unpleasant experiences. Taroon was one of the most feared men in Afghanistan, for good reason."

On being escorted through the door by armed bodyguards, visitors would have to proceed, like supplicants, across a large, dimly-lit approach to the commandant's desk at the far end of the room. The desk was large and imposing, perched on a riser one foot above floor level. Once seated, visitors would find themselves looking upward into the malevolent glare of Afghanistan's chief secret policeman. Flanking the commandant were pictures of "The Great Leader," President Taraki and Taroon's patron, Amin. But pride of place was given to a striking black and white image positioned high on the wall directly behind the desk. This was a portrait of Fidel Castro, savoring a cigar. Taroon, himself a chain smoker, emulated the macho Cuban dictator by languidly puffing on a long black cigarette holder.

If the commandant's manner and office décor weren't enough to unnerve visitors like Mike Malinowski, Taroon had another favorite plaything to deploy. "The guy had this chrome plated Kalashnikov. No shoulder stock, just the firing mechanisms and clip. It was an ugly thing, lying there on the front edge of the desk. He'd play with it, spinning it this way and that. Then he'd stop it, pointing it straight at your head. If he really wanted to make a point, he'd stroke the trigger with his finger. The guy gave us the creeps."

Taroon was still more of a threat for Afghans. Like some medieval tyrant, he kept a number of dungeon-like cells in the basement of the Interior building. A private stairwell led from his office to this bespoke prison. The torture and abuse committed in those cells was an open secret in Kabul. Taroon was rumored to have personally committed some 30 murders there. Alarmingly, this paled in comparison to the scale of brutality inflicted at the Communist regime's other detention sites, including Pul-e-Charkhi prison on Kabul's eastern outskirts.

Lacking any legitimate degree of public support across Afghanistan, the PDPA instituted terror as a means of strengthening its hold on power. Although the regime sought to develop a culture of dependency on their administration among left-leaning Afghans, everyone else was threatened with nighttime raids and imprisonment, torture and execution. Conservative estimates place the number of Afghans murdered by the Khalqist regime under Taraki and Amin at 12,000 souls by the time of the Soviet intervention in December 1979. Even rival Parcham Communists lived in fear of the deadly duo, who purged the Afghan military of Parchamist officers.

In the early stages of this bloodbath, the U.S. embassy's political officers were approached by a Kabul physician. He told the Americans he represented a group of doctors. As professionals and humanitarians loyal to their country, they were forming an underground front to overthrow the Communist regime. All they needed, the doctor said, was guns and money from the United States. In short order, the Carter administration instructed Embassy Kabul to respond with an unequivocal "no." Political officer Jim Taylor understood Washington's reasoning. "We didn't want to get involved in any plot against the government with people about whom we knew nothing other than what they said they represented." Despite this setback, the doctors continued plotting. One year later, Taroon's spies uncovered the operation. Most, if not all, of the physicians were rounded up and executed.

Another basis for the Americans' discomfort over the doctors' plot was the increased activity of the Soviets in Kabul. Doug Wankel began seeing Soviet advisers skulking around the interior ministry's counter-narcotics offices. This coincided with his Afghan contacts in the ministry beginning to exclude him from their operations. At the same time, word was reaching the capital of attacks in the countryside by gunmen opposed to the regime. Soon to gain renown as the Afghan *mujahideen*, or holy warriors, the Islamic resistance to Communism had drawn first blood from the Soviet-backed government.

"That is where we first detected a growing Soviet participation with the regime," Jim Taylor later recalled. "The (Afghan) military and the security forces had been virtually all trained in the Soviet Union, except for a minuscule number who went to the United States, Pakistan or India. When the opposition started growing, Soviet active participation on the security side became evident."

By the time of Spike's arrival as ambassador, reports were reaching the embassy of Soviet military advisers turning up in distant provinces. In Kabul, as well, the Soviets were taking an active role in Amin's reign of terror. According to Taylor: "The Soviet activity on the security side came to the point where they were participating in some of the arrests, interrogations, torture and killings," though mainly it was Taroon's officers who were actually "pulling the triggers."

CONFRONTED BY these factors, Spike Dubs realized the U.S. had a steep uphill slope to climb in attempting to salvage some measure of influence with the PDPA regime. The opposition movement in the provinces was accompanied by a nationwide economic crisis. Both factors increased the Communist administration's dependence on the Soviets. The Americans were witnessing more and more propaganda about the "great brotherhood of friendship" between the Afghan and Soviet people—and increasing anti-Americanism, too.

Spike wrote to Lindsay:

> I can't quite describe the brand of Marxist-Leninism that this regime is in reality. Professions of independence and nonalignment abound, yet one can't help but wonder how beholden to the Soviet Union this regime feels itself to be...
>
> One cannot ignore that this people is ferociously independent and deeply religious, characteristics which must give any regime pause if its intentions are to impose an alien ideology upon this nation...
>
> Rumours of resistance, especially in the tribal areas, are rampant... While the outward atmosphere is calm, one senses disquiet below.
>
> One good thing—there's an 11 p.m. curfew. Embassy personnel are enjoined to be off the streets by 10 p.m. to ensure against untoward incidents. For myself, I'm generally in bed by 10 p.m. with a book. It's been a long time since I've gotten so much sleep...

What Spike Dubs had no way of knowing, in these early

stages of his ambassadorship, was that one of the most effective, hands-on executors of Soviet operations in Afghanistan was an intelligence officer who would one day seize control over Spike's destiny—and his life.

LT. COL. Sergei Gavrilovich Bakhturin was a highly experienced, 45-year-old officer in the Soviet KGB. On arrival in Kabul, he had been revealed or "declared" to the Afghan regime as an intelligence operative by the Kabul *rezident*, or station chief, Viliov Osadchy. As a result, Bakhturin served as a legal Soviet spy in Afghanistan. This was necessary due to his much more visible profile as the Soviet embassy's head of security, with overall responsibility for the safe conduct of the mission's duties and all its personnel. Nevertheless, Bakhturin operated under a code name, Volgin, issued by KGB headquarters in Moscow. This spoke to his proficiency in the KGB's dark arts, such as intelligence gathering, subversion and sabotage, as well as the crafting and dissemination of disinformation.

Like Spike Dubs, Bakhturin spent the formative years of his career on the frontiers of the Iron Curtain. In 1961, aged 28, he was posted to Berlin. He arrived just as Communist East Germany began to construct its infamous wall to isolate Germans living under Soviet rule from their countrymen in the democratic West. Bakhturin's cover was as an employee of NIIMash, the Soviet Union's Research and Development Institute of Mechanical Engineering, specializing in rocket engine design. Much later, in his retirement years, Bakhturin would admit with a smirk that rocket science was hardly his strong suit. He considered himself a soldier, first and foremost. He was a professional combatant, recruited by the KGB from the ranks of the Red Army to do battle with the Motherland's capitalist foes.

After Berlin came a major shift in Bakhturin's pursuit of the espionage trade. The KGB's First Chief Directorate, the division responsible for foreign intelligence, informed him he would be posted to the Soviet mission in Tehran, the Iranian capital. He and his wife would be allowed to take their daughter along, with the family undertaking at least a seven-year posting in the region. "I took this idea to my wife," Bakhturin would later recall. "She said: 'of course.' She agreed immediately." The prospect of escaping Moscow's grey winters and bare supermarket shelves more than made up for the uncertainty of moving to an unfamiliar city in Asia.

Iran turned out to be a successful start for the Bakhturins abroad. Sergei earned a promotion, and an onward posting to Pakistan. In immediate succession, he served in KGB units going toe-to-toe with two of the U.S. Central Intelligence Agency's most active and sensitive overseas stations: Tehran and Islamabad. He witnessed firsthand the CIA's support for the infamous, pre-revolution regime in Iran. In Islamabad, he saw the CIA developing close ties with the Pakistan military's Inter-Services Intelligence branch, the ISI.

In September 1977, Bakhturin and his family moved to Kabul. This would prove to be an especially astute assignment by his KGB masters. Bakhturin was both a seasoned spy and a practical, resourceful fixer. No longer on the outside looking in, as he had been with the American-allied regimes in Iran and Pakistan, Bakhturin would work in Afghanistan as an insider, within both a larger KGB station and an allied Communist regime, functioning openly. When the PDPA seized power some seven months into his posting, Bakhturin was ideally situated to deliver results as never before. "The composition of the new Afghan government and Communist party leadership quite suited us," he later recalled. "These were persons known to the Soviet embassy and the KGB residency."

As his embassy's security officer, Bakhturin swiftly earned the trust of his ambassador, Alexander Mihailovich Puzanov. The Soviet mission was a jumbled, ever-expanding complex of structures located on Darulaman Road, the main artery leading to Kabul's southwestern outskirts. Bakhturin secured Moscow's approval to strengthen the perimeter, install new generators and a closed-circuit TV monitoring system, and construct a bomb shelter large enough to house the mission's leadership and their families. The Soviets were uncomfortably aware of their client regime's unpopularity among much of the Afghan populace. There was no guarantee the violent clashes taking place in the countryside would not migrate to the capital. As the Communists' sponsors, the Russians needed to prepare for the worst: direct attacks by insurgents.

This is not to say Soviet personnel were living scared in Afghanistan. To the contrary, Bakhturin was able to devote his expertise to his ambassador's recreation as well. Puzanov loved nothing more than heading off just after Friday lunch for the Naghlu Dam, a hydro-electric project built in the 1960s by the Soviets. Russian engineers continued to supervise its operations. These expeditions began with a scenic hour-long drive to the east on a well-surfaced roadway, down the steep switchbacks and chasms of the Kabul Gorge and into the town of Surobi. At Bakhturin's insistence, at least two vehicles would make the journey, with his Mosckvich sedan riding shotgun on the ambassador's Volga. "We preferred a place in the calm water of the lower reservoir, not far from the village of Soviet specialists. By one o'clock, the ambassador would invite us for lunch. There was always a snack and a bottle of Stolichnaya."

On one occasion, the Czech ambassador and Bulgarian trade representative joined the group. There they were, the *tsars* of Kabul's East Bloc diplomatic community, dangling their fishing poles over the tranquil waters, taking in the splendid mountain scenery, and toasting one another with vodka. It was only a matter of time until someone's line was tugged: on Puzanov's orders, the reservoir was kept stocked with trout.

Bakhturin fit comfortably within both the Soviet diplomatic

and intelligence enterprises in Kabul. This was no mean feat, given the sheer size of Moscow's footprint in Afghanistan. The KGB had at least 100 Russian officers serving in Afghanistan, either mining intelligence or acting as controllers. The controllers ran a vast number of in-country agents, mainly Afghan nationals serving in the regime's ministries and the military. For instance, at the Ministry of Interior, the PDPA's secret police, the Soviets had more than 200 agents providing information and clandestine services. As well, some 50 or more Soviet advisers were attached to the much-feared internal spy agency KAM, the Security and Intelligence Organization, later known as KHAD.

"FOR SURE, the Soviets had the place wired," says Warren Marik, a 33-year-old CIA case officer who served at Embassy Kabul during Spike Dubs ambassadorship. "They were everywhere. They could be aggressive, and sometimes downright clumsy." A former college football lineman, Marik liked a tough contest. More than once in his playing days he threw himself into the formidable form of Dick Butkus, the future star linebacker for the Chicago Bears. So he could handle the average Soviet spy. "Right after the '78 coup they placed a bug in my house. They did it with two visits. First, an Afghan officer accompanied a Russian to recruit my house man—they thought. They told him: You're working for us and you'd better not tell the American.

"Then they came back a second time. He watched them plant the bug under a table. It was a wooden box, about 4 by 8 inches and an inch or so deep. My house man took me out in the yard and told me about it, so I would know it was there. I left it where they planted it, almost to the end of my posting." The device eventually wound up in a tech lab at the CIA's Langley, Virginia headquarters.

Misadventures aside, many of the KGB's schemes

succeeded. This was mainly due to the sheer number of illegals, or secret operatives, fielded in Kabul. "Our undeclared department was many times larger than the residency," Bakhturin says. "It performed all the functions of the KGB, with some assignments led by generals." To say the CIA was outnumbered and outmuscled is an understatement.

"The agency was still recovering from Vietnam and Watergate," explains Warren Marik's former Chief of Station. "We were at a low point when I reached Kabul." The CIA occupied only six desks at the embassy, including a secretary. "I had no specialists, no analysts. We were starting from scratch. What we did have was a lot of paper, 15 safes full of it. I ordered it all destroyed. If it's worth anything Washington will already have a copy. I told the team we don't want to keep anything more than we can burn in five minutes. That's how long I figured we'd have, because the regime could have overrun the embassy anytime."

By contrast, Bakhturin and his bosses were challenged by an embarrassment of riches in resources, especially the human variety. Early on in his tour, a prickly issue arose at the Soviet embassy: exactly who should the KGB residencies, both legal and illegal, report to in Moscow? The answer, Bakhturin says, came from the top. The KGB's steely chairman and future Soviet leader, Yuri Andropov, directed Kabul to communicate directly with Lieutenant General Boris Semyonovich Ivanov, Andropov's most senior adviser on intelligence matters. To ensure the signals exchanges moved smoothly between the KGB Center in Moscow and the residencies in Afghanistan, a communications team from the Soviet defence ministry was dispatched to Kabul to install and maintain the necessary hardware. Bakhturin says the highest priority was placed on these connections. "During the Great Patriotic War, there was a saying: If the battle is won, then well done tankers! When it is lost, the fools are the communications officers. The fault is theirs."

As for his personal record in Afghanistan, Bakhturin has no doubt about his greatest achievement. "There was no treason in the column on my watch." He insists that during his time in Kabul, not one KGB officer, or agent or informant, turned traitor and compromised the mission. Ambassador Puzanov simply let the KGB get on with its work, providing whatever assistance Andropov's spies might require. "Alexander Mihailovich (Puzanov) regarded me as both security officer and assistant ambassador. But regarding everything concerning intelligence, he knew I had to obey first and always the KGB in Moscow. This was perceived and understood with no problem, because such orders usually came behind the scenes."

On Puzanov's part, this had nothing to do with favors for a fishing buddy. He knew, or at least suspected, that Bakhturin had a role in rooting out traitors. This meant Sergei liaised with Directorate K, the KGB's counterintelligence branch, responsible for unmasking spies and rooting out corruption in the ranks. Naturally it would follow that Bakhturin would monitor the Soviet ambassador's actions and communications, all under the steely oversight of the Kabul *rezident*, Osadchy.

These were the cold realities of existence within Soviet officialdom. Trust had a flip side of suspicion. Authority was exercised under a shadow of fear. Bakhturin's relations with Puzanov were warm and collegial, but both men knew the colonel was a cog in the KGB's machinery of oppression. He was a soldier dedicated to preserving his masters' all-encompassing power over each and every citizen in the U.S.S.R. In practice, Puzanov was a zealous servant of Moscow's Afghan agenda, so these concerns were largely academic. Still, the ambassador took care to remain in his security officer's good books. No Russian diplomat wished to see the KGB's teeth, much less feel them.

PART TWO

CHAPTER 4

DECIPHERING IN THE DARK

SPIKE DUBS' official State Department photographs depict a pleasant, reserved and bookish man in middle age. No-one who really knew Spike describes him that way. This was a man with an upbeat, engaging presence, and a physical one. His natural athleticism led him to seriously consider a career in professional golf. At ping-pong, he was a notoriously keen racket hand and virtually unbeatable. Get-togethers in his spacious ambassador's residence in Kabul inevitably included lengthy sing-alongs. Anywhere Spike found himself, all he needed was a handful of people and a piano, and soon he would be rolling out show tunes and gospel songs and leading the chorus. At work, too, even in the face of the Soviets' infamous intransigence, Spike got by with what colleagues described as "unflappable good humor."

Given Spike's nature, Afghanistan and its people moved him on many levels. This was more than just another diplomatic outpost. Like countless newcomers before him, he found himself awash in a flood of sensations. He marveled at the sights and sounds of the capital city and its inhabitants. The place was dramatic and primitive, as if from another age; yet open and inviting. This was a country and a people that fired the imagination. Afghanistan stoked the outsider's curiosity, sparking a hunger to know more, to understand. It was a civilization that wore mysticism, fable and legend on its face. To journey there and explore, for any length of time, leads inexorably to the people who inhabit this strange land.

In dress and countenance, "biblical" is a word that comes too readily to mind. Because the more often an outsider visits Afghanistan and journeys around the country, the more they realize they have to learn. From religion and ethnicity to culture and history, the Afghan people are impossible to comprehend in simple descriptors and raw numbers. True, there are constants. A majority of the population is profoundly Islamic. But even this aspect leads to complexity, since in addition to the Sunni majority, the country's Shia territories help define Afghanistan as a whole. In the same way, the Hazara, Tajik, Uzbek and Turkmen people resist the Pashtun majority's history of seeing themselves as the dominant ethnic group. But nobody, and nothing, dominates Afghanistan except uncertainty. Especially in terms of who rules: whose flesh and bones, whose race and creed, will occupy the throne.

"As many as twenty-five ruling dynasties have swept through Afghanistan over the past three millennia," author and journalist Edward Girardet reminds us in his 2011 book, *Killing The Cranes: A Reporter's Journey Through Three Decades of War in Afghanistan.* He writes: "One cannot help but be overwhelmed by Afghanistan's past. It has repelled, absorbed, or simply let pass through those who invaded, rampaged, or marched across its borders." Girardet's book stresses one of the country's very few constants, namely the ruin the land and its residents will inevitably visit upon any invader silly enough to try to establish a foreign dominion over the Afghan people.

Yet well-meaning newcomers are welcomed with warmth and hospitality—and protection. Imagine being stalked by a gang of bandits in the countryside. If you're wise enough to have an experienced guide, he'll quicken your pace towards the next village. There, you encounter a tall figure in white, a bearded man wearing a lordly turban. He's walking towards you, his hand extended in greeting. The village mullah is signaling his and his peoples' greeting—and a warning to the bandits that you are a welcome visitor, a guest whose safety the village will protect at any cost. This is their duty as devout followers of the Prophet. No newcomer who finds himself rescued in this way will ever forget the comforting guardianship of mullah and mosque. It was this reporter's salvation on my very first day in Afghanistan.

Naturally, Spike Dubs wanted to experience the countryside and the people living there. He asked his new aides at Embassy Kabul to take him somewhere special, far from the prying eyes of the regime. The choice was easy. The Ajar Valley in Afghanistan's central Bamiyan Province is one of the most spectacular places on earth. It was King Zahir Shah's hunting reserve until his overthrow in 1973. Spike could meet Afghans leading much the same lives as their ancestors. The wildlife included Siberian Ibex mountain goats, and he might see a few wolves or jackals, perhaps even a snow leopard.

Spike jumped at the chance. Keeping the lowest possible profile, the party was kept to just a few vehicles. He chronicled the journey in a letter to Lindsay:

> The route goes up over the Salang Pass, at an elevation of about 12,000 feet—Kabul lies at 6,000. Once we turned off the main road, the going was rough but the scenery quite spectacular. Of greatest interest was seeing what life was like in the deep countryside. It seemed pretty primitive in some respects, but I couldn't help but feel that the people were getting along all right, on land that has been farmed for centuries.

The new American ambassador and his aides relished the same pastime as Spike's opposite number at the Soviet embassy: fishing.

> The end of the valley where we fished was beautiful, sunny and quiet. The stream in which we fished was crystal clear and came gushing out of a tranquil, deep blue lake upstream which had been formed as a result of a landslide some time ago. We had good luck fishing. Four of us caught about 125 trout of varying sizes.
> It was great having trout for breakfast lunch and dinner. Fortunately, we brought along our own cooking equipment and some canned food such as soup. On the way up, we had purchased potatoes, carrots, cucumbers, etc., so our diet wasn't too bad.

The country and its people made a deep impression on him. Its spell was only enhanced by the landscape's tranquil, mesmerizing beauty. He told Lindsay: "Spending hours by oneself walking up and down a trout stream provides wonderful opportunities for quiet contemplation and reflection." This came as no surprise to Lindsay. "He had a reputation, when we were in the Soviet Union and also in Yugoslavia, for really getting out. He wanted to see the country and learn about the people. Shop in the marketplace, meet all these interesting people."

The embassy's local hires were the first Afghans the ambassador got to know. He peppered his driver, Gul Mohammed, with questions about every facet of his family's life. Gul was a seasoned wheel man who knew every thoroughfare and back road of Kabul and the surrounding area. He was also familiar with the roads to distant provincial capitals, many of which featured steep, switchback passages through mountainous terrain. The Americans had provided Gul with basic instruction in tactical driving. With a new ambassador on post, the embassy's security officer, Chuck Boles, ensured Gul Mohammed regularly changed routes for moving around the capital. A rugged former Marine, Boles was responsible for Spike's safety and that of the embassy in general. Though not a spy, he was Sergei Bakhturin's opposite number in security matters. As such, he soon found himself having to broach safety concerns with his new boss.

At issue was Spike's free-wheeling approach to getting around. The ambassador's vehicle was a tan-colored 1976 Oldsmobile Ninety-Eight Regency. Spike loved the big four-door sedan. At nearly 5,000 pounds, it was one of the biggest cars ever to roll out of Detroit. Unlike an uptight posting like Moscow, Kabul enabled Spike to take the wheel himself, cruising across town with Old Glory flying from a flagstaff on the passenger side front fender.

Chuck recalls the occasion that finally caused him to confront the ambassador over his use of the Olds. Spike's secretary had been on home leave and was flying back into Kabul Airport. The terminal building was one of the more heavily-guarded sites in the capital, ringed by armored vehicles and troops of the Communist regime. None of this made Spike blink an eye. With Stars and Stripes flying, he wheeled the massive Olds up to the police and military checkpoints, one after the other. At one of the roadblocks, the interior ministry police insisted on inspecting the vehicle. Spike got out and opened the trunk. Eventually he was allowed to proceed to the terminal, where he parked the car and strolled inside to greet his returning assistant.

Learning this, Chuck sounded the alarm. He reminded Spike neither the regime's police nor armed forces had the right to halt a foreign mission's official vehicle, much less search it. To Boles, the incident underlined two imperatives. First, Spike's delegated driver, Gul Mohammed, or an American member of staff, should handle chores like an airport pickup. Second, the ambassador should get used to being a back-seat driver, rather than taking the wheel. There were reasons the

Olds was partially armored and equipped with special purpose communications hardware. It was called enhanced protection. Embassy Kabul had been issued the car to protect its lead diplomat. To that end, Chuck recommended Spike be accompanied by an escort vehicle when in transit, or at least a bodyguard, preferably one of the embassy's contingent of Marines.

Chuck tried to be convincing. But he was getting to know this ambassador, and realized the man was set in his ways. "He listened politely enough. But he wasn't having any of it. He was a very private guy, and humble. He didn't want to be seen as some big-shot foreigner. He wanted to avoid that kind of attention. If possible, he wanted to mix freely with ordinary people in the street."

Spike made personal contact with the Afghan people as often as his schedule would allow. To this end, he quickly became one of the most active and approachable diplomats on the Kabul scene. He followed up on his initial introductions to regime notables with return visits. Many of these Communist office holders were taken aback by the easy-going American envoy, who represented the dominant power of Western capitalist-imperialism. Spike found one of the best ways to break the ice was to be fully versed on world news—and to share the headlines generously with the cloistered regime officials.

He devoured every scrap of daily news available to him. "I get up at 7 a.m. most mornings," he wrote Lindsay, "and immediately turn on Voice of America, which has a good news summary at 7:30. When I get to the breakfast table, a wireless file is awaiting me five days a week, in addition to a copy of the *Kabul Times*." The venerable local paper was now a party organ, featuring "precious little news on international developments." But it covered the regime's leadership at great length, especially the activities of "The Great Leader" of the Afghan people, President Nur Mohammed Taraki, and Hafizullah Amin, "the distinguished Vice-Premier and Minister of Foreign Affairs."

On his chauffeured drive to the office, Spike would study the latest editions of the *Herald Tribune* and *Washington Post.* Events in Afghanistan rarely made the foreign sections, let alone the front pages. Still, as 1978 turned from summer to autumn, Spike and his foreign service officers had their work cut out for them, trying to fathom the inner workings of the People's Democratic Party of Afghanistan. Spike's letters to Lindsay speak to his analyst's mind picking through the chaotic functions of the regime:

> ...this past week has been fairly quiet, even though the revolution appears to be in the process of devouring some of its participants. About a week ago, the Politburo decided to remove the Minister of Defense, Abdul Qader. He was in charge of the aircraft which bombed the Palace during the coup of April 27 (1978), and there is little doubt that he played a crucial role in bringing down the old government.
>
> Now he and some other officers and civilians are accused of conspiring against the leadership, headed by Noor Mohammed Taraki and Hafizullah Amin. This purge of what I consider to be rather nationalistic elements within the leftist leadership follows a purge of more radical elements known as the Parchamists. This syndrome is reminiscent of the purge of Trotsky and then the rightists in the early years of the Communist Party of the Soviet Union.

This was a syndrome that spelled trouble to any seasoned Russia hand:

> I'm afraid that the present ruling group is communist by background and intention. It hopes to bring about a radical economic social and political transformation of

> society not, unfortunately, by democratic means but via a tightly organized and disciplined party which will do everything possible to maintain a monopoly of political power.
>
> Whether this government can maintain a semblance of independence from the Soviets is not yet quite clear. Our problem is to do those things which help Afghans become self-reliant and resilient and thus confident enough to ward off undue and perhaps harmful pressures from the outside.
>
> The task for us here is not going to be easy, for the present leadership is by inclination quite pro-Soviet and, conversely, suspicious of the West.

Try as he might, Spike was unable to really engage with the Afghan regime's senior leadership. President Taraki impressed most Western representatives in Kabul as detached from reality. He shunned face to face contact with them, and on the few occasions a British, German or American diplomat might corner the president at an official function, they would be treated with speech-excerpts every bit as dry as the tracts dutifully reproduced, page after page, in the *Kabul Times*.

Amin was equally enigmatic. True enough, he granted Spike access. But this was more in the nature of some Grand Wazir receiving a supplicant. Spike would be treated to an obligatory period waiting in an outer office. Then he would be ushered through oversized doors and into the Great Man's chamber. Amin took the American Ambassador's polite deference as a signal to start boasting about the regime's sterling accomplishments, primarily his own. Spike came to sense what every other foreign envoy, from West or East, had discerned within weeks of the revolution. This preening, doctrinaire Afghan Marxist really believed he was the Man Who Would Be King.

Spike realized he and his entire embassy team needed to

raise their game if they were to pierce the PDPA's realm of propaganda. He had just the player/coach in mind. Professor Tom Gouttierre had made an indelible impression on Spike during his pre-assignment briefings. Not only had the expert from the University of Nebraska worked magic with Afghanistan's national basketball squad, he had also once been a member of the same Dari language poetry club frequented by Taraki. Tom also knew Amin, and one of his former students was an up-and-coming leader of the PDPA's Parcham faction, Mohammed Najib. Eventually, Najib would be installed by the Soviet Union as Afghan president.

Gouttierre needed no coaxing to make a return visit to his home away from home. At Spike's invitation, he flew to Kabul in mid-November 1978. The two men met in Spike's residence and formulated a plan. During his two week stay in Kabul, Tom would renew his old contacts, staying first at the home of the American representative of the Asia Foundation, then moving to Spike's residence. Tom would work every friend and acquaintance in the capital to arrange informal, one-on-one meetings with as many regime office holders, notables and supporters as possible. He would offer assurances their discussions were strictly off the record. In this way, Tom would take measure of the PDPA figures who would offer the best chances of engagement by Ambassador Dubs in follow up meetings.

Gouttierre relished the opportunity to dive into the deep end with the upstart Communist government's ruling elite. Within days, however, he felt a chill run down his spine, the chill that had come over the entire Afghan capital. It became clear that the numerous reports of arrests, detention and summary execution had, if anything, understated the full scope of the PDPA's reign of terror. At ministry after ministry, Tom found doors closing in his face, perhaps more politely given his popularity as the wonderful "Mr. Tom" of basketball fame, but closed nonetheless. Even his warmest Afghan friends were visibly upset in his presence. It was clear their own safety, and that of their families, hung in the balance, day in and day out. "Some told me that even to know Americans could put them at peril." One week into his stay, a friend in the Ministry of Foreign Affairs reached out to him with a clandestine phone call. Tom's elation at being contacted by a potential source so well placed in the regime firmament quickly turned to disappointment. "He told me my safety was at risk. That it would be best if I left Afghanistan right away. Then he hung up."

By this time, Gouttierre didn't need an explanation. When he brought the news to Spike's desk, the ambassador took immediate action. He ordered up a car and driver, and soon Gouttierre was on his way up the Khyber Pass and into Pakistan. The next afternoon, Spike's houseman sounded the alert. Commandant Taroon and a squad of his Interior police had breached the entrance to the residence compound and were storming up the driveway. Spike went to the front door to meet them. Taroon puffed out his chest and gave the ambassador a perfunctory salute. Kindly produce the American, Mr. Thomas, he demanded: he is wanted for questioning. Spike suggested the commandant take his inquiries to Peshawar, as Mr. Thomas was long gone. Fuming, Taroon chose not to invade the premises. He turned on his heel and led his men away.

The episode further complicated Embassy Kabul's perplexing task of trying to figure out what lay in store for Afghanistan under the PDPA. Given Taroon's tight relations with his ministry's Soviet advisers, could the Russians have been party to the regime's overreaction to Gouttierre's mission? Clearly panic had run hot through the paranoid upper reaches of the PDPA machine. Had each of Tom's Afghan contacts reported his approaches to the authorities? Or were the regime's secret police more capable of monitoring its ministries than the Americans suspected?

Ironically, the Americans weren't alone in massaging their furrowed brows over the ghoulish excesses of Taraki, Amin and Company. The Russians, too, had abundant cause to fret about the future of their client regime. On the surface, Ambassador Puzanov was happy enough to lap up the PDPA leaders' Marxist pronouncements and pass them along to Moscow and the office of Foreign Minister Andrei Gromyko. For instance, President Taraki made the following pledge to Puzanov and a visiting delegation from Moscow: "The leadership of the Democratic Republic of Afghanistan are using the wealth of experience of the Soviet Union and their support to make the dreams of the Afghan people come true."

Amin, ever eager to outdo his mentor and boss, told Puzanov and a group of Russian scientists: "The Soviet embassy always helps us in times of trouble, and this is key to the victory of our revolution... We have no secrets from our Soviet friends, because we always sought to teach the members of our party the four basic qualities: patriotism, Marxism, Sovietism and internationalism.

Meantime, the veteran despots of the Soviet Communist Party's Central Committee could see through the regime's frothy declarations. This was in no small part due to the spying on the PDPA conducted by Lt. Col. Bakhturin's KGB colleagues in the Kabul residence. The result was a growing sense of alarm among the Soviet Union's top leadership in Moscow. This is evidenced by a most revealing entry at the end of September, 1978, in the diary of Anatoly Chernyaev, the Central Committee's deputy director of the International Communist Movement. Chernyaev's boss was Boris Ponomarev, effectively the policy chief of the worldwide Communist Bloc. Chernyaev wrote in his diary that Ponomarev had just returned from Afghanistan:

> He went there with a secret mission—to warn Taraki that if he keeps slaughtering people who made the revolution,

> we will turn away from him. Already people are pointing fingers to blame us for the mass repressions. People's anger is turning towards Soviet specialists, whom Taraki invited by the hundreds.

Even the Soviets had difficulty assessing the full extent of the PDPA's reign of terror, both in terms of its bloody internal rivalries and the regime's sweeping repression of perceived opponents in the population at large. By the end of 1978, Western diplomats and military observers in Afghanistan agreed many thousands of Afghans had been summarily executed by the Communists. At the same time, reports of armed clashes in the provinces were coming in more frequently. "Power is really exercised through having control of the gun barrels," Spike commented in one of his Sunday dispatches to Lindsay. Although things were calm on the surface in Kabul, "we know that the government continues to encounter problems in the tribal areas."

The embassy's modest CIA detachment was made aware by their colleagues in Islamabad that Pakistan's freshman President, Muhammad Zia-ul-Haq, was supporting the Islamic opposition to the Kabul regime, the mujahideen. The previous year, as army chief of staff, Gen. Zia had overthrown his predecessor, Zulfikar Ali Bhutto. Zia had Bhutto tried for murder and hanged. It had been Bhutto who initially permitted Pakistan's army to provide safe haven to mujahideen groups from Afghanistan. Now, on Zia's orders, this support went into overdrive. Arms, training and logistical support from Pakistan began to transform the rag-tag Afghan guerrilla groups on the Northwest Frontier into a potent resistance movement.

As a result, the Taraki regime felt the walls closing in on all sides. Paranoia and fear stalked its politburo meetings. Spike and his embassy team became accustomed to the government's undiplomatic cold shouldering. The ambassador noted the regime "is not very interested in having a lot of American technicians or Peace Corps volunteers in the country," but remained "intensely interested in having money and material help from the U.S. Officials have taken the view that they have all the human resources necessary to implement specific assistance projects, i.e., engineers, architects, mechanically trained personnel, teachers, etc... So it may well be that we will have to assume a low-profile posture for a spell."

A LOW U.S. PROFILE in Afghanistan suited the Carter White House to a T. In fact, as 1979 beckoned, few officials in Washington, DC spared even an occasional thought for the Southwest Asian backwater. Instead, the Carter administration was intensely focused on coaxing along negotiations with the Soviet Union over the SALT II strategic arms treaty. Carter was also promoting human rights around the world, and combatting global poverty. He ended U.S. support for the regime of Anastasio Somoza in Nicaragua, and visited sub Saharan Africa, the first sitting American president to do so. In Rhodesia, he helped press Ian Smith to put his white minority rule to democratic elections. Few other foreign policy issues did anything but heighten disagreements within Carter's divided team. What position should the U.S. adopt to rising tensions among Vietnam, Cambodia and China, three years after the American retreat from Saigon? As for the Soviet Union, should Carter opt for Secretary of State Cyrus Vance's approach, favoring détente over confrontation? Or should he take a tougher line with Moscow, as advocated by Zbigniew Brzezinski, his national security adviser?

Meantime, the administration was confounded over Iran, on Afghanistan's western border. Protests against the U.S.-backed Shah, Reza Pahlavi, had been growing all year. Most Iranians despised the Shah as a corrupt, incompetent American puppet. Strikes were crippling the country. At Embassy Tehran,

Spike's counterpart, Ambassador William Sullivan, was feeling the walls closing in. A hugely popular Iranian cleric, Ayatollah Ruhollah Khomeini, came to be viewed as the opposition's leader-in-waiting, biding his time in exile as the Shah's regime disintegrated. As rioting worsened in November, Sullivan telegrammed Washington, broaching the possibility of the United States turning its support away from the Shah. Once again, Vance and Brzezinski differed on the issue. Brzezinski flatly rejected abandoning the regime, while Vance advised the Ayatollah might eventually bring democracy to Iran. Carter wavered, unsure of his options. Khomeini seemed unstoppable. By December, the Ayatollah was calling for the Shah's overthrow. The Iranian revolution was underway.

In Kabul, Spike and his embassy staffers could do little more than watch as history was being made to the west. The CIA's Warren Marik, for one, had no illusions about his post's place in the intelligence scheme of things. "Afghanistan wasn't on the radar," he recalls. "Langley (his agency's headquarters) was focused on Iran. Same at State and the White House. Tehran was where the action was."

As geopolitical dramas unfolded elsewhere, Spike relished the prospect of an overdue reunion with his family. In mid-November, Mary Ann arrived in Kabul for an extended Christmas holiday. Lindsay would join them at the beginning of December. Until then, Spike kept his daughter up to date with his weekly letters:

> Mary Ann and I are off to Kandahar and the Helmand Valley tomorrow for a four-day trip. Over the years, much of U.S. assistance has gone into dam and irrigation projects in the Helmand Valley. At the moment, we have about eleven families in the area, and it's time that I got down for a visit and a chat with them. I have the feeling that they see themselves as being quite isolated

and in need of some recognition for the good work they are doing.

With minimal escort, the couple journeyed safely some 400 miles from Kabul to the remote USAID posts in Afghanistan's desert southwest. Their return trip was also without incident. After Lindsay's arrival, the trio embarked on still more travels. From the Afghan capital's landmarks and bazaars, north and west to Bamiyan, and then east to Jalalabad and over the Khyber Pass, Spike ensured Mary Ann and Lindsay saw as much of the land and its people as possible.

"We travelled all over the place," Lindsay says. "And I was delighted with this country. It was just fascinating to me." Like her father, she was deeply moved by the warmth and hospitality of the Afghan people. "My father's house was very comfortable and lovely, and I felt very relaxed. Things felt really happy." For Christmas, Spike invited the embassy's staff to a four-hour open house at his residence. Before long he was at the piano, leading his foreign service officers and their families in carols.

During their visit, neither Lindsay nor Mary Ann sensed an inkling of trouble on the horizon. Spike seemed entirely at ease six months into his mission to Afghanistan. Eagerly, he had taken on the role of Andrew Carnes in the Kabul Amateur Dramatic Society's production of *Oklahoma!* In early March, he would shed his diplomat's persona and belt out a full-throated rendition of *The Farmer and the Cowman*. This promised to be a real treat for expatriate audiences craving distraction from Kabul politics—especially Americans yearning for home:

Territory folks should stick together,
Territory folks should all be pals.
Cowboys dance with farmer's daughters,
Farmers dance with the ranchers' gals.

Meantime in the real world, the PDPA regime was applying pressure to Embassy Kabul by way of the mission's local hires. In mid-December, an aide named Ghulam Jailani Ashrat quit his job after being roughed up by Taroon's men. An AID worker, Adilah Loynab, was arrested and held for two days. Terrified by the ordeal, she nonetheless returned to work and told her American colleagues what had happened.

To Spike and his section chiefs, these were serious breaches by the host government, but manageable. Overall, the ambassador was tremendously upbeat about the year ahead. In early January, he would fly to the Sri Lankan capital, Columbo, for a chiefs of mission conference. Then he would return to Kabul with a renewed sense of purpose. Somehow, he and his embassy team would find ways to connect with the Afghan government's ministries. If that meant promoting financial aid, reminding the regime of Washington's unrivalled capacity to provide material support, so be it. The United States would not allow the Soviet Union, or the PDPA's leadership, to diminish the American presence in Afghanistan.

Above all, Spike would strive to convince his colleagues at the State Department, and throughout the Carter administration, that one priority should be placed above all others in American policy on Afghanistan. The U.S. should do nothing that might force the Afghan regime even deeper into the Soviets' embrace. Washington enjoyed a competitive edge in resources. The U.S. had the wealth and ingenuity necessary to rebuild America's historic ties with Afghanistan and its people. This was a massive advantage over the Soviets. But it would be squandered if the U.S. simply gave up on the Afghan regime and its leadership. The administration, and Embassy Kabul, had no option other than to keep seeking engagement with the PDPA, as thankless as this task was proving to be.

Chapter 5

By Persons Unknown

FOR PRESIDENT Jimmy Carter's representative to Afghanistan, there was nothing unusual in the wintry dawn of Wednesday, February 14, 1979. Like every working day, Ambassador Spike Dubs was awakened at 7 a.m. sharp with a knock on his bedroom door by his houseman, Serajuddin. This 51-year-old Afghan domestic servant had been in the employ of the U.S. government since 1954. He listened a moment to ensure his knock had been heard. There it was: the sound of the shortwave radio coming to life beside the ambassador's bed. Hearing this, Serajuddin went to the kitchen to prepare breakfast.

Also at 7 a.m. sharp, Spike's driver, Gul Mohammed, arrived at the entrance to the residence's driveway. The guard on duty, Abdul Akim, another trusted U.S. Foreign Service National, greeted the chauffeur and waved him through. Gul Mohammed walked to the garage and began his morning ritual. First, a walk-around of the big Oldsmobile sedan. Then he checked the oil and radiator, and started the powerful V8 engine. He backed the car into the drive to let the engine warm up.

Meantime, Spike was listening to the news on Voice of America. Iran dominated the day's international headlines. The spiritual leader, Ayatollah Khomeini, had returned from exile two weeks earlier to a euphoric welcome in the streets of Tehran. The hated Shah and his family had fled abroad. Remnants of the last government formed under the monarchy were trying to hold on, but on February 11th the army deserted the old order and returned to barracks. The Ayatollah was now effectively in control of the entire country. His revolutionaries seized all government buildings and crowds of adoring citizens surged through the streets of Tehran. The White House and State, Spike realized, would be consumed with the task of engaging Khomeini and his Islamic government. Not to mention protecting Embassy Tehran and its staff.

Shortly after 8 a.m., Gul Mohammed finished polishing up the Olds and strolled into the house for a coffee. The cook, Nawroz, had water on the boil. He helped the driver prepare a cup of instant before setting out the ambassador's breakfast in the adjacent dining room. At 8:15, Spike took his place at the table and began scanning the *Kabul Times*. The headlines reminded him the Iraqi foreign minister had arrived in Afghanistan. Spike's lips must have spread into a knowing smile. Dominating the front page was a photograph of his prime interlocutor in the Afghan regime, Hafizullah Amin, greeting Dr. Saadun Hammadi as he emerged from his Iraqi Airways plane.

Spike knew the Afghan foreign minister well by now. Amin would bask in the spotlight for the duration of the official visit, ushering Hammadi and his aides from place to place, followed closely by official photographers and an obedient scribe or two from the *Times*. It was doubtful the week would end with any other local news eclipsing the visit of Iraq's Foreign Minister. After all, he was the envoy of an emerging military strongman in the region named Saddam Hussein. The visit would amount to a splurge of authoritarian backslapping. At event after event, Amin and President Taraki would heap praise on Saddam's envoy, who in turn would commend the accomplishments of the heroic People's Democratic Party of Afghanistan,

Top: Afghanistan's Bamiyan Valley in 1978, a safe destination for Afghans and foreigners alike.
Bottom: Doug Wankel fishing in the Salang River, and left, his trusty driver, Ewaz Ali.

Top: Spike with first wife, Jane Wilson Dubs, and daughter Lindsay in Moscow in 1962.
Bottom: A Soviet intercontinental ballistic missile in Red Square.

The U.S. Embassy Chancery Building, Kabul, Afghanistan in the 1970s.

Main: Dari language training in Washington, DC. Top row, second from left, Spike with Mary Ann Dubs. David Litt bottom center, with wife Beatrice standing second from right.
Bottom: in the Defence Attaché's aircraft, Jeannene Cramer, left foreground, with Mary Ann and Spike Dubs in the middle row.

Main: Spike Dubs with his 1976 Oldsmobile Ninety-Eight Regency sedan.
Bottom: Spike with staff outside the embassy canteen and speaking at the American School.

Center: Nurse Jeannene Cramer outside the USAID dispensary in Kabul.
Roadside assistance: Afghan National Army soldiers help Jim Taylor repair a flat tire on Jeannene's Bug.
Inset: An ANA crew decorate their Soviet-made T-34 tank.

Top: Ballerinas Catherine and Elizabeth Rigamer (center) with classmates from India, Turkey, Iran and Yugoslavia.
Center: The American International School in Kabul Scorpions, with Steve Rotz back row, third from left.
Bottom: American School second graders in a backyard treehouse.

Kabul scenes by photo student Steve Rotz.
Top left: Steve's mother Marlene shops in a street bazaar.

Top: Tom Gouttierre with son Adam in Kabul in the summer of 1971.
Bottom: Coach "Mr. Tom" with Afghanistan's basketball stars of the mid-1960s.

Karen and Mike Malinowski pictured in 1978.

Top: The gatehouse of the U.S. Ambassador's residence compound.
Main: Rear view of the residence.

Bottom: The Hotel Kabul as seen from Pashtunistan Square.
Top left: An ANA soldier on patrol.
Top right: Looking down on Pashtunistan Square, with the Hotel Kabul on the left, and opposite, Da Afghanistan Bank.

its Great Leader and his esteemed Vice-Premier. This would go on for days.

In fact, the rest of the month held out little prospect for anything unexpected happening in Kabul. Even the pending release in Washington of the State Department's report on human rights in Afghanistan seemed unlikely to make waves. The regime's leadership knew the report was coming and was bracing for a stinging rebuke from the Americans. They would likely just ignore it. Embassy Kabul was by now accustomed to the Communist regime's dystopian posturing. Any revelation, no matter how strong the evidence, would be smothered with bare denials and bellicose torrents of Marxist-Leninist claptrap. Some ten days earlier, Spike wrote to Lindsay: "We keep plugging along here, and keep wondering when this regime will become more assertive along Afghan rather than leftist lines."

WHILE SPIKE was finishing breakfast, his administrative chief, Bernie Woerz, was already at the embassy. His February 14th commenced with a look at the latest cables sent to his attention. A regular weekly staff meeting was scheduled for 9 a.m., and his immediate boss, the embassy's Deputy Chief of Mission, Bruce Amstutz, might well have a request arising from the overnights. So Bernie wanted to have the decks cleared and ready.

Meantime, the DEA's Doug Wankel still hadn't made it out the front door. He was helping Marilyn with preparations for the Valentine's party they were hosting in their home that evening. It was shaping up to be a grand occasion. With help from Karen Malinowski, Marilyn had combed the Chicken Street bazaar for anything resembling Valentine's Day greeting cards. Red paper and cardboard was the best they could do, so almost all the decorations for the living and dining rooms were made by hand. As well, Marilyn had picked up enough red cotton cloth in the bazaar to fashion Valentine-themed local clothing for herself and Doug, the loose-fitting Afghan tunics and trousers known as *shalwar kameez*. There would be plenty to eat and drink, a house full of good friends—it would be an all-American Valentine's Day party to remember.

Unlike Doug, Mike Malinowski was ahead of time with his morning routine. At 8:00 a.m., he kissed Karen so long for the day and headed off for the embassy in the couple's old Toyota Land Cruiser. Being February, there was little chance the young consul would be confronted with anything unexpected during the day, much less an emergency. It was highly unlikely an American backpacker would turn up in low season, much less fall into the custody of Commander Taroon's thugs with a pocketful of marijuana, or a bag of black Afghan hashish in his pack. Still, Mike wanted to be early: he, too, would be attending the staff meeting.

Jeannene Cramer, meanwhile, was right on time reaching the dispensary in the AID compound across town from the embassy. She looked forward to telling her colleagues at the clinic about her excursion into the bazaar with Ambassador Dubs the previous day. It had been her turn to put in the nurses' weekly afternoon shift in the small examination room at the embassy. As it turned out, the only "patient" who dropped in was Spike. "He said he'd had a few Mai Tais the night before, and would it help if I gave him some oxygen. He was just messing around. We talked for about 20 minutes and then he left. But he came back and said 'do you want to go carpet shopping with me?' Absolutely, I said." With Gul Mohammed at the wheel of the Oldsmobile, they headed off for the bazaar.

Another embassy staffer spent time with Spike on February 13th: Dr. Elmore Rigamer, the mission's psychiatrist. An MD and conscientious objector to the Vietnam War, Rigamer had gone to Liberia with the Peace Corps in 1971. Prior to this, he studied neurology and psychiatry at Cornell. Embassy officers in Liberia told him he was the first psychiatrist to set foot near their mission. Later, back home in New Orleans, the State Department asked Rigamer if he might be interested in serving as their first overseas community psychiatrist. Based in Kabul, he would serve the American missions in Pakistan, India, Nepal and Sri Lanka, as well as Afghanistan. Elmore eagerly accepted.

Soon after arriving in Kabul, he and his wife Anna were befriended by Ambassador Dubs. Spike came to their house for dinner on February 11th, and volunteered to give piano lessons to one of their daughters. On the night of the 13th, just hours after carpet shopping with Jeannene, Spike invited Elmore and Anna to be his guests at the Embassy of the People's Republic of China. There, an opera company from Beijing performed for the capital's diplomatic corps. The performance went on and on, seemingly without end. Now, bright and early the morning after, Elmore was on the road to Pakistan. He had appointments scheduled at Embassy Islamabad the following day, Thursday the 15th.

About the time Elmore was leaving Kabul, Jim Taylor was dropping off his wife Louise at the American Cultural Center. With a wave, Jim drove off and headed for the embassy, just minutes away. With snow on the ground, there would be no tennis today. Less than a week earlier, during an unseasonably warm spell, Spike invited Jim and two Marine guards for a lunchtime doubles game at his residence.

"Having taken an hour to split two sets, Spike asked if we could spare time to play a third." Unanimously, the men agreed. "After trashing us 6-1 in the rubber set, Spike took in the blue sky, the surrounding mountains and warm sun, and remarked: 'Life is simply too short not to seize the good times when they come your way.'"

By the time Jim reached the embassy, security officer Chuck Boles was already inside, beginning his work day. Two weeks earlier, he had conducted his monthly threat assessment.

This meant touching base with all the embassy's department heads and key sources of security information, and circulating an updated evaluation of local conditions. In mid-February of 1979, there was no threat to report, much less adapt to. Embassy Kabul remained one of the most secure American overseas posts in the world. Within the hour, all of that would change dramatically, and forever.

JUST AFTER 8:30 a.m., Gul Mohammed emerged from the ambassador's residence and returned to the Oldsmobile. Retrieving two flags from the trunk, he went to the front of the car and slipped the banners onto its front fenders: the American flag to the left, the driver's side, and the ambassador's on the right.

Spike appeared at the front door and walked to the car. He wore slacks with a sport jacket over a lightweight turtleneck sweater. Copies of the *Washington Post* and *Herald Tribune* were tucked under his arm, along with two letters to be sent home to DC. Before getting into the car he greeted Gul Mohammed warmly in Dari. As customary in Afghanistan, this was a prolonged affair. "Salaam Alaikum" (Peace be upon you), followed by "Chetoor hasta?" (How are you). Then came a stream of friendly queries and responses. Are you feeling strong today? How is your family, is everyone well? And so on.

Gul Mohammed opened the right rear door of the Olds and Spike eased into the seat. "Embassy, please," he said. The driver closed the door and dashed back behind the wheel. He tripped the electronic locks, securing all four doors. Then he pressed the keying device, a transmitter button on the car's custom radio. This sent a signal to Abdul Akim in the guard shack, letting him know it was time to open the gate. As the Olds approached, both Abdul and Gul checked their watches and noted the time: 8:40 a.m. The big car rolled through the gate and turned left. Spike opened the *Post* and began to read.

ON THE other side of town, Steve and Christie Rotz were aboard their Blue Bird school bus. Steve frowned out the window at the snow on the ground. There'd be no football or baseball that afternoon. But there was always basketball to break up the day. By this time their father, Dr. Lloyd Rotz, had arrived at the USAID dispensary, not far from the school and also on Darulaman road. He drove himself to work in the only vehicle available for the family's use until their Chevy Blazer arrived from Michigan: a converted Chevy station wagon, adorned with red crosses and a light bar on the roof. This was Embassy Kabul's ambulance, equipped with first aid gear, oxygen and room in back for a stretcher.

Heading inside, Lloyd bid good morning to nurses Jeannene Cramer and Marjorie Yamamoto. Then he settled in for another day familiarizing himself with the clinic and its resources. The equipment was rudimentary and in some respects outdated, such as the decades-old X-ray machine. But overall the facilities were more than adequate to provide the services of a small hospital. There was a procedure room with a table, enabling everything from physical examinations to delivering babies. Beyond this, critical injuries or other emergencies required an airlift to the larger U.S. hospital in Islamabad.

THE AMBASSADOR'S tan-colored Oldsmobile glided past the Kabul Post Office, then the interior ministry. In five minutes or so, Spike would be climbing out of the car and striding into the embassy. The sleek Olds 98 seemed enormous, cruising among old Datsuns and Toyotas and VWs—and hand-carts heaped with firewood, drawn by swarthy men in turbans and robes. On this morning, Embassy Kabul's CIA station chief happened to be driving in the same uniquely Afghan stream of traffic, making the school run with his daughters. For a time, they were just two car lengths behind Spike's vehicle. They could see him clearly in the back seat. Then they turned off to the right, heading south towards the American School. Gul Mohammed took the Olds the other way, turning left onto a street named Sher Ali Khan Wat.

The traffic was now heavy and slow moving. Up ahead on the right was the American Cultural Center, located within the U.S. International Communications Agency compound, known simply as the ICA building. To the left was the Afghan government's Prime Ministry, one of Amin's offices. It was on that side of the road that Gul Mohammed first saw the figure: a tall policeman, perhaps 25 years old, in the uniform of a sergeant. He was dodging through the traffic, walking directly towards the Olds sedan at a distance of about 50 feet. When that gap closed to about 15 feet, the policeman, looking directly at the Oldsmobile's driver, raised both his arms in the air and began waving downward. Stop, he was signaling. Gul Mohammed did so. He noticed a stationary blue-gray delivery van immediately to the right, blocking traffic in that lane.

Spike looked up from his newspaper. Gul Mohammed explained what was happening. "Find out what he wants, please," Spike told him. The driver lowered his window about three inches. The policeman approached, then leaned in towards him. In Dari, Gul Mohammed asked what he wanted.

"I want to search your car," came the reply. "I have orders from the government."

"This is the American ambassador's car," Gul told him.

"I know. But these are my orders from the government. I must look in the car, just quickly."

As a foreign envoy, Spike had no obligation to heed the cop's demand. But the situation looked routine enough. Spike waited for Gul's translation, then nodded. "It's all right. Let him look in the car."

Gul Mohammed unlocked his door; only his door. The sergeant opened it and with his right hand checked the driver's waist and legs, as if looking for a weapon. Then he turned slightly, reaching awkwardly with the same hand behind Gul Mohammed and pulling up the lock on the left rear door. In an instant, the sergeant's left hand flashed into view—holding a small handgun, a revolver. He thrust the weapon into Gul Mohammed's stomach. "Don't speak and don't move," he said.

Three other men appeared on the left side of the car. Opening the back door, they ducked inside, one after the other. The first man knelt on the floor, facing Spike. Another climbed into the front seat on Gul Mohammed's right. He stuck a gun into the driver's side and said, "Be still." The police sergeant joined the others in the back seat, slamming the door behind him. He pressed his revolver into the back of Gul's neck.

"Shoot the driver," Gul heard a voice say in the back of the car. But the gun just jerked against his neck, and the cop said: "Go ahead, drive." The Olds moved forward, the lane ahead now clear of traffic. Through all of this, Spike sat calmly, and silently, at the right side rear door. Gul Mohammed assumed that he and the ambassador were being arrested by the security police for some reason. "Do you want me to go to the police station?" he asked.

"No. Go to the Hotel Kabul," came the reply. As the car passed the foreign ministry, the traffic light in the distance turned red. "If you stop at that light, I will shoot you," the man in the front seat said. Shortly after, another voice said, "Shoot him now." But nothing happened. Then Gul swung the vehicle onto Ebn-e-Sina Road. The pale green expanse of the hotel appeared on the right. Directly opposite was a huge three-story building. "Da Afghanistan Bank," the sign said. No buses or cars were parked in front of the hotel, so Gul Mohammed brought the Olds to a stop at the building's entrance. The awning above the front doors was crowned with simple, elongated metal letters, announcing: "Hotel Kabul."

Gul noticed an elderly man standing there in a dark coat

and pillbox hat: the doorman. But then the gun behind him pushed his head all the way forward until he was staring at the floor between his knees. The other man's weapon was still pressed to his side. Now they're going to shoot me, he thought. He heard the back doors open and a scramble of bodies leave the car. Then footsteps on the sidewalk, then a voice shouting, "Open the door!"

The gun was removed from his neck. The man beside him got out of the car and yelled over his shoulder: "Go now and tell the people at the embassy."

Gul Mohammed started breathing again. He tried to get his bearings. Across the street in front of the bank, a traffic cop was walking along, looking at the ground with his hands in his pockets. Gul's eyes swept back to the right, he leaned over to check the hotel entrance. There was no one in sight. The ambassador, he realized, had been taken inside. At gunpoint.

He put the car into drive and pulled away. What else could he do but go to the embassy and report what had just happened? Then his training kicked in. He stopped the vehicle and quickly removed the ambassador's flag from the right fender. Driving the official car with the flag displayed but no ambassador in the back—well, that could get an Afghan arrested for theft in the People's Democratic Republic of Afghanistan.

In the lobby, now, Spike was hurried along by the trio of abductors. The front desk manager and several clerks noticed the group turning immediately to the right towards the main stairway. Forced upstairs to the second floor, Spike found himself being taken across an open landing, then to the left and down a corridor. They were now treading a carpeted floor directly above the main lobby. Passing several numbered doors on either side, the gang pulled him to a halt. He faced a door bearing three numerals in tarnished brass: 117.

Then the three men holding him began to fuss and curse amongst themselves. Spike must have sensed their confusion.

Did he laugh out loud, or realize he was in even greater danger than he feared? Because his abductors were at a loss to open the door to room 117. Somehow, they had forgotten to get a key to their own hideout.

Chapter 6

The Dead End Gang

WHILE THE SCENE outside the Hotel Kabul was unfolding, the wife of one of the U.S. embassy's military attachés happened to be making her way along the sidewalk not 30 yards away. Nancy Sandrock was heading for the post and telegraph office, located next to the hotel and facing Pashtunistan Square. Nancy spotted Spike's unmistakable figure and wondered, momentarily, why three local men would be escorting him to a meeting in that hotel. 'Modest' or 'budget' were polite ways of describing the sprawling, weather-beaten old inn built in 1945. But there seemed nothing sinister about the scene, so Nancy continued into the post office. Perhaps that evening, over a Valentine's cocktail, she would mention the sighting to her husband John, the embassy's U.S. Air Force attaché.

At Embassy Kabul, the Marine guards on duty spotted the ambassador's Oldsmobile speeding into view just before 9:00 a.m. They scarcely had time to swing open the front gates before the vehicle roared past and came to a stop, tires screeching, at the embassy's main entrance. Gul Mohammed leapt from the car and ran into the lobby. He burst through the first door he saw. This was Mike Malinowski's post, the Consular Office.

"Suddenly Spike's chauffeur was there before me, and he was very upset. He told me the ambassador had been arrested by some policeman. At gunpoint." This made no sense to the young consul, but the terror in the Afghan driver's eyes set his own pulse racing. This was an emergency, a red alert. Taking Gul Mohammed by one arm, Mike rushed him to the security office, alerting Chuck. The three of them continued upstairs and into the office of Spike's DCM, his deputy chief of mission, Bruce Amstutz. Hurriedly, Gul Mohammed recounted everything that had happened.

At the hotel, meantime, one of the three kidnappers reappeared in the lobby. He stalked up to the front desk, his brow beaded with perspiration. Pausing a moment to catch his breath, he asked for the key to room 117. My friends have a guest waiting upstairs, he explained. "Once they're able to enter the room, I will come back down to register."

A manager was summoned. The nervous man repeated his request. The manager reflected for a moment, then called a bellman over and gave him the key. "Let them into the room, but get names. Get all the names. And bring this man back to check in."

AT EMBASSY KABUL, Bruce Amstutz realized he could not afford to waste time pondering the many unknowns of the predicament confronting him. A seasoned, 50-year-old career diplomat and Asia specialist, Amstutz realized his first priority was to scramble his best officers to Spike's aid. The Americans had no clue what this apparent arrest was all about, but at least they knew where Spike had been taken. Amstutz ordered Bruce Flatin, his senior political counsellor, to go immediately to the Kabul Hotel (as the Hotel Kabul was commonly referred to by Westerners). Flatin was a steady hand on his second posting to Afghanistan: from 1957 to '59 he served as a junior counsellor. He would take Chuck Boles with him to the hotel, along with Mike Malinowski. As consul, Mike could invoke the Geneva and Vienna conventions to demand access to any American citizen, not least the U.S. ambassador.

Before leaving Amstutz's office, Chuck managed to get a call through to Commandant Taroon. Nothing happened in Kabul without the regime's secret police chief knowing about it. "He sounded surprised. He made it sound like this was the first he was hearing about the situation." The exchange only deepened Chuck's sense of dread. Taroon, denying any knowledge—somehow it just didn't add up. The commandant asked Chuck to put Gul Mohammed on the line. Come to the Ministry of Interior at once for questioning, the driver was told. Bruce Flatin waited for the call to end, then ordered one of Mike's consular staffers to take a detailed statement from the chauffeur, typing it in full, before letting him leave the building.

Upstairs, DCM Amstutz was trying to connect with the regime official best positioned to resolve the crisis: Amin. His call was answered by one of the Foreign Minister's aides. Eerily, the functionary echoed Taroon's surprise. The affair at the hotel was all news to the Vice-Premier and his staff. Before Amstutz could be transferred to Amin, the connection was broken. Not for the last time that day, the American deputy chief was left staring into a telephone receiver, droning out a lost signal.

In the hallway outside room 117 of the Hotel Kabul, the bellman was taking his time putting the key in the door lock. He wanted to get a good look at the four figures waiting there. The foreigner's white face stood out in the darkness. American or British, the bellman thought; a pleasant looking man, well dressed and wearing glasses. He looked calm compared to the other three. These Afghans were from the provinces, probably Afghanistan's north, the bellman thought. Their clothes were poor and rumpled; jackets and trousers looking as though their owners had slept in them. Like the man who had come for the key, the other two were anxious, their faces wet with perspiration. They held the foreigner tightly by both arms.

Finally, the bellman turned the key and opened the door. He was pushed instantly aside as the foreigner was thrust into the room. One of the men slammed the door in the bellman's face, but not before revealing a revolver in his hand. The bellman staggered backward. By now the third man, the one who had come for the key, was running away, dashing down the corridor for the stairs. The bellman hesitated, then ran after him.

At the front desk, the manager and clerks heard footsteps drumming towards them on the stairs. A figure emerged, moving fast across the lobby for the door. "Stop him!" the bellman's voice echoed in the stairwell. "They're criminals!" One of the clerks managed to step in front of the fleeing man and a wrestling match ensued. The bellman and another clerk threw themselves on top, and the would-be escapee was forced to the floor, only steps from the hotel's double front doors.

The manager was already on the phone. He was calling the only authorities still trusted, to any degree, by the people of Afghanistan's capital city: the Kabul Police.

BY THIS TIME, Spike was taking stock of his surroundings. Pushed through the door of room 117, he found himself facing an interior wall; he was in an entryway of some kind. To his right, a door opened into a bathroom. He might well have glimpsed a mirror and sink before his captors jerked him sharply to the left. He was thrust through another open door, this one made of glass set in metal framework. Once through this interior threshold, a turn to the right and three or four paces down a narrow hallway brought the ambassador and his captors into the main room. Spike was ordered to sit on a straight-back wooden chair, located well away from the window overlooking the street. He was sitting literally with his back to the wall. Very likely he would have realized this was the other side of the partition that confronted him right after being pushed in from the corridor. This meant the outer door to room 117 was directly behind him, beyond that wall.

It was a small room. Aside from the chair the only furniture consisted of a double bed, an old wooden dresser near the entryway and a table beneath the window. Next to the table was an iron radiator, painted the same drab green as the walls, and throwing off heat as water coursed noisily through its thick, cylindrical conduits. There was no sign of a telephone or radio. The only light was the grey cast of a winter morning, filtered through the curtains. Peering through these was the gunman who had given commands from the front seat of the car. The other man stood by the dresser, keeping watch on the little entry hall, the only exit from the room. Both men had guns in their hands—revolvers, pointed in Spike's direction.

Meantime at the embassy, the first responders decided to ride together in the ambassador's Olds sedan to the hotel. Chuck Boles got behind the wheel and swung the big car though the front gates. Beside him sat Mike Malinowski. Bruce Flatin, the political counsellor, was in the back, along with Chuck's locally-hired assistant investigator, Abdul Ghafari. This 35-year-old Afghan was far more than a trusted interpreter. He was the embassy's chief security liaison with the Afghan government, and an invaluable authority on the dysfunctional inner workings of the PDPA regime.

As Chuck leaned hard on the accelerator, Bruce Flatin noticed Spike's newspaper on the seat beside him. Beneath this were two letters with DC addresses. Bruce tucked them into the breast pocket of his suit jacket for safekeeping. The Americans were armed only with Chuck's two-way Motorola radio. None of them carried weapons. Mike began running through the possible causes of the emergency. "There we were, rushing over to the hotel, wondering what this could possibly be about. At first, we were thinking it might be our Human Rights Report. It was due out that day and it was going to be very critical of the PDPA and their sorry record on human rights. And we were thinking: 'those bastards!' We worked hard to get everything right in this human rights report, and this is their ham-fisted response!"

On reflection, this scenario made little sense, even for a nonsensical regime. There had to be a better explanation. But why the Hotel Kabul? It was a government owned facility in the regime's back yard, the very heart of the capital. "So then darker thoughts entered our minds," Mike says. "We didn't talk about it, but we all had a bad feeling for what might be waiting for us at the hotel."

IN HIS OFFICE on the embassy's upper floor, Bruce Amstutz and his team were working Kabul's antiquated phone system to little effect. It was the opposite of the kind of communications technology needed in a crisis. For instance, the embassy's phone directory included this plea under "Telephone Procedures":

> When you get a busy signal, please hang up the receiver. <u>DO NOT JIGGLE THE RECEIVER</u>–this blows the fuse.

Amstutz's only success had been to reach the regime's number two at the foreign ministry, Shah Mohammed Dost, the Afghan government's principal contact for all foreign legations. Dost promised he would remind his boss, Amin, that the emergency required his personal intervention. But Amstutz was taking nothing for granted. He ordered political officer Jim Taylor to get over to Dost's office, while administrative officer Bernie Woerz would try to buttonhole Amin himself. The regime must be left in no doubt. The safety of Ambassador Dubs was paramount. His staff was standing by to take him into their care and protection. The Afghan government must ensure this take place without delay.

Next, Amstutz checked with the embassy's communications

officers. How were they doing with that flash cable to Washington? The answer was as predictable as it was exasperating: Amstutz's initial emergency communication was still a work in progress. In fact, the term "flash cable" was a misnomer. This was, after all, the pre-digital era of American diplomacy. Rapid communications, not to mention instant messaging, were still the stuff of science fiction. Alerting the State Department that one of its ambassadors had been abducted was a painfully slow process. First, Amstutz dictated the brief message. This had to be typewritten on a State telegram form, then carried to the secure communications vault, where the comms team would retype it into a telex machine. The console would spit out a punch-hole tape of the message, which then would be fed back into the system. Inch by inch, the tape would chatter along through the teeth of the feeder. Once the last punch-hole was through, the signal was on its way–if all went to plan.

As a result, at 9:20 a.m. in Kabul, some 20 minutes after learning that Spike was being held in a room at the Hotel Kabul, Amstutz and his staff still had not communicated a word to the State Department in Washington. It would be another 25 agonizing minutes until Embassy Kabul's first alert reached a telex machine located in the 7th floor Operations Center at the State headquarters complex, known by the name of the historic DC neighborhood in which it is located: Foggy Bottom. There, it was now 15 minutes past midnight. In Kabul, it was 9:45 a.m., some nine and one half time zones ahead of Washington.

THE FIRST RESPONSE by local law enforcement came in a ramshackle cohort of Kabul city policemen. Two and three at a time, the cops wandered hesitantly past the Hotel Kabul's doddery doorman and into the lobby. The manager hurried out to greet them, only to discover the cops had no idea why they had been ordered to the scene. He started to explain. This drew a crowd of guests, including several Europeans and at least two American tourists. They wondered why the front desk clerks were off in one corner, struggling to restrain a short, slight, panic-stricken man who was fighting desperately to break free. Soon they had their answer: he's one of the gang from room 117, the manager told the police.

Outside in the street, another clutch of policemen was making way for a big tan-colored car with a U.S. flag on the left front fender. The Oldsmobile pulled to a stop, its doors flying open. The Americans hurried into the hotel, with Bruce Flatin in the lead, followed by Chuck Boles, Mike Malinowski and Abdul Ghafari. Mike recalls the melee that awaited them. "When we got inside there was massive confusion. The hotel people were upset, but they were able to tell us some kidnappers had taken an American up to a room on the second floor."

Bruce Flatin realized he had to act swiftly. The American, he told the Afghans, was in fact the Ambassador of the United States of America. He had been brought there against his will. At this, there was even more disorder. Even the city cops had the sense to realize this wasn't a routine public order complaint. They began rushing about in no particular direction, jostling Mike aside. "Suddenly there were a lot of guns being waved around. It was clear nobody was really in charge. We tried to get some kind of order but it was very chaotic."

Then a squad of uniformed men armed with bolt-action rifles stomped into the hotel, followed by the grand figure of Kabul's police chief, Lal Mohammed. This put many of the younger cops even more on edge. Something truly serious—and dangerous—must be happening. No sooner did the hotel manager repeat his story for the chief than a calamitous uproar from the street interrupted the gathered throng. The double doors flew open to reveal an advancing troop of soldiers. Behind them, a convoy of Afghan National Army trucks was filling the street. The vehicles' cargo streamed onto the pavement and began thundering into the lobby: squad upon squad of Afghan regime troops, all bearing Soviet-made assault rifles, Kalashnikovs.

Two officers emerged from the throng and strode over to where the hotel manager and his clerks were briefing the Americans. Chief Lal Mohammed realized rank would soon be pulled. These were not army officers. Their closely-tailored uniforms were those of the Ministry of Interior police. They were Commander Taroon's men. The hair beneath their peaked hats was meticulously groomed, as were the thick black moustaches, bristling up from closely shaved cheeks and chins—the notorious affectation of devoted Afghan Communists. Clearly, these were two of Taroon's most senior officers. Whatever role Lal Mohammed and his men might perform, it would be on the instructions of these men, acting for the ruthless paramilitary arm of the PDPA regime.

Moments later, a third officer appeared, a tough looking character, also mustachioed, and with a sinister-looking scar on his right cheek. He wore civilian clothes, a suit. Mike whispered to Bruce, "It's Taroon's chief of staff, Major Saifuddin." Dangling from one of the major's hands was a large bag, a clear plastic one. Inside were canisters of some kind. "Tear gas," Chuck said.

Then another figure appeared before them, a specter of a man making his way through the uniformed horde with long, confident strides. He was slim and tall with a long black overcoat draped from his shoulders. A black, narrow brimmed hat, tipped low, all but concealed his blue eyes. These were deeply set and watchful, staring out from the man's pale face with a cold intensity. A Russian, the Americans realized; one that might have been sent by central casting. The figure crossed the room to where Taroon's officers were standing. The Afghans seemed to know the Russian well. They greeted him as if resuming an earlier conversation.

Taking in the scene, Mike couldn't help thinking of the *Spy vs. Spy* comic strip in Mad magazine. Was the Russian more than just another diplomat from the Soviet embassy? Was this the Soviets' intelligence service materializing before their eyes? The KGB? To Bruce Flatin, it was a secondary consideration. The Americans' priority was to insist every measure would be taken by the Afghan authorities to ensure Ambassador Dubs' safety. With Ghafari at his side to help translate, Bruce confronted Major Saifuddin. The major denied the government had any role in Spike's abduction. The Russian, as it happened, spoke some German, one of Bruce Flatin's languages. So, in German, English and Dari, the Americans stressed the need for calm, for caution in handling the situation. The Afghan officers nodded. We understand, they appeared to be saying. The Americans just stood there, a good deal less than reassured.

ACROSS TOWN, the telephone at the USAID dispensary rang just before 9:30 a.m. The embassy was on the line. Could Dr. Rotz please come to the phone immediately to speak with the deputy chief of mission? Lloyd's conversation with Bruce Amstutz was one he'll never forget. "He was calm but he said, 'Lloyd, the ambassador has been taken by armed men to the Hotel Kabul. We don't know why. I want you to go there and try to talk your way in. Take some help and medical supplies with you. Just in case.'"

Lloyd had to ask him to repeat the request. The call lasted less than a minute. Amstutz had other phones going and not a scrap more information to impart, other than that a number of embassy officers were already on the scene and ready to assist, should the need arise. Lloyd replaced the phone on its cradle. He took a deep breath, then summoned his team. He selected Marjie Yamamoto to come with him to the hotel; she was the nurse with the most critical care experience. Jeannene

Cramer and the others would stand by at the clinic to help out at Lloyd's direction. "Marjie grabbed an IV stand and some fluids. We jumped into the ambulance and headed across town."

Though they were driving into the unknown, at least Dr. Rotz and Nurse Yamamoto were in motion. Bernie Woerz and Jim Taylor were hitting one brick wall after another at the Ministry of Foreign Affairs. Bernie was unable to get past minister Amin's outer office. Instead, he was provided with a time-honored Afghan bureaucratic nicety. He should sit down, please. And wait. In the hours to come, Bernie would make repeated efforts to see the great man but to no avail. Finally, he returned to the embassy empty handed.

Jim Taylor didn't fare much better. True enough, he achieved the first objective set for him by DCM Amstutz: he was received by Amin's deputy, Shah Mohammed Dost. One of the more agreeable personalities in the Afghan Communist firmament, Dost assured Jim the minister would contact the U.S. embassy as soon as possible. All efforts would be made to secure the safe release of Ambassador Dubs. Taylor later wrote that Dost's expressions of support "were virtually meaningless" and left him with a sense of "complete futility." The reason: Dost's lack of political influence was well known among foreign diplomats in Kabul. His role was to deflect approaches from foreign envoys and, if possible, to block them entirely.

Checking in with Amstutz by radio, Taylor suggested he should go to the Ministry of Interior. It was time to find out what Commandant Taroon knew of the kidnapping, and what he intended to do about it. "In security matters, Taroon was second only to Amin. He was a rough customer, often described simply as a thug." However, this emergency, and any possible resolution of it, was in that particular thug's domain.

Meanwhile, the U.S. embassy's warden system was circulating an alert to the entire American community. Every residence and facility in the Afghan capital was equipped with a two-way radio. The handsets were to be kept switched on at all times and secured in their chargers. Each home or office was issued a call sign. Once a month, a Marine guard would work down the list to ensure everyone was contactable. Could they hear and be heard by central security? Anyone failing to respond to the test signal was reported to Chuck Boles, who would follow up with the offender.

The first alert was broad and general, since the Americans were still trying to determine the nature and gravity of the emergency. All personnel and family members should remain in their homes or places of work if possible. Police and troop movements were taking place in central Kabul, so no one should commute within the center until further notice.

Steve Rotz and his classmates knew something was up. "The whole mood in the school changed. The local workers made sure the gates were closed. They wouldn't open them for incoming traffic. We went into lockdown." Steve's classmate Mark Flatin was one of the first students to learn what was going on—and that his dad Bruce was involved. Mark's mother, Kay, was a teacher at the school. "She came to me and said: 'the ambassador's been kidnapped and taken to the Kabul Hotel—and your father is with him.' That was the first message she got. So we thought, oh no, does that mean he's been kidnapped too?" Only later in the day were they to learn Bruce had been sent to negotiate *after* Spike was taken.

One of the boys' teachers was Jim Gurnett, a Canadian who brought his family to Kabul in 1975. They had enjoyed three years of relative calm in Afghanistan, even hiking in remote countryside. Then came the Communist coup. They had been on alert ever since. "We had drills to be ready for emergencies like this. It was sometime after 10 a.m. we were told there was trouble at the Hotel Kabul. These were just vague reports, but it was decided everyone should head home. We had about 250 students, so getting them all on their buses wasn't a problem.

The school was evacuated by noon." Jim's own kids, one in kindergarten, the other a third grader, were among the last to leave. "I remember driving my motorbike home on the Darulaman Road, my two kids on the bike with me. After what we'd all gone through in the April '78 revolution, it wasn't surprising there was some kind of other disruption."

AT THE HOTEL KABUL, the Americans were joined by another embassy colleague, economic officer Jay Freres. Bruce Flatin noticed Jay had a notebook in hand, and asked him to start a log, a continuous record of events as they happened. In all the confusion, it was vital to document the developing crisis. Jay gazed around the lobby, wondering where to begin. Nobody seemed to be in command.

Still, the identities of a number of the senior officers had been established. The two smooth-looking Interior officers turned out to be Commander Taroon's executive secretary and the chief of the anti-smuggling unit, Yousuf Sahar. Taroon himself was nowhere in sight. As for the city police, the chief had left the scene. In his place, the head of the Criminal Investigation Division, Mohammed Andar, was now questioning members of the hotel staff in the lobby. Also nosing around was the Russian in the black coat. The Americans, as yet, had no way of knowing this man was Alexander S. Klushnikov, a declared officer of the Soviet KGB working within the Afghan interior ministry. In other words, a Soviet advisor to Commandant Taroon.

Despite all the bodies and noise, it seemed to the Americans that little was being accomplished in terms of resolving the crisis. Like the rest of the group, Mike Malinowski was growing more apprehensive. "Our priority was getting the ambassador to safety, number one. Then secondarily, if something went wrong and he was injured, we had to be able to take him to get medical care as quickly as possible."

That grim prospect became all too real when Lloyd Rotz and Marjie Yamamoto arrived. Lloyd carried a collapsible stretcher; Marjie was pushing an IV stand along before her. Tubes dangled from a bottle of plasma, swinging from a chrome hook atop the contraption. Its wheels squealed and scratched across the lobby floor. "When we got inside the hotel," Lloyd recalls, "Chuck Boles was assessing the situation with Bruce Flatin. And they asked me, 'Do you think the ambassador could withstand tear gas?' And I said 'Why are we talking about tear gas?'" The explanation was nearly as incomprehensible as it was frightful. A gang of armed men had seized Ambassador Dubs. Now a captive at gunpoint, he had been brought by his kidnappers to a place in walking distance from several Afghan police and army installations. Spike and his captors were now surrounded, cornered in an upstairs room with no telephone. The gang had no means to communicate their demands. And one of them had been caught after losing the key to their lair.

Taking all of this into account, anything was possible. The police or army might try to flush the culprits out with tear gas—despite Bruce Flatin's repeated appeals that no action be taken that might place the ambassador's safety in jeopardy. For the time being, they decided, the only course open to them was to head upstairs. Somehow, they had to get to their boss, to their friend, Spike Dubs.

Lloyd ordered Marjie to set up the IV in the lobby and wait there. Then the Americans worked their way through the horde of uniforms. Bruce Flatin, Mike Malinowski and Chuck Boles led the way, with Lloyd Rotz following along with the stretcher, and Jay Freres with his log.

SPIKE'S OFFICERS could only guess at the circumstances confronting their ambassador at that moment. In fact, the treatment meted out to him behind the door of room 117, and Spike's responses to his captors, have never been revealed in any meaningful detail. Yet the people who had come to know him best expected that Spike Dubs would use all his knowledge and interpersonal skills to make a connection, somehow, with the two men holding him. His State colleagues regarded him as exactly the kind of man to turn to in a deathly emergency. Spike wouldn't shy away from his abductors. He would respect the gun barrels pointed his direction, but would use reason to see past them. He would seek eye contact with the kidnappers, as direct and as prolonged as possible.

Tom Gouttierre shared many intense briefing sessions with Spike in Washington and Kabul. "I knew him to be ingenious and engaging. He was very much a take-charge guy. He would have tried every means that came to mind to get out of that mess–his captors with him, since they were trapped in that room, too." Spike's foreign service officers agree. As a captive, he had only his words to work with. He would have reached out to the kidnapper said by Gul Mohammed to speak halting English. Spike would have appealed to the kidnappers' own sense of survival. He would have tried to buy time, to persuade the gunmen he was their best hope of coming out of that room alive.

PART THREE

CHAPTER 7

RUNNING OUT OF TIME

ON THE OTHER side of the world, the graveyard shift in the State Department's 24-hour Operations Center was having difficulty getting Embassy Kabul on the phone. Several more flash cables had been received, dispelling any doubt that Spike's "arrest" could be anything other than an abduction. The ambassador was being held hostage by persons, and for a purpose, as yet unknown.

Night watch managers Leo Wallemborg and Jeffrey Buczacki notified the department's director of the Office for Combatting Terrorism, Anthony Quainton. Next, they contacted the staff assistants of the building's top floor "principals," including Cyrus Vance, the Secretary of State. Stirred from his sleep at home, Vance processed the news, then got out of bed and prepared to head in to the office. Before leaving home, he dictated a cable to Embassy Kabul, authorizing Amstutz to inform the PDPA regime's leadership, on express behalf of Secretary Vance, that no action be taken that might put Ambassador Dubs at risk.

Hurriedly, an Afghanistan working group was set up in the Operations Center to manage cable communications and to continue trying to connect with Kabul by phone. Tables were rearranged and phone lines shifted. Officers of the Bureau of Near Eastern and South Asian Affairs set up shop opposite the department's Afghanistan desk officers. A duty secretary was assigned to the group. All of these professionals were accustomed to keeping watch on an unruly, complex world. But no one was prepared for what happened next.

At 2:17 a.m. Washington time, a call came in from Dick Matson, the duty officer in the White House Situation Room. He told the State operations team: "We have another serious problem." Through unofficial channels, a request had been received from American personnel in Iran. All telegraph traffic should be halted to Embassy Tehran. The reason: an armed crowd had breached the compound's walls. The embassy was under attack.

At almost the same moment, the Operations Center's Iran working group answered a telephone call from Iran—on a public land line. A Marine guard was calling in. Embassy Tehran, he told the ops team, was in danger of being overrun. In the background, gunfire could be heard.

The previous day, Ambassador Sullivan and his staff were warned of dire consequences if they failed to lower the embassy's American flag and replace it with the Iranian revolutionary banner. Now machineguns were raking the perimeter walls. Bursts of gunfire sounded over the Operations Center's loudspeakers. On the other side of the world, Embassy Tehran's 19 Marine guards were taking direct fire. Sullivan ordered the guards to lay down tear gas against any intruders and use their shotguns only if their lives were at stake. Then the ambassador directed the rest of his staff to prepare to destroy sensitive hardware and documents. An outpost of American diplomacy might soon go the way of the Alamo.

A THOUSAND MILES to the east, in Kabul, it was well after 10 in the morning. The kidnapping crisis was into its second hour. Bruce Amstutz paced the floor, stopping now and then to stare out his office window in the direction of the Hotel Kabul. The pressure was becoming unbearable. He was the point man of the American response to the emergency. Spike's life was in the balance. Yet his attempts to make contact with the local authorities had come to nothing. Now a sickly wave of desperation was washing over him, a sense of helplessness. But he could not give in, he must not falter. He was Spike's deputy; it was his leadership the embassy's staff were relying upon now.

He dictated another cable to Washington, suggesting an expert in hostage negotiation be rushed to Kabul. "The terrorists," he advised, "could be holed up with Ambassador Dubs for days." Then Amstutz continued deploying his officers. He got Doug Wankel on the phone. The DEA agent should link up with his CIA counterpart, Warren Marik, and get over to the hotel at once. Together, the two big men would lend considerable muscle to the American presence. They would also bring unique skill sets to the most urgent task at hand, namely ensuring their ambassador's well-being.

By this time, Jim Taylor, too, was redoubling his efforts on Spike's behalf. He breezed into the Communist regime's imposing Ministry of Interior building and made his way upstairs. Taylor knew the narrow halls and passageways from previous visits. Hostile glares from uniformed men greeted him as he passed, but no one attempted to stop him. Soon enough, there he was again, crossing the threshold of the outer office of Sayed Daoud Taroon, Commandant of the regime's secret police.

The room was filled with men in uniform. Some sat behind desks, others stood guard. All were wearing side-arms and the guards had rifles slung over their shoulders. One of these paramilitaries advanced on Taylor, blocking his path to the door on the far side of the office, a door adorned with plush black leather, crisscrossed in gold-colored studs. Taylor asked to see the commandant. It was an emergency. One of the seated officers motioned to an empty chair. Sit down and wait, the gesture said. Commandant Taroon, he explained, "is busy with the situation."

For a moment, Jim weighed trying to barge his way past the guards, but he thought better of it. "Taroon was known to have even more heavily armed bodyguards with him at all times. I had no choice but to give a hastily-written version of the U.S. position to one of the receptionists..."

This proved helpful, at least in better understanding what Taroon was up to behind that tacky, ostentatious door. Because when the desk officer went through to deliver Taylor's message, the American caught a quick glimpse inside. Taroon was seated at his desk, holding a radio headset to his ear. Beside him was a tall man, a foreigner in a black suit. He was hovering over Taroon, hectoring him. Aside from the few words Taylor overheard, the foreigner's clothing and pale complexion left little doubt about his nationality. Taroon was indeed "busy with the situation"—busy in the company of a Russian diplomat, or intelligence officer, from the Soviet embassy.

AT THE HOTEL, Chuck Boles saw something, or someone, that made him check his watch and take note of the time. It was 10:25 a.m. Coming the Americans' way, up the stairs from the lobby, was one of his opposite numbers in Kabul's diplomatic community: the security officer of the embassy of the Union of Soviet Socialist Republics. Unlike Chuck, who was strictly a State Department employee, Lt. Col. Sergei Bakhturin was a senior officer in the KGB. His day job was spying. "We had met at various diplomatic functions. He spoke good English and was easy going. We got to be on a first name basis. He wasn't aloof at all. Just a smooth operator, real smooth. A guy you wanted to beware of."

Bakhturin wore his trademark black leather coat, mid-length and belted at the waist. His greying hair was crowned by a fedora-like hat, also black. The hat was followed, one after the other, by no fewer than three others almost identical to it. Because trailing Bakhturin on the stairs was the tall Russian,

Klushnikov, plus two other Soviets wearing nearly identical overcoats and headgear. Might as well be uniforms, Mike was thinking as the quartet reached the second floor foyer. "It was just so obvious they were KGB. But we noticed right away that just the sight of these guys seemed to settle the Afghans down. There had been so much chaos to this point, we had been worried that people might start shooting by mistake, or dropping weapons and having them go off. So at first we hoped having the Soviets on the scene might be helpful."

One of the four Russians was a good deal shorter than the others. This man was carrying a duffle bag, large and heavy-looking. He had to step quickly to keep up with Bakhturin and the others. Unknown to the Americans, this was Major Yuri I. Kutepov of the KGB, code name "Krabs." Kutepov was a weapons specialist of the KGB's Ninth Directorate. Declared to the Afghan regime, his cover in the foreign diplomatic community was second secretary at the Soviet embassy. In reality, he was in charge of security for the Afghan regime's leaders, including Taraki and Amin. Kutepov's duffle emitted a dull clicking sound, metal upon metal, with each of his hurried steps. The Soviets filed past the Americans without a word and continued down the corridor towards Taroon's officers, who had staked out the door to room 117. Warily, the Soviets traversed the empty space in front of the doorway. Then they formed a huddle with their Afghan counterparts, keeping their voices to a low murmur, as if the kidnappers might be listening through the keyhole.

By this time, the Americans had received word from the embassy about Secretary Vance's instructions. Bruce Flatin decided there was no time to waste. He strode down the hall and interrupted Bakhturin in mid-sentence. Bruce introduced himself, then cautioned both the Soviets and Afghans: under no circumstances should anything be done that might place Ambassador Dubs in danger. "This was the theme we repeated all morning. I kept telling the police that our embassy was trying to reach Hafizullah Amin with a special message from Secretary of State Vance, urging that there be no precipitous action."

Bakhturin listened politely, then turned on the charm. He claimed he and his "security associates" were there simply to assist the Afghan authorities. No one had any intention of taking drastic measures. The Russian seemed sincere. Bruce felt Vance's message had been received and understood. "I was assured by the Afghans and the Soviets that they would not endanger the ambassador, (that) they were going to do their best to negotiate." Later, Flatin advised Washington in a cable that Bakhturin "promised that he would personally defend the ambassador with his own life." Still, he wrote: "I also got the impression that one of Bakhturin's principal jobs was to watch us and clam us." In other words, contain the Americans; keep them out of the way.

Bakhturin next turned his attentions to another pressing duty. International incidents aside, he was also the Soviet embassy's security chief. A good many Soviet citizens were guests of the Hotel Kabul on that day. The place was favored by visitors who couldn't afford to stay at the newer Intercontinental on the capital's western outskirts. Among the Russian nationals were several senior officials from Moscow. And so, armed with a list prepared by the front desk, Bakhturin and one of his men went to each floor and wing of the building, asking Soviet passport holders to leave at once. Embarrassingly, the only snag the KGB duo encountered was adjacent to room 117. Bakhturin had to knock repeatedly to get a response from the person inside: the wife of a Communist party functionary. Her husband had reported for work earlier that morning at the Soviet embassy, so she was alone in the room. The woman refused to open the door, despite the KGB officer's pleas. She had heard all the commotion. With armed men in the building, she wasn't going anywhere.

Bakhturin was reduced to ordering a group of Afghan officers to move closer, shielding the farcical scene from the view of the Americans further down the hall. After some time, he was able to reassure the frightened woman. She opened the door and was swiftly evacuated down a rear stairway. She joined scores of other Russian guests, pushing and elbowing through the armed camp in the main lobby. Many of the unhappy evacuees were weighed down by holdalls and suitcases stuffed with clothing and tobacco and electronic devices, purchases from Kabul's bazaars, treasures they could seldom find at home in Russia. The exodus of civilians underway, Bakhturin was finally able to return to the second floor—and to his true professional calling: spycraft.

AS CONFUSION reigned at the Hotel Kabul, the State operations team in Washington was coping with multiple quandaries. The Iran and Afghanistan working groups were scrambling to handle competing emergencies, both aggravated by intermittent, often unintelligible communications. For a time, in those anxious early morning hours, the Carter administration's top foreign affairs officials were forced to consider if there might be a connection between the storming of Embassy Tehran and Spike Dubs' kidnapping in Kabul. The last thing the operations teams needed were still more conundrums to decipher. Yet there was no way, at that early stage, to simply dismiss the possibility that the crises were commingling, not just coincidental.

By 2:30 a.m. one breakthrough had been achieved: establishing a telephone connection to Embassy Kabul's communications vault. Trouble was, the line was weak, all but drowned out by waves of static and distorted noise. Shouting from either end proved useless. Still, the line was kept open, and from time to time voice messages were passably audible. As well, the State operations team took heart from one of DCM Amstutz's recent cables from Kabul. This stated that the Afghan regime officials at the hotel had expressed no intention of storming the room where the ambassador was being held.

The department's anti-terrorism chief, Anthony Quainton, was now at work in the operations center. His team was in the early stages of identifying and dispatching a seasoned hostage negotiator to Kabul. Quainton also contacted the Pentagon to see if the Defense Department's aircraft and pilots based in Islamabad could stand by in the event they were needed. As well, he directed the Afghan working group to contact Spike's wife. This was a tough assignment. It was a cold winter's night, many hours before dawn. Stirring Mary Ann Dubs from a deep sleep, the State officers could tell her little more than her husband had been kidnapped and was being held hostage. The place was surrounded and there was no reason to believe any harm had come to him. The news, they could tell, hit Mrs. Dubs very hard. She asked to be kept informed. Then she reached out to Spike's daughter, Lindsay.

"I received a phone call, I can't remember exactly when, sometime in the middle of the night. Mary Ann was very upset, and she said, 'oh, they've kidnapped your father.' That was stunning news to try to absorb, and of course we knew nothing more. That's all she was able to tell me. And so, I put down the phone. I was kind of numb and stunned." Lindsay had already been on edge. The previous evening, she had gone to see a movie with friends. It was the political thriller directed by Costa-Gravas, State of Siege. The film was based on the 1970 kidnapping and murder of a U.S. embassy official in Uruguay, Dan Mitrione.

Spike had always made an effort to be frank with Lindsay about the dangers posed by representing the United States far from home. Six years earlier, the American Ambassador to Sudan, Cleo Noel, was abducted and killed by terrorists. In a letter to Lindsay on March 3, 1973, he wrote: "...we cannot afford to give in to the ransom demands made by thugs who direct such organizations as the Black September Group. I personally don't like to think of being any kind of a martyr; but if I were ever taken in a situation such as that which occurred in Khartoum, I would want Washington to understand that I would rather sacrifice my life than to have someone capitulate to the demands of terrorists."

IN KABUL, it was 11:15 a.m. on Valentine's Day, 1979. Chuck Boles and Bruce Flatin were in the main floor lobby of the Hotel Kabul. An Afghan officer had just told them a policeman in the bank across the street had been able to get a brief look through the window of room 117. The ambassador appeared to be all right. Now the Americans were searching for a quiet corner to confer by radio with the embassy, someplace out of earshot of the Afghan and Soviet officers crowded into the corridor upstairs near room 117. Soon, however, Col. Bakhturin came stalking their way. "What languages does your ambassador know besides English?" he asked.

Bruce Flatin replied that Russian was Ambassador Dubs' most fluent foreign language, but he also spoke and understood German very well. "Do you know German?" Bakhturin asked. Flatin answered yes. At this, the KGB officer headed back upstairs. Bruce and Chuck managed a brief radio exchange with the embassy, but they had to cut this short when a plainclothes Afghan police officer approached. Flatin recognized him. It was a policeman by the name of Azizi, who years earlier had been assigned to protect a previous U.S. ambassador. Azizi asked Flatin to come back upstairs. "He said we'd like to have you talk to your ambassador in German so that the people inside the room will not be able to understand what's being said."

Flatin agreed and they headed for the stairway. In the

foyer upstairs they passed Jay Freres, writing an entry in his notebook. Mike stood nearby with Lloyd Rotz, holding the stretcher. Proceeding down the hallway, Flatin noticed the door was open to the room next to 117. He asked Azizi if he should try to speak through the wall of the adjoining room. The policeman told him, "No, it's best if you talk right through the door into the suite where the ambassador is being held."

Flatin took a deep breath. He stepped into no-man's-land, closer to the solitary, silent doorway. Bakhturin was nearby with his men, watching. Bruce turned to the door, his eyes level with the three brass numbers, 117. Then he looked at the doorknob, and the keyhole just above it. "I could imagine myself swallowing a bunch of bullets. I knelt by the keyhole, and I said in German, 'Good morning, Mr. Ambassador. How is it with you?'"

Spike's voice came back to him. It was clear but strained. "Mir geht es gut." I am all right. Azizi whispered in Flatin's ear: "Now ask him what kind of weapons they have." Bruce thought a moment, then asked: "Welche Waffen haben sie?"

Spike answered. But his response included the words "pistole" and "revolver." Even in perfectly accented German, this gave the game away. "Stop this conversation!" a voice shouted from inside the room. "We won't stand for any tricks. There'll be no further conversation."

Now Azizi began appealing to the kidnappers through the door. Let's keep the conversation going, he shouted. In response, only silence. The aborted keyhole exchange would stand as the one and only time one of the captors' voices was heard by a representative of the United States government.

Bruce returned to the American end of the corridor. Taroon's officers followed him, with Bakhturin in tow. Major Saifuddin told Bruce Flatin: "Tell your ambassador that exactly ten minutes from now he's either to try to go to the bathroom, or he is to fall to the floor." Flatin was dumbstruck. "I replied,

'Just a minute, I want to talk to you elsewhere.' So we went down to a cross hallway where I said, 'We've spent the whole morning telling you that we don't want any precipitous action here, and you're now telling me to help you light a fuse that's going to go off in exactly ten minutes?' I said, 'I want to repeat once again that we're trying to find Foreign Minister Amin to deliver an urgent request from Secretary Vance that there be no attack on this room.'"

Saifuddin shrugged his shoulders. "I have my orders," he said. At this, Flatin turned to Bakhturin. "Once again, I want to tell you we don't want any precipitous action here." Bakhturin nodded and steered Major Saifuddin towards room 117, speaking quietly into the Afghan's ear as they made their way down the corridor. This led Flatin to believe he had bought more time. He would soon discover this would be measured in minutes, not hours.

IT WAS 11:45 a.m. in Kabul when Doug eased his green and white Land Cruiser to a stop at the police cordon blocking access to the Hotel Kabul. Warren Marik was in the passenger seat beside him. Armed officers rebuffed their attempts to get the vehicle any closer, so Doug found a parking space and the two men walked the rest of the way. Approaching the hotel's entrance, they spotted movement on the building across the street. A squad of uniformed riflemen, regime soldiers, were jostling for elbow room on a cramped balcony, just below and to the left of a sign reading "Da Afghanistan Bank." On the sidewalk in front of the hotel, some firemen and soldiers were standing by with a ladder. They looked confused and uneasy, as men do when they discover the orders they've been given have no chance of success.

Entering the lobby, the two Americans were challenged by Taroon's officers. This time, Doug and Warren were able to talk their way through. They made their way upstairs. Doug found himself dodging bodies rushing his way. "Soon as we reached the second floor, as I round the corner there, I see a guy, an Afghan, being dragged down the hall by two Afghan police officers. And they're whipping on him pretty good, kicking him and he's yelling. And they dragged him down the stairs and out of sight."

Chuck Boles filled in Doug and Warren about the prisoner's misadventure with the room key. They all agreed that taking one of the kidnappers alive was progress, but that's where the good news ended. Before them, the second floor corridor looked like an armed showdown.

Crowds of uniformed men were drawn up on either side of room 117. In front of that door and for several feet on either side was an empty space, a kind of no-man's-land. From the foyer end of the hallway, the Americans looked out over the heads of the Afghan troops and police gathered around them, and across no-man's-land to the soldiers on the other side. Prominent among those troops were Bakhturin and his KGB team. It was a classic Cold War set piece, a standoff in a drafty old hotel in Nowheresville, Southwest Asia. Americans on one side, Soviets on the other, with the Russians' Afghan proxy forces scattered throughout.

Doug realized the Embassy Kabul team had few options. "We just knew that we needed to try and communicate, talk to the men holding the ambassador. Drag this thing as much as we could, see what we could find out." But how to communicate? So far, neither Taroon's men nor their army counterparts had taken any measures to get a telephone or radio into the room. The only exchanges going on were among the Russians and the Afghan regime's officers, along with radio chatter in Dari, which the Americans presumed were communications from police and army headquarters. The old hotel was claustrophobic and dark—the police had ordered the hotel's power to be cut. "There was a sense of helplessness and frustration to some degree, because we did not feel that we had control. We didn't feel we had the authority, or the ability to take charge to do something. The Russians made it clear: they were there, and they were talking, huddling with the Afghan authorities. Whatever action that was going to be taken, it was up to them.

"No-one was talking to the Americans from the Russian/ Afghan side. There was no attempt to invite ideas, opinions, thoughts or wishes, anything that we wanted. At the same time, you had the sense that these Russian guys were also on radios or telephones, getting something as well from their leaders, somewhere in Kabul. There was a lot of that going on, but there wasn't a meshing of communications at all."

A MILE OR SO from the hotel, in the anteroom of Commandant Taroon's headquarters, Jim Taylor was enduring the same communications blackout. His vigil outside the secret police chief's office had gone on for more than two hours. Several times he had prevailed on Taroon's guards to take his written messages into their boss. Each time the leather-clad door swung open and closed, he caught sight of Taroon and the smartly-dressed Russian leaning over him. "I could hear constant radio chatter from Taroon's office," Taylor later recalled, "and several voices responding as Taroon directed the actions of his security forces at the hotel."

Elsewhere in Kabul, preparations were well underway in case the unthinkable should happen, namely that Spike Dubs would fall victim to some kind of injury. Immediately after Dr. Rotz and Marjie Yamamoto left the dispensary for the hotel, Jeannene Cramer and her colleagues went into action. "When we're at a post like Kabul without a ready blood supply, we had what we called a walk-in blood bank. Of course we had the ambassador's blood type, so we got ready." The call went out among the American community. Within two hours, three units of blood were at the ready. Stephen Thomas, another

AID physician, took the blood and additional IV fluids over to the hotel, where he joined Marjie Yamamoto on standby in the lobby. The medical team hoped and prayed these steps would remain nothing more than contingencies.

Still, an unnerving air of apprehension was taking hold, not least inside the U.S. embassy complex. Very few people in the building were being briefed as the emergency unfolded. But it was clear that something major had disturbed the orderly conduct of the day's business. This began with the awkward postponement of the embassy's regular weekly meeting. Economic officer David Litt was among staffers who had gathered, at 9 a.m. sharp, in the big second floor conference room between the ambassador's and deputy chief's offices. But neither Ambassador Dubs nor DCM Amstutz had shown up. As usual, it was a fairly full house. There were staff in attendance from the political, economic and administrative sections, as well as defense, USAID and the Peace Corps. They all waited for a time, but when it became obvious the meeting was a scrub, everyone went back to work.

Only later in the morning did David Litt and the others learn there was some kind of incident underway at the Hotel Kabul, one that involved the ambassador. Then, at 11:30 a.m., David suddenly was brought into the loop. A caller was put through to his extension, a Belgian banker named Jean-Phillipe Briffaux, one of David's contacts in the capital's expat business community. In breathless, staccato phrases, Briffaux began relating the drama unfolding before his eyes. He was in his office at Da Afghanistan Bank, directly across the street from the hotel. On the sidewalk, near the hotel's front doors, were three Kabul city firemen wielding a ladder. With them were three soldiers, armed with assault rifles. It looked like they intended to position the ladder under one window in particular, the window of a room on the second floor.

David grabbed a pen and tried to keep up. Briffaux said he

would continue watching the scene until noon, when he had a meeting down the hall with the bank's governor. When the call ended, David immediately got the DCM's office on the line. Amstutz thanked him for the update.

Briffaux called again at five minutes past noon. The bank governor had cancelled their meeting. Things had changed outside in the street: the place was now deserted. There was no sign of the firemen. As for the army, there were now Afghan soldiers in the bank. Five of them, with AK-47s, were positioned on a balcony overlooking the street, not far from where Briffaux was standing. He estimated the balcony was at an offset of five to six windows' distance from that room on the hotel's second floor, at just about equal height.

David thanked Briffaux and asked him to stay on the line. Then he switched over to the DCM's assistant. She put David through to Amstutz and he relayed the latest information from the bank. A squad of riflemen, Amstutz reflected. At the ready, but for what? Could it be possible the regime's leadership was simply ignoring the Americans' repeated appeals for caution, for buying time, for seeking a peaceful resolution to the crisis? Amstutz had only just received word his most recent cable had reached Washington. In it, he reported Flatin's account of the assurances given by the Soviet and Afghan officers at the hotel, that force of arms was not an option. Now he would have to send an update to DC. Because room 117 of the Hotel Kabul was in the crosshairs. It was targeted, from inside and out.

Chapter 8

The KGB's Order to Fire

In the State Department's Washington operations center, the local time was now 3 a.m. The officers in the Iran working group were scrambling. The phone line they had been keeping open to Embassy Tehran had gone dead—just as Secretary of State Cyrus Vance arrived on the floor. The two working groups briefed him, one after the other. The situation in Iran, already out of control, had now gone dark. Embassy Kabul, meantime, had still not communicated with the Afghan Communist leadership. True, a measure of reassurance had come from the police. DCM Amstutz's most recent cable reported that "Commandant Taroon informed us by telephone they have no intention to break into the room by force." The Afghans, the cable went on, would "do everything possible to get him released unharmed." Trouble was, Taroon's promise was belied by the evidence on the ground. The kidnappers' lair was now ringed on all sides by a deployment of armed forces that continued to grow in size and armament.

Vance conferred briefly with his deputy, Warren Christopher. They decided to summon Anthony Quainton, their counter terrorism officer. Quainton was to continue his search for a hostage negotiator. He must also solve this puzzle: in the void of communications with the Afghan regime's most senior leaders, how might Embassy Kabul be assisted in playing for time? Was there some way to draw out the standoff at the hotel? This might give President Carter an opportunity to engage the Soviets and Afghans directly. The Americans hoped additional time would create more options.

Vance then headed to his office to call the White House. He could wait no longer to wake the president and break the bad news on both fronts. On his way out the door, he ordered the Iran desk to get through to Khomeini's headquarters in Tehran. Political officer Dave Patterson was already doing just that, seeking assistance from the Iranian spiritual leader's staff. Vance also had a final instruction for the Afghan working group. Get another message through to the embassy. Re-emphasize our demand: nothing is to be done to endanger Ambassador Dubs.

The officers on the Afghan desk complied. They succeeded in getting the Secretary's message through over the phone. Embassy Kabul, in turn, relayed the communication to the foreign ministry, but only to the lowly Shah Mohammed Dost. Minister Amin, the Americans were told, was too busy with the Iraqi Foreign Minister to come to the phone. Embassy Kabul was unable to confirm any senior authority in the PDPA regime had received Secretary Vance's appeals. Not that morning, nor for the rest of the day.

ON THE SECOND FLOOR of the hotel, the Americans sensed a heightened tension among the Afghan soldiers and police. Bakhturin strode down the hallway to where Bruce Flatin was standing. Leaning close, speaking in a low voice, the Russian said the police had informed him the kidnappers had set a 1 p.m. deadline. For what, Bruce asked? A deadline for what, exactly? There were no demands on the table, no negotiations under way. How could there be, since there had been absolutely nothing in the way of communications, direct or otherwise, between the men holding Spike and any U.S. official or authority. Bakhturin offered nothing by way of explanation.

Instead, the Russian spy gestured towards Lloyd Rotz. By now the doctor had opened the stretcher to its full width and was holding it upright at his side. "Please have your medical personnel at the ready," Bakhturin said. "The matter is out of our hands."

The Russian backed away and rejoined his men. As he did so, Taroon's executive officer was handed a photograph of Spike Dubs by one of his men, an undercover cop in civilian clothes. The officer began showing the picture to the soldiers positioned closest to room 117. Doug and the other Americans didn't like what they were seeing. "We were just there on the periphery, we were witnesses, we were bystanders. Our pleas for going easy, for restraint—they just weren't hearing it. There was no room for discussion, it's final."

They watched as three Afghan soldiers emerged from the crowd on the Soviet side of no-man's-land. The men wore helmets and flak jackets. All three held AK-47s, and held them in a way that made it obvious they intended to use the weapons, and soon. Taroon's executive officer displayed Spike's photograph to each man in the trio. Were these commandos some kind of breach squad, the Americans wondered? What were they going to do, just burst into the room with rifles blazing? Then something else caught Lloyd's attention. "We saw this plainclothes Afghan officer show up again, speaking broken English. He was the guy who brought the black and white photograph of the ambassador. Now I saw that same officer talking with the Soviets."

Chuck was at Lloyd's side. Both men watched as the tall KGB officer waited for the shorter spy beside him to fish an object out of the duffle bag. It was a handgun, a small pistol. The tall Russian took it into both his hands and turned to the plainclothes Afghan Interior policeman. Chuck got a good look at the weapon. "The pistol's an automatic. It loads from the bottom, with a sliding magazine. The Soviet loaded it. Then he cocked it and put a round in the chamber. And he gave it to the Afghan."

From where Doug was standing, he couldn't make out whether the tall KGB officer had armed the pistol. But he, too, saw the Russian pass the weapon to the Afghan secret policeman. Then the man vanished into the crowd of uniforms on the far side of room 117. Mike Malinowski witnessed the handoff as well and saw other hardware being pulled from the short Russian's duffle bag. "He was a much younger guy, very pale faced. It looked like he had percussion grenades, or something else very heavy in that bag. He gave the bag to his senior officer, who then distributed the items to the Afghan commandoes."

At this point, with the clock approaching 12:50 p.m. Kabul time, one of the three flak jacketed soldiers knelt on the floor. He stretched out into a prone position, immediately in front of room 117, and levelled his rifle at the door. As he did so, the other two commandos positioned themselves on either side of the doorway. They pressed their backs to the wall and held their rifles at the ready. Waiting now, all the commandos fixed their eyes on the same figure in the black leather coat: Lt. Col. Sergei Bakhturin. The Russian gestured to the men with one open hand. "Hold there," he seemed to be signaling. Then Bakhturin swiftly crossed no-man's-land towards the Americans.

"He comes over to us and says 'We are going to rescue your ambassador now,'" Doug says. "And we're going, 'no, no, no.'" Bakhturin was ready with his reply. "We are in charge. We're going to send some of the Afghan people in to rescue your ambassador. So please stand back." Then he breezed by and made his way to the window of the foyer. From there, Bakhturin could see the bank building opposite the hotel. And, with a wave, he ensured the riflemen on the balcony could see him as well.

Horrified, Mike saw what happened next. "Bakhturin stood at the window with a handkerchief in his hand. It was obvious he was going to give the order for the operation to begin." Across the street, the troops on the balcony trained their rifles on the window of room 117. Then their eyes turned to the right, to the larger window directly opposite them. They were watching the white handkerchief, hanging from Bakhturin's hand.

THEN IT BEGAN. The gloomy tension in the hotel corridor was pierced by a shrill command, shouted in Russian. At this, one of the standing commandos spun round to face room 117. With one great heave of his boot, he kicked the door open. Then he leapt back out of the way, taking cover against the wall. The prone commando opened fire into the doorway, unleashing an explosion of sound and flame.

At the same instant, thirty feet up the corridor, Bakhturin's arm swept downward. Now five more Kalashnikovs began firing on full automatic from the bank balcony. Everyone in the hallway–American, Soviet, Afghan–threw themselves to the floor. The noise was concussive, beyond deafening. The floor quaked; the entire building was shaking. Mike felt the breath being forced from his lungs. "The firing went on and on, and my feeling was there were so many bullets going in it was hard to imagine anybody was going to be alive when this was over."

The prone commando got to his feet, changed magazines and charged the open door, firing as he advanced. The other commandos followed, vanishing into the smoke billowing from the room. Meantime, Bruce Flatin had his face pressed to the floor, sheltering his head with both hands. He looked at his wristwatch, inches from his eyes. "The floor just shook with the gunfire... When the whole thing was over there could not have been one cubic centimeter in that room that didn't have a bullet pass through it. A gnat flying in that room would have been hit." He checked his watch again. It had gone on for 40 seconds–the combined fire of eight AK-47 assault rifles.

In Doug's estimation, the firestorm was shorter in duration.

"I don't think it was 40 seconds, but it was a long time. Perhaps 15 seconds. Which if you think about it, and I've been at a few shootings as a law enforcement officer, and I can tell you that if you have 15 seconds of semi-automatic or automatic gunfire, that's a lot. A lot of gunfire." Their ears ringing, the Americans took in the scene in the corridor. Smoke wafted through the door of room 117 and floated out above the huddled bodies on the hallway floor. Then shadows emerged, figures stumbling through the doorway. "I saw the three guys come backing out of the room," Doug says. "One of them was crying, he was obviously very upset, distressed by what he had participated in, by what he had seen."

Slowly, the Americans got to their feet. They stood together as a group: Mike, Doug and Chuck, with Warren Marik and Lloyd Rotz holding the stretcher between them. Bruce Flatin and Jay Freres stepped aside, clearing the way for the stretcher bearers. "We had decided to get into that room as quickly as possible, whenever the circumstances allowed," Mike says. "We wanted to give the ambassador the best chance to get out of this. We were all poised like a relay team..."

For a long moment, their eyes searched into the smoky gloom of the corridor. The Soviets and Afghans beyond the room were still crouched low to the floor. Some of them were coughing. The weeping commando continued to wail as his comrades dragged him off to the far end of the building.

Lloyd held out the stretcher. It was time to move. Mike, Doug and Warren each found a free handle. Chuck led the way, with the stretcher bearers falling in behind him. They were running, now, but the 30 feet they had to cover looked like a country mile. "Thank God the people I was with were all strong officers," Mike says. "I mean, we helped each other out. And I remember going down that hallway, and just yelling: "Let's go let's go let's go!"

They had taken only a few strides when more gunfire

sounded. They stopped cold.

"We heard: 'pop pop pop, pop pop,'" Lloyd says. "The words just came out of my mouth—the only thing I could think of saying was, 'Tell 'em to stop shooting, there won't be anyone left alive!'"

Mike froze on the spot, waiting to see if anything else was going to follow those four or five phantom gunshots. "They were small caliber shots, not as loud as the rifle fire, but coming from the room. We were frightened as it was. What else was waiting for us in there? We were worried that we'd walk into that hotel room and get blown up. But we stopped for just a couple of seconds. We knew we had to keep going. The ambassador was in there."

They all leaned into it again, charging for the door. Chuck was now ahead of the four stretcher bearers by two or three paces. Dense blue smoke billowed out to meet him, full in the face. He turned left, into the open doorway, and took a tentative first step inside. Before him was a small space, a dressing area with coat hooks on the wall. The main bedroom was still somewhere ahead, down a short passageway.

Something moved to his right. Chuck turned his head in time to get a good look at him, the lone figure, framed by another doorway. It was the entrance to the bathroom, Chuck realized. There was no mistaking the man standing there. It was the Afghan secret policeman, the plainclothes cop who was given the pistol by the KGB officer. "It was him, all right, standing in the bathroom door." Chuck didn't have time to wonder when and how the man got there. He had only one priority, an urgent one: to locate Spike and get him the hell out of there. So he quickly turned to the left, turned away from the ghostly figure, who was stepping backward, disappearing into the darkness of the bathroom.

Now another obstacle lay in Chuck's path: the shattered remains of yet another interior door, one made of glass set into a metal frame. Mike and Doug were now on his heels, tilting the stretcher sideways to make it in from the corridor. They, too, noticed the bathroom on the right, but by now it was just a dark void; by the look of it, empty. Lloyd and Warren, following behind, struggled to see through the haze. Hot water was cascading underfoot from somewhere up ahead, and an eerie hissing sound, like rushing steam, filled the blinding space before them. Doug, by now at Chuck's side, was struggling to find a way forward. "The smoke, the gunsmoke was so acrid but also so intense that your eyes were watering, and you really couldn't see."

Lloyd found the choking fog getting thicker with each step forward. "There was that swinging door, half glass, and the glass had been shot out and was all over the floor. Then there was a short passage to the room itself. And with the gunfire, there was water all over the floor. The radiator had been hit, and it was gushing out all over the place."

"The room itself was extremely confusing," Mike says. "The rifle fire from across the street had shredded the drapes. Bullets had come right through the wall and struck the radiator pipes. The light was scattered, kind of stabbing into the smoke through the holes in the wall and those shredded curtains. The air was thick to breathe, painful to breathe."

Then, one by one, came the gruesome discoveries. Stumbling like blind men, the Americans came across the bodies of the two kidnappers. Mike felt them underfoot. "I can still remember the feeling of stepping on those bodies. It was awful. We had to step over them to go any further into the room." Finally, they made out a shape some 10 or 12 feet from them, near the back of the room, away from the window and the ruptured radiator. It was motionless, still as death. The five of them stared for a time, unable to speak. That shape was their leader, their friend. Spike Dubs.

"The ambassador was sitting upright in a straight-back

wooden chair next to the bed," Lloyd says. The men rushed forward. Spike was slumped forward but not tied up or restrained in any way. "I mean I took one look at him and thought, he's dead. There was no movement from him whatsoever. No response."

Doug's heart sank. "I knew he was dead. He was shot in the head, shot in the chest. It was pretty obvious he was dead." Still, the team didn't give up. Silently, they lifted Spike's body onto the stretcher and rushed back the way they had come. They carried him over the bodies of the dead men, through the passage and shattered door, turning finally into the corridor. There, the Soviets and Afghans were back on their feet. They all stood there, motionless. The ambassador's body passed directly in front of Taroon's men, then three of the Soviet spies. At the top of the stairs, the body passed beneath the gaze of Sergei Bakhturin. The Russian took one look. Then he walked away, as if something more important needed his attention.

The Americans kept on moving, carrying the body down the stairway. Doug felt a profound sense of duty, binding them together. "It was important, at that point, for Ambassador Dubs, for his family, and for the United States, that we recover his remains, and treat the body with reverence and respect. So we all were very quiet, there wasn't much said. Everybody was just wanting to make sure that they did their piece, that they took care of Ambassador Dubs, got him to where he needed to be, where he would no longer be in harm's way."

When the stretcher team reached the ground floor lobby, Lloyd began searching over the heads of the soldiers and policemen gathered there. "I'm looking for Marjie and the IV stand and she wasn't there." Instead, the nurse and Dr. Thomas were waiting with the ambulance, where they had taken cover from the gunfire. The stretcher was eased into the back of the vehicle, with Lloyd scrambling in after it. In a desperate attempt to save Spike, he started cardiopulmonary resuscitation.

Above left: Hafizullah Amin, the Communist PDPA's ambitious Vice-Premier and Foreign Minister.
Right: Nur Mohammed Taraki, leader of the People's Democratic Party of Afghanistan and the first Communist President of Afghanistan.

Top: Soviet foreign minister Andrei Gromyko with his Afghan counterpart Hafizullah Amin in 1978.
Below: Gromyko and Soviet leader Leonid Brezhnev, right, receive Afghan President Taraki in Moscow.
Inset: Amin was notorious for his bellicose speeches.

Top: Hafizullah Amin, left, with the Soviet Union's Ambassador to Afghanistan, Alexander M. Puzanov, far right.
Bottom: Lt. Col. Sergei Bakhturin, left, with the KGB's Kabul rezident, Viliov Osadchy, and Commandant Syed Daoud Taroon, chief of the Afghan Communist regime's secret police.

Top: Sergei Bakhturin with KGB colleagues in Kabul, Afghanistan.
Bottom right: Bakhturin at a 1980 diplomatic reception in Kabul.
Bottom left: Viliov Osadchy, KGB rezident or station chief in Kabul.
Right background: Soviet Spetsnaz special forces soldier in Afghanistan.

Yuri V. Andropov served as Chairman of the Committee for State Security, the KGB, for some 15 years. He succeeded Leonid Brezhnev as Soviet leader.

Bottom: KGB Zenit special forces troops following Operation Storm-333.

Background: the KGB's Lubyanka headquarters.

The corridor outside room 117. "The Russians made it clear—whatever action was going to be taken, it was up to them."

ILLUSTRATION BY GREG BANNING

Communist regime soldiers take aim from a balcony across the street. A nearby sign reads *"Da Afghanistan Bank."*

ILLUSTRATION BY GREG BANNING

The KGB colonel could see the bank, and with a wave, he ensured the riflemen could see him as well.

ILLUSTRATION BY GREG BANNING

Arming the shooter. "The pistol's an automatic. The Soviet loaded it. And he gave it to the Afghan."

ILLUSTRATION BY GREG BANNING

The prone commando got to his feet, changed magazines and charged the open door, firing as he advanced. The other commandos followed.

ILLUSTRATION BY GREG BANNING

The shape before them was motionless, still as death. It was their leader, their friend. It was Spike Dubs.

ILLUSTRATION BY GREG BANNING

Jimmy Carter, the 39th President of the United States.
Carter with Secretary of State Cyrus Vance.
Zbigniew Brzezinski, Carter's National Security Advisor.

Thomas sensed there was little hope. "There was no pulse, no respirations, and both pupils were widely dilated and fixed." Still, Lloyd continued with chest compressions. This was Spike Dubs in his care, a United States ambassador. He had to keep trying, however slim the chances.

By this time, the rest of the American foreign service officers were gathered on the sidewalk, dazed and exhausted. They could see Lloyd through the side windows of the ambulance, working on Spike's chest, bending to give him breath, mouth-to-mouth. Chuck Boles climbed behind the wheel of the old Chevrolet wagon and it roared away from the curb. The others watched it round the far end of the hotel. Then it vanished into Pashtunistan Square, speeding to the southwest towards the dispensary.

MINUTES EARLIER at the interior ministry, Jim Taylor and Commandant Taroon's bodyguards heard a faint, dull rattle of gunfire in the distance. "As soon as it stopped, a man in civilian clothing—a Soviet as I believed then and so reported—emerged from Taroon's office. He turned at the door and spoke, in Russian, back into the office. He had been with Taroon for at least an hour and forty minutes."

Next, Taroon emerged with several bodyguards, all carrying AK-47s. The commandant and his men brushed past Taylor without a word. "When I caught up to him and asked what had happened, he replied, 'It is over.'" Taylor pursued Taroon all the way downstairs and out of the building. He asked the commandant to stop a moment and speak with him. "I'm too busy," came the reply. Then Taroon was ushered into the back seat of his black Volga. As he settled in, the commandant was handed a machine pistol by one of his men. Taroon rested it on his knees. Then he nodded to his driver and the car sped away.

AT THE HOTEL KABUL, the shooting was over and the

cover-up had begun. After watching the ambulance drive off, the Americans re-entered the hotel and went upstairs. Doug felt a sense of defeat washing over him. "You know, this was such a trauma for everyone, it was like a battlefield, a wartime setting or situation. We felt we had failed, I guess, to do what we needed to do, what we wanted to do, through no fault of our own. But nonetheless we did not achieve what we wanted the result to be, obviously."

Doug and Warren headed back into room 117 to take a better look at the place now the smoke was clearing. Going in, they stood aside as the bodies of the two kidnappers were dragged out into the corridor. Bruce Flatin was standing nearby. "Those two men, they were brought out and dumped at my feet. One was probably dead, and the other one looked definitely dead; they were taken away." The third man, however, captured and repeatedly beaten by the Afghan police, was still alive. "They put a brown bag over his head and took him away screaming and kicking. Then I went downstairs and saw the police official in charge and said, 'I just want you to know our Ambassador is dead.' He's the one who had kept assuring me that if anything happened there would be a very small chance of any problem. He said, 'I'm very sorry.' He did not sound very convincing."

The policeman named Azizi appeared, holding Spike's sport jacket and glasses. Bruce held out his hands, expecting the personal effects to be handed over. The tall Russian, Klushnikov, had other ideas. The items were needed for "police examination," he said. The Americans eventually succeeded in recovering the belongings. As well, Bruce had the presence of mind to pick up two shells lying on the floor, Kalashnikov rounds, one expended, the other live.

Mike and Warren, meantime, inspected the shattered room. An inch of water covered the floor. They found no weapons or bullet casings. As well as removing the kidnappers' bodies, the Afghan police had already swept the room for physical evidence. Doug noticed "seven to nine bullet penetrations" in the ceiling and wall near the position Spike's body was found. The angle of the holes suggested to him the bullets had been fired by the riflemen across the street.

All the Americans knew for sure was that nothing about the scene made sense. Spike was found seated on a chair, unbound. There were no signs of a struggle, or any indication he had tried to take cover once the shooting started. Did this mean the ambassador was shot at the outset of the shooting? At the time, Doug thought so. Yet it was the regime's Kalashnikovs, all eight of them, that fired first. The force and fury of that storm of fire had cut down the two kidnappers where they stood. Their bodies were sprawled on the opposite side of the room from Spike. How could they have crossed the room when the shooting started, reached their captive and shot him repeatedly, then returned to the other side of the room to die? It seemed impossible.

The foreign service officers weren't the only Americans trying to make sense of the crime scene. Sandy Stiebel and her husband Mayer were tourists from Highland Park, Illinois. They'd been planning to check out of the Hotel Kabul that afternoon. Instead, they found themselves shuffled into a disused restaurant off the main floor lobby—and hitting the floor when the shooting started. Now they had luggage to retrieve, and a flight to make. Sandy ventured into the lobby in time to see the third man being hustled away. "He was brought down the stairs fighting and kept trying to raise a leg to kick one of his captors in the groin." Mayer, meantime, went up to get their bags. The stairs were a bloody mess. Smoke was still in the air. He looked into room 117 and saw shattered glass and bullet holes in the walls. "It was a demolished room afterward, filled with gunsmoke with a lot of blood on the floor."

IT WAS NEARLY 1:20 p.m. Kabul time when the ambulance

reached the AID compound and screeched to a stop in front of the dispensary. Hearing the commotion, Jeannene Cramer ran to the door. "When they came in, Dr. Rotz was helping carry the stretcher. He was just shaking his head. And he said, 'I think it's too late, his pupils are blown.' But we rushed upstairs to the operating room because we had to try. We knew we had to try to resuscitate the ambassador."

Feverishly, Lloyd continued doing CPR. "Really, there was no question, Spike was unresponsive. And looking at him, it looked like the killing wound was a bullet wound in his chest. He had a sweater on, and there was blood right over his heart area. Oddly enough there was almost no bleeding from his head." The team removed Spike's sweater and shirt, both soaked in what they assumed was blood. Lloyd inserted a large-bore IV catheter under the clavicle and persisted with CPR. Jeannene watched for signs of life. "I remember Chuck Boles at one point came over to me and asked if the ambassador was coming around, or if he was going to make it. Because when Dr. Rotz did the chest compressions, you could see it on the monitors. I think Chuck knew. He must have known that it was over. But he was hoping."

He certainly was. But the looks on Lloyd's and Jeannene's faces finally convinced Chuck he could wait no longer. He left the room and spoke quietly into the two-way radio, reporting in to Bruce Amstutz. "There's nothing more they can do. The ambassador is dead."

As a nurse, Jeannene found herself having to take a step back from the tragic reality before her. She couldn't allow her personal feelings to inhibit her effectiveness as an emergency caregiver. "I was just doing what needed to be done, and kind of removing myself at the time. You just kind of dissociate yourself. This isn't someone you know, that you had just spoken to yesterday. This is a person who needs your help. You just keep doing what you have to do. Later, it just kind of all hit me. It was hard. It was very hard."

A floor below the procedure room, the dispensary's staffers were dealing with another potential crisis, one taking shape just outside the front door. A squad of regime soldiers had come onto the compound. Several of the AID workers blocked the building's entrance. They asked what the troops were after. The answer seemed unfathomable. The Afghan Communist regime was after Spike's remains. The body, an Afghan officer stated, should be turned over at once. It was "evidence," necessary for the forthcoming police investigation.

The soldiers' demands were relayed by phone to Embassy Kabul. Amstutz and his officers could scarcely believe it. These were the same regime "authorities" who had refused, throughout that horrible day, to communicate, much less consult. U.S. Marine guards were sent across town to order the Afghan troops off the AID compound. The regime was trespassing, a flagrant breach of diplomatic protocol. It was, in every sense, an affront beyond belief. The Communist regime was actually seeking to kidnap Spike Dubs all over again.

IT WAS SHORTLY after 3:30 a.m. in Washington when a cable came through stating an armed assault had been staged on room 117. "FLASH: Hotel group reports that break in is scheduled in one minute" the message began, followed immediately by "FLASH: They went in and firing is over."

Just minutes earlier, the State operations team learned Embassy Tehran had been completely overrun. The clock was nearing 4 a.m. when a voice could be heard from the adjacent Office for Combatting Terrorism, Quainton's office. The voice loudly called out: "The ambassador is wounded?" The staffers realized this was being shouted down the phone link to Kabul. The voice repeated the question. Then this: "You say the ambassador is seriously wounded?" There was a long pause. Then a statement, not a question; one pronounced slowly, and with some difficulty. "The ambassador is dead."

A few minutes later, the telex machine clattered out a confirmation from Embassy Kabul. Spike Dubs was gone. Cyrus Vance was informed. He called the White House to tell the president his envoy to Afghanistan had been killed. Jimmy Carter had only a few minutes to process the news. Once again, the crisis in Iran intervened, this time with a degree of promise. Khomeini's people were promising to do everything possible for the Americans in Embassy Tehran. Word reached the State operations center that the Ayatollah's deputy prime minister had shown up at the embassy with a megaphone, ordering the attacking mob to leave the compound. At 5:00 a.m. Washington time, the Pentagon was able to inform the president that Khomeini's forces had retaken the embassy. Two Iranian embassy employees were dead, and a Marine guard was wounded. But the Americans had been saved.

The president's relief on that front was short lived. In Kabul, another imperative needed to be addressed, a sad one: what to do with Spike's remains. Carter directed Vance to have the body repatriated to Washington without delay. Quainton's office was to transition from rescue to recovery. The mission would be flown by one of the U.S. Air Force's blue and white 707 jetliners, the aircraft used by the president and vice-president. It fell to Quainton to break the terrible news to the ambassador's family. Once again, his office contacted Mary Ann by phone. And once again it was left to her to inform Lindsay.

"It was right when day was breaking in DC. Mary Ann called back and she said, 'well, they've killed him.'" Reeling from the blow, Lindsay struggled to pull herself together. Her mother Jane, Spike's first wife, would need to know. "I was sort of stunned and trying to figure out what was going on, I did not immediately pick up the phone to my mother." Lindsay felt she needed to be with her mother. Face to face, the news might not come as such a shock. "I rushed over to her house to tell her in person, but by the time I got there, she had already heard about it on the news, over the airwaves. That was not good."

After comforting her mother, Lindsay drove to her father's apartment in Bethesda, Maryland. By the time she arrived, the place was already crowded with her father's colleagues. "The room was full of foreign service officers. Everyone was dumbfounded, just in a state of numbness." It was decided Mary Ann and Spike's brother Al would travel with the official State delegation to Kabul. They would formally identify the body and escort it back to the U.S. "She and I talked and she felt pretty strongly that I shouldn't come, that it would be better for me to stay in DC and be here to greet them when they got back." Lindsay agreed, but only after making a promise to herself. She would make sure that Jane Wilson Dubs, her mother, would be there, too. She and her mother would witness her father's body returning to U.S. soil. On that day, Lindsay wanted her family to be together again.

Chapter 9

Horror and Loss

AT THE DISPENSARY in Kabul, Lloyd set about the grim business of confirming the facts of Spike's death as best he could. "We didn't have telephones, so I cabled Washington and specified the time when I pronounced him dead. I got a cable back from Washington almost immediately. To begin with, they said: 'Are you sure he's dead?' And I thought, well who did they think they sent here to take care of all the American foreign service officers and their dependents? I thought it was just a crazy question to ask. But then they proceeded to say we'd like you to do an autopsy, which I'd never done before. And we'd like you then to embalm the body, which I'd never done before. And they asked was the equipment there for the embalming."

Lloyd confirmed there was enough formaldehyde in the dispensary's supply room. But there were limits to what he could accomplish in Kabul. "When they said, we want you to do an autopsy, I cabled them back right away and said we will do a trunk autopsy, but I will not touch the skull. Because I was thinking about it, shades of JFK, where even with a pathologist doing it, a sloppy job was done. And that only raises questions about how well it was done, and what wasn't done." Lloyd welcomed the help of a top physician at the CARE/Medico charity teaching hospital in Kabul, Dr. William Neal. Together, with Jeannene assisting them, the doctors began the process of identifying each wound in the ambassador's body. Hopefully this would establish cause of death.

But a surprise awaited them. "The ambassador had two wounds in the chest," Lloyd recalls. "Interestingly enough, the one I thought might have been the killing wound, right over his heart, we opened that up. There was a bullet there, but it hit the rib and slid right along the rib. It never even entered the chest. The rib was cracked, but the bullet actually slid along it. In other words, the rib deflected the bullet. It had probably gone through a window or something, and most of the impact of it was spent. We did find that bullet."

Though not a fatal wound, this was the cause of much of Spike's blood loss, along with the second wound on the right side of his chest. "That bullet did penetrate the chest and enter his lung. He had some blood in that lung, but very little. And that bullet, for some reason we couldn't find it. There was no exit wound. We weren't forensic pathologists. If we had kept digging around we could have probably found it. It was probably buried in his lung."

While Lloyd recorded each step of the procedure, Jeannene kept her own notes. In a letter the following day to her best friend back home, she noted that in addition to the two chest wounds, they found bullets had struck Spike in the left hand, the right arm and elbow, and his right shoulder. But most of their attention went to the small-caliber bullet wounds they found in the head: three to the left temple, two on the right.

In all the smoke and confusion in room 117, Lloyd had scarcely noticed the head wounds. Using the dispensary's old X-ray machine, they discovered five bullets deep in Spike's brain. This only made sense, since there were no exit wounds in the head. "By this time, I wasn't surprised by anything. I think we were all kind of in a state of shock. I reported the killing wounds were in the ambassador's skull, and those I would not touch." As a result, Lloyd left the fatal rounds exactly where the murder weapon or weapons had placed them. Removal and analysis of the bullets would be left to specialists back in the U.S.

As the autopsy neared completion, the embassy's psychiatrist, Elmore Rigamer, arrived at the dispensary. He was exhausted. Earlier that afternoon on his way to Islamabad, he had stopped in at the U.S. Consulate in Peshawar. His colleagues there broke the bad news: his ambassador had been kidnapped. That's all they knew. Elmore rushed back to Kabul. Now he was standing at the threshold of the procedure room, speechless and numb. "I can still see it vividly. Ambassador Dubs' body was there, stretched out on the table, nude. Lloyd Rotz was finishing the preliminary autopsy. They were washing the body, it was really quite gruesome. I didn't go in. I was really horrified."

Less than 24 hours before, Elmore and Anna had been with Spike at the Chinese embassy, taking in that interminable opera performance. Now the ambassador was dead, slaughtered by gunfire. It was too much to take in. Yet soon, perhaps that very night, Elmore would be called upon to help the entire U.S. mission in Afghanistan absorb the shock and the horror of this calamity—and to continue functioning somehow. He felt confident he could meet the challenge, but not just yet. Not the way he felt at that moment. No, Elmore needed to be with his wife and kids, and right away. He left the dispensary and headed home.

Lloyd and the team gathered up the autopsy records, together with Spike's clothing and effects. Then they moved on to embalming the body. Finally, mindful of the regime's earlier intrusions, Jeannene and her colleagues placed the remains in a safe place. "We had what we called a morgue, which really was just a small cold room we could use as the morgue. It was on the AID compound, in the grounds behind the dispensary. We took him over there." Throughout these final stages of the ordeal, Jeannene's discipline, her sense of professional detachment, was tested to the extreme. Like Elmore, she had been with Spike only the day before, strolling through the carpet bazaar, sharing the exotic sensations of Kabul's street life. Now she was handling his mortal remains. Concluding the letter to her friend, she wrote, "It was a terrible experience. Unbearable."

ACROSS TOWN at the embassy, Spike's surviving foreign service officers were also struggling with the unbearable. Doug Wankel worked with Bruce Amstutz's assistant, drafting a lengthy cable to State in Washington setting out the day's key events. Meantime, Mike Malinowski was downstairs in the consular section compiling his own report. "It was important we reconstruct what had happened and the time frame of it all." He began by debriefing Spike's driver, Gul Mohammed. This took a good deal of time, and not only because Mike pressed the chauffeur on every detail of the bogus traffic stop, the armed hijacking and the men behind the guns. Each question had to penetrate a thick pall of grief because Gul Mohammed, too, was grappling with his emotions. He had served Ambassador Dubs loyally, faithfully. Every bit as much as Spike's American staffers, Gul Mohammed loved the man.

Confronted by all of this, Mike had to dig deep to get a hold on himself. He was not alone in this. All his colleagues spoke of being in daze leaving the hotel, of looking out on the empty streets of the Afghan capital with gunfire still ringing in their ears. When Mike entered his office, his deputy drew back in horror the instant he laid eyes on him. Only then did Mike look down at his shirt. It was covered in blood. "So I took it off and asked my vice-consul to take it home and get me a clean one. Well, my wife Karen was at home. And she had heard the security radio throughout the day, so she knew something was going on. And we lived close enough she had actually heard the gunfire. So she already knew something terrible had happened.

But when my deputy showed up at the front door with the bloody shirt, well, it was a bad day, a terrible day for her, for all of us. It was the worst, the strangest day of my life.

"The ambassador was more than just a father figure to everybody at the embassy. He's the top official, the president's personal representative. To have anything happen to him was a shock to all of us. Plus, he was extremely well liked, and everyone knew that he was one of our best officers."

Doug, too, was struggling to regain any sense of composure. "We were all pretty much in shock. The embassy was buzzing with communications. Upstairs they were busy letting everyone in the American community know what had happened. Everything functioned all right, people were professional. But there was just an aura of shock. It was bad." In particular, Doug is haunted by the memory of returning home that evening. "My wife Marilyn and I had scheduled a big party that night at our house. Keep in mind, this was Valentine's Day. So that was cancelled. And we wound up just sitting there amongst all the food and the cake and decorations. It was an air of despair and despondency, like nothing I had ever experienced before. That obviously was the worst day of my life, to that point, and even to this point today. It's something I never got over."

At their residences across the Afghan capital, American families were coping as best they could. Steve Rotz was waiting as his father came through the door that evening, far later than he had ever returned before. "He just plopped down on the couch and shook his head, as if to say: 'unbelievable.' Then he started questioning everything he'd done." Steve, his sister and his mother listened as Lloyd tried to come to terms with what had happened. There had been no inkling of a warning. Then sudden violence struck at the core of their new community. "I believe he was thinking: I've put my family in harm's way. Into an area embroiled in the the Cold War. I'm sure that was racing through his mind. Then he was talking about what happened that day. And he was second guessing himself, every move that he'd made. Kind of like a cop, who's in a compromised moment, and it's dark, and someone pulls something out, and he's got a millisecond to respond and any delay could cost someone their life. He just sat there and he was questioning everything he'd done. How he finally removed the ambassador from the hotel and that room. How he put him in that Chevy Impala and took him to the dispensary. And everything he did there."

At the Flatin household, Mark had been standing by since early afternoon with his mother and younger brother. Relieved as they were to have learned, some hours earlier, that the head of the family had never been in the kidnappers' clutches, everyone heaved a sigh of relief when Bruce walked through the door. "I just thought 'wow!' I was so impressed. I remember him sitting down and recounting the events, and I just couldn't believe he had lived through all that. Speaking through that keyhole in German—we knew it had been a really harrowing day."

The Flatins and Rotzes weren't alone in rerunning the terrible events of the day over and over in their minds. At the embassy, lights burned late into that black Valentine's night. The process of debriefing everyone who had witnessed the bloody scenes in and around room 117 had established only one definite result: a shared feeling of disbelief and hopelessness. Each and every foreign service officer had answered the call, rushing headlong into the emergency. Yet they had been powerless to act. They failed to save Spike's life. They lost their ambassador.

At 8 p.m., just as many of the grief-stricken staffers prepared to head home for the night, the ordeal took another bewildering turn. A call came in from the Ministry of Foreign Affairs. One of his Amin's aides was on the line. He was switched through to Bruce Amstutz, still in his office. With him were

Bruce Flatin, Mike Malinowski and Chuck Boles. Listening in on the call, Chuck found himself needing to sit down. "They had an invitation for us. Would we care to visit the military hospital and view what they called the 'four dead terrorists involved in the killing of Ambassador Dubs?'" For the first and only time that day—but far too late—the regime was purporting to offer a measure of cooperation.

Amstutz accepted. Chuck, Mike and Bruce Flatin got in their cars and made their way across town. Enforcing the curfew, the regime's soldiers were on edge after the day's events. The Americans had to negotiate safe passage through checkpoint after checkpoint. Finally, they pulled up at a drab, hulking shadow of a building. This was the capital's military hospital, which boasted some of the best equipped surgeries in the country. But it wasn't a care ward the officers were escorted to by a major of the Afghan National Army. It was to the squalid subterranean reaches of the complex.

In a silent procession, trailed by armed guards, the Americans walked the dimly lit basement corridors. Eventually they arrived at a pitch-black passageway the lights could not reach at all. The major tripped a switch on the wall. A sickly green fluorescent glow flickered overhead. They were in the morgue. Or to be exact, in the hallway leading to the morgue's open door. Inside, cadavers were visible, laid out on gurneys. Some of the bodies were exposed, pale vestiges of humanity. Others were partially covered by sheets, cast haphazardly over the remains. But it was the four naked bodies at the Americans' feet the major wanted them to see. Four dead men, laid side by side on the concrete floor.

Chuck knelt down for a closer look at the corpses. "We recognized two of the bodies as the kidnappers we found inside the hotel room. Each of them had multiple gunshot wounds to the torso." Mike gasped when he recognized the third body. "It was the Afghan the hotel staff had grabbed and subdued, the one beaten up by the police. The last time we saw him at the hotel he was very much alive. But now he was dead, and with a head that looked like a huge golf ball. Later I was told that sometimes when a bullet is fired into someone's head at close range the gasses expand and can cause that dimpled effect. It appeared that man had been summarily executed."

The fourth body had a face the Americans had never seen before. In Chuck's estimation, the corpse was clearly dissimilar to the other three. "The skin tone was more pale and waxen looking. He'd taken a single gunshot to the back of the head. It was obvious that body had come from somewhere else."

After allowing the Americans a good long look, the major snapped to attention. He spoke as if reciting a prepared script. "These are the four criminals who killed your ambassador in room 117 of the Hotel Kabul." Chuck felt the room spinning. Mike leaned into the Afghan officer's face, ready to explode, but the major spoke first. "The bodies of these criminals were all taken from the room where your ambassador was held. The government of Afghanistan very much regrets his killing by these terrorists."

The Americans stood there, dumbstruck by the audacity of the official lie. They stared at the four dead men. Their lives were gone, and so too were their secrets. Any information they might have possessed was running off in trails of blood, reaching off across the floor and trickling down the drain.

PART FOUR

Chapter 10

A Comedy of Liars

Steven Rotz woke in the pre-dawn darkness of February 15, 1979 and reached for his short-wave radio. Steve was an avid listener of the BBC and Voice of America, and he wanted to hear how the ambassador's murder was being reported in the outside world. "At that time we didn't have digital tuners, so you just sort of tuned across the dial. When you heard British English, that was the BBC. That morning, I just kept tuning until I heard what sounded like North American English. I assumed it was Voice of America. The program was all about the events of the day before. How Ambassador Dubs was abducted in Kabul. How the local officials did everything possible, and how they mounted a rescue mission. But unfortunately, in the whole fusillade of gunfire, the ambassador was injured. The announcer said Ambassador Dubs was removed by the American medical team and taken to the American dispensary, but due to the Americans' incompetence, they were unable to save his life."

Hearing this, Steve threw off his covers and jumped out of bed. "I thought: that's not what happened. The ambassador was dead at the scene. Then all of a sudden, the identifier comes on: 'You're listening to Radio Moscow.'"

The report was not a mistake. It wasn't some rogue broadcast soon to be corrected with the truth. What Steve Rotz heard that morning was an introduction into what was destined to become one of the most focused and intense disinformation campaigns of the Cold War. It was a coordinated effort by the Soviet government, and Afghanistan's Communist regime, to conceal the true circumstances of the kidnapping and murder of Spike Dubs—forever.

In fact, the process commenced the day before, only two hours after the bloody assault at the Hotel Kabul. That was when the regime chose to make its first official statement on the matter, issued by none other than Hafizullah Amin. After spending the day cold shouldering the Americans, rebuffing all of their pleas to communicate, the Afghan Vice-Premier reverted to his long-winded self. The venue was Kabul Airport, where the Iraqi Foreign Minister was beating a premature departure from the troubled Afghan capital.

After farewell handshakes staged for state-controlled media, Amin turned to the handful of dignitaries from Kabul's diplomatic corps who had turned out for the ceremony. He told them that Ambassador Dubs' kidnappers had demanded the release of three prisoners of the regime. He refrained from explaining how those demands were communicated, or to whom. Neither did he name the alleged prisoners, much less any of the abductors. Later in the day, a conflicting account went out over state-controlled Radio Kabul. Only one individual was sought by the gang, the report said: a leftist political activist from Badakhshan named Bahruddin Bahes.

Once again, there was no mention of how and when negotiations were conducted. And within days, even Amin was contradicting himself on the matter. In contrast to his statements at the airport, he now confirmed it was only Bahes' release the kidnappers sought. His alleged "three prisoners" simply disappeared, much like the four corpses displayed at the morgue for the Americans. Gruesome pictures of the dead men were all that remained of the gang. The images were published on the back page of the February 15, 1979 edition of the *Kabul Times*.

Arguably no one examined these pictures more intently than Chuck Boles. At his desk in the embassy's security office, he pored over the macabre forms. For the photo session, the bodies had been cleaned up and placed on stretchers. Shrouds covered the dead men from the waist down. Cotton wads concealed gaping head wounds. The cadavers were squeezed together; arms crossed over midsections; fingers gnarled and lifeless; faces expressionless masks of death. There were no names beneath the images, only this run-on caption: "The enemies of the people and the assassins of H.E. U.S. Ambassador to Kabul Adolph Dubs killed in gun battle."

Some battle, Chuck thought. He had been told by Doug and Warren what they'd seen on their second look around room 117. All the damage to the walls and ceiling appeared to have been done by the breach team and the rifle squad at the bank. There were no bullet holes evidencing return fire, no sign the two kidnappers in the room had been able to get off so much as a single shot at their attackers. What did exist, and in abundance, were questions. Why execute the third man? Couldn't Taroon have beaten even a name out of him? Why not question the wretched survivor for days if necessary? And if the regime's claim about Bahes had any truth to it, why wasn't the third man's confession of the gang's motive obtained? Why was there to be no show trial—an opportunity for the regime to demonstrate its implacable and courageous stance against terrorism?

There were too many unanswered questions to count. Yet Chuck had no option but to knuckle down and try to answer each and every one of them. "It was my job. As security officer, it made sense for me to do the investigation. That's how State wanted it." His regional supervisor, Ron Kelly, was on his way from Embassy Islamabad to assist. Backing them up would be a young State security officer, Al Golacinski, ordered by Vance to temporarily rebase to Kabul from his post in Rabat, Morocco.

A central strand of the investigation would be guided by Abdul Ghafari. Exercising extreme caution and under cover of night, he dropped in to see friends and contacts with jobs in the middle echelons of the regime's ministries. These were apolitical public servants who had no love for their doctrinaire Communist overlords. But the fear cast by the Taraki-Amin leadership was profound. Few of Ghafari's sources dared speak with him, and none had any clues as to the origins of the kidnapping, much less the ruthless manner in which the episode was brought to an end. Still, Embassy Kabul's local investigator persevered. He did so with remarkable bravery: Abdul Ghafari was acutely aware of the price he would pay if he fell into the deadly web of Taroon's spy network.

For his part, Chuck was struggling to balance the weight of responsibility in heading the investigation with his personal sense of grief. He realized he hadn't yet worked through even the first stages of mourning. "Spike was my friend, not just my boss. He was killed on my watch. That was tough to get to grips with. And it's bothered me ever since."

THE LATEST WORD from Washington only seemed to deepen the sense of loss and helplessness felt by everyone at Embassy Kabul. Vance's deputy, Warren Christopher, had summoned Soviet Ambassador Anatoly Dobrynin to the State Department. The diplomat was made to endure a "strong protest" over the role of Soviet advisors to the Afghan police in the storming of the hotel room. Trouble was, Soviet envoys didn't come any tougher or more calculating than Dobrynin. Christopher might as well have waved a feather duster at the man. Dobrynin, perhaps more than any other Russian official, was someone Spike had identified to his daughter Lindsay as a dangerous adversary.

"I actually remember Mr. Dobrynin myself, because I think I had met him and his wife several times, because the work of diplomacy happens at parties and receptions and over dinners and I had been around for some of that. And I know that my dad had a relationship with Mr. Dobrynin. I think he respected him, but he wasn't fooled by Dobrynin. Dad knew that he was a consummate tactician."

In much the same vein of official protest, Malcolm Toon, the U.S. Ambassador to Moscow, confronted the Soviet Foreign Minister, Andre Gromyko. But Gromyko, too, was one of the toughest old school autocrats ever produced by the U.S.S.R. In terms of Cold War conflict, Washington's protests over the murder of one of its brightest diplomatic lights were tepid at best.

Against this, however, President Carter made an effort to ensure the American people appreciated Spike's sacrifice for the nation. He also said: "...the manner of his death redoubles our dedication to the struggle against the kind of senseless violence which took his life." Less public emphasis, if any, was placed on redoubling the administration's dedication to solving the crime. The president ordered American flags to be flown at half-mast on all government buildings throughout the United States and its possessions, and at U.S. embassies, consulates and military installations around the world. Secretary of State Vance stated: "He has given his life serving his country. His bravery, self-sacrifice and personal sense of duty are qualities of which we are proud and which we all strive to emulate. His death only confirms us in our determination to work to eliminate the mindless violence which threatens our world community."

None of this moved the Communist regime in Afghanistan. To the contrary, Taraki and Amin appeared set on pouring salt into the excruciating emotional wounds suffered by the American community in Kabul. A day after the conflagration at the Hotel Kabul, a bitter Bruce Amstutz reported to Washington that "no high-level official in the foreign ministry or Afghan government has troubled to phone the Embassy to express the government's regret over the ambassador's death."

This callousness expressed itself in a material way, as well. From the start, Chuck's investigation was stonewalled by the regime. He assured Bruce Amstutz that, given time, he and the security team would find ways to push their inquiries forward. Before they could get into full swing, however, Chuck was assigned another difficult mission. He would be among the first embassy officers to meet the State delegation on their arrival from Washington on Friday, February 16. He would brief the officials on arrangements for their visit, then accompany Mary Ann Dubs to the ambassador's residence, the home in which, just weeks earlier, she and Lindsay shared a fabulous Christmas holiday with Spike. Later in the day, the residence would host a memorial service open to the entire Embassy Kabul family.

Chuck wasn't alone in feeling the impact of Spike's violent death increasing with each passing hour. David and Beatrice Litt found it difficult to come to terms with the tragedy. "There was a sense of immense grief and loss. It was like losing a family member, or a very, very close friend, a friend of long-standing. It was a similar feeling with Spike. Not just because of his personality, although that was a huge part of it. And it wasn't really the affront caused to the United States. It was the loss of his incredible leadership at our embassy. Like someone had just lopped off the top of this entity called the United States embassy. That was just a tremendous loss for me personally, and I suspect for everyone else as well."

On the eve of the memorial service, Elmore Rigamer was also dealing with traumatic aftershocks. Yet as the community's psychiatrist, he realized he needed to pull himself together and go to work. "One gets a hold of oneself. It was really just the first 48 hours or so that I was really upset. People were in shock and mourning. The most I could help people do was identify their feelings. So you would allow people to talk. You'd tell them what you're feeling yourself to sort of normalize it, then help them identify what they feel. This was my first introduction to a situation of this kind. And it marked the rest of my career in the foreign service on how to talk with communities and how to work with ambassadors who were under threat of terrorism."

Jeannene Cramer coped in two ways: continuing to do her job and writing home to the States. "I wrote about everything we'd done, about the X-rays and taking the body to the morgue. How I told one of the Afghan soldiers who came into the dispensary to leave." Remarkably, considering the regime had tried to seize Spike's remains, it was left to Jeannene, in her blue Volkswagen Beetle, to deliver the autopsy records, X-rays and Spike's clothing and personal effects. "Looking back, it seems a little crazy. But yes, it was me in my little Bug taking all of those things over to the embassy." Luckily the transfer came off without a hitch. The autopsy records, the recovered bullet fragments, each item of Spike's clothing—all of these were vital pieces of evidence. Together with Spike's body, that evidence would be repatriated to Washington, DC for a formal autopsy.

WHILE THE AMERICANS mourned, the Afghan Communist regime shifted its disinformation machinery into higher gear. The objective: to persuade the world the killing of Spike Dubs was the unintended consequence of a valiant rescue mission by the Afghan authorities, acting entirely on their own. To this end, the initial coverage in the regime-controlled press was rushed and superficial. A single sentence of some 30 words appeared on the front page of the Thursday, February 15th edition of the *Kabul Times*.

The headline above this was crowded into a single column: "Flags at half mast today on US envoy demise." The ambassador's name was misspelled as "Dubz." The same error was made on the back page beneath the photos of the dead alleged gang members, as well as in a brief biographical sketch of His Excellency "Adolph Dubz," who "was assassinated, regretfully, by a number of terrorists and enemies of the people of Afghanistan." An editorial on page two proclaimed: "This savage and inhumane act is totally rejected and condemned by our Khalqi government and our noble people. And we are sending curse upon those who have committed such a cruel act..."

With no paper published Friday, the Muslim holy day, the next issue of the *Times* appeared on Saturday, February 17th. By then, the regime's portrayal of the incident had gained a sharper focus—and better editing. At last the ambassador's name was spelled correctly. And the regime's empathy was put on display. In a picture story running down the right side of the front page, Amin's deputy Shah Mohammed Dost was quoted at run-on length after laying a wreath at the U.S. embassy the previous day. "Adolph Dubs was an extremely good personality and talented diplomat and had great interest in strengthening the relations between Afghanistan and the United States of America and we are sorry that His Excellency is not among us... Our remorse is more than others because the incident has occurred regretfully in Kabul." The story continued: "The Deputy Minister sought patience and courage for Madamme Dubs and his other survivors. In return Bruce J. Amstutz, Chargé d'Affairs of the US Embassy in Kabul was moved by this action of the Minister..."

Nothing could have been further from the truth. Amstutz tolerated Dost's display of crocodile tears, but through gritted teeth. He had been appointed the mission's chargé after Spike's death. In this new role to have snubbed the regime's representative's request to sign the embassy's book of condolences would have been to slam the door permanently on bilateral relations with the Afghan government. That would make Chuck's investigation even more difficult at a time when both State and the White House wanted answers, and wanted them quickly. So the charade continued, most notably on Mary Ann Dubs' arrival with the official party from Washington on Friday, February 16.

At 2:45 p.m., the iconic blue and white profile of the U.S. Air Force 707 taxied to a stop at Kabul Airport. Once again Foreign Minister Amin was absent. In his stead, several deputies turned up. A large contingent from Embassy Kabul was assembled on the tarmac, led by Bruce Amstutz and all the mission's section chiefs. The regime gave in to Amstutz's demands and waived all passport and visa formalities, in part because the official party was expected to be on the ground in Kabul for only 16 hours. The delegation was led by Harry Barnes, the Director of the U.S. Foreign Service, and President Carter's personal envoy, Charles O'Keeffe. There were assistant state secretaries and deputies, escort officers and Spike's older brother, Alexander "Al" Dubs. But it was the sight of Spike's widow that riveted the attention of the crowd on the tarmac; the dark, attractive young woman descending the gangway at Chuck Boles' side.

With a minimum of delay, Mary Ann was whisked by motorcade to the ambassador's residence. There, plans were discussed for the memorial service that evening. At her request, she was taken on a drive-by of the kidnapping site and the Hotel Kabul, followed by a briefing at the embassy. Then, at 6 p.m., an interdenominational service began at the residence. The home so widely known for Spike's singalongs and backyard pool parties was filled to overflowing. It was a somber, grieving assembly of some 600 people. Virtually the entire American community in Kabul was there, the Rigamers among them. Elmore found himself having to keep at least one professional eye dry in case he was needed. "It was quite emotional as you can imagine. And beyond the grief, people were afraid of what might come next in Kabul."

Teacher Jim Gurnett was there too. More than once his

family had been guests at the residence, and met Lindsay there during her Christmas visit. "Ambassador Dubs had seemed like such a good man to me, and we were thinking of Lindsay and what this was meaning for her. I think it was just that human response—that this was just a horrible, unnecessary, unexpected thing and you wanted to be with other people at that time, and be around to share the emotion of it."

All the foreign embassies were represented, led by none other than the Dean of the capital's Diplomatic Corps at that time, Soviet Ambassador Alexander Puzanov. Standing a respectful distance from his American counterpart's coffin, Puzanov was a model of decorum and politesse—and deception. Nearly two decades would pass before the secret would be revealed of his embassy's role in initiating, and expanding upon, the cover-up of Spike Dubs' murder.

Heavy with anguish, the atmosphere in the residence became suffocating. Midway through the 20-minute service, one of the Marine honor guards collapsed at the foot of the casket. It was a bad fall, a shocking one. The call went up for a doctor. Luckily, Lloyd Rotz had just arrived. "It was either emotion or just the heat or whatever, a combination of everything that was going on. The Marine passed out and came down on the terrazzo floor right on his face. He fractured his jaw and was bleeding from his ear. That can indicate a basilar skull fracture, and if you overlook it he could have a brain abscess and die." Jeannene Cramer helped Lloyd get the young man out of the house and over to the dispensary. "We were quite worried about him. I stayed with him through the night and in the morning, took him out to the plane." Lloyd and the injured Marine would hitch a ride with the departing official party to their refueling stop in Spain, where the man could be hospitalized.

The departure from Kabul Airport was no less poignant than the memorial service the previous evening. A cortege with police motorcycle escort crept through the frigid February dawn. Mary Ann sat with Bruce Amstutz in his car, following the dispensary ambulance carrying the flag-draped coffin. At the wheel was David Litt, who volunteered to drive the makeshift hearse, accompanied by two Marine guards. The pallbearers' van was next in the procession, followed by a stream of U.S. embassy cars.

The cortege passed through several Afghan army checkpoints before finally maneuvering to a stop on the apron beside the Air Force 707. A crowd of 500 watched as the pall bearers lifted the coffin from the rear of the vehicle. Carefully, they placed it on a cargo lift to be hoisted up and into the Boeing's fuselage. Earlier, Embassy Kabul informed the government it must "waive the Afghan police and health requirements concerning the preparation of the body, the closing of the casket and its transportation to the USAF aircraft." Reluctantly, the regime agreed and the plane was loaded without incident. Already on board were Spike's personal and household effects. These had been inventoried and packaged by Bernie Woerz and his admin team, a duty he found extremely sad and difficult.

The American foreign service officers who were present for the plane's departure remember the silence and the cold air, and most of all the stunned sadness among Spike's friends and colleagues. There was palpable grief, as well, etched on the faces of diplomats from countries all over the world. And, once again, there were the granite features of Alexi Puzanov, Moscow's standard bearer in Afghanistan. Notably missing were senior officials of the Afghan regime. Western envoys interpreted the Communist leadership's absence from the airport, and the memorial service the previous day, as calculated insults to the United States government.

The crowd watched Mary Ann Dubs climb the stairs to the plane. At her request, Jim Taylor would accompany her and represent Embassy Kabul at Spike's funeral in Washington,

DC. There, preparations were underway for two very different receptions. One would be public, with President Jimmy Carter receiving his fallen ambassador. The other would be private, consigned to the precincts of science and ballistics and forensic pathology: a formal autopsy of Spike's remains, together with a detailed review of the preliminary evidence gathered by Lloyd Rotz and the medical team in Kabul. Questions needed to be answered, and urgently. Questions that posed potentially explosive consequences in the already strained relations between the United States and Soviet Russia. Most crucially: what, exactly, was the cause of Spike Dubs' death, and who was responsible?

WHILE THE AMERICANS craved answers, the Afghan regime was desperate to extinguish the smoldering embers of the slaughter at the Hotel Kabul. In service of that agenda, Taroon finally agreed to an interview for Chuck Boles' investigation. Chuck's regional supervisor, Ron Kelly, and Abdul Ghafari accompanied him to the commandant's office. There, they found themselves sitting like supplicants, looking up at the man seated throne-like behind his elevated desk. As ever, Taroon held his cigarette holder in one hand while stroking his chrome plated Kalashnikov with the other. Replying to Chuck's questions in any meaningful way was the last thing on his mind.

"Do you know why the ambassador was kidnapped?"

"We don't know because all the persons involved are dead."

"Do you have any information on the background of the people involved?"

"No, because they probably used false names."

"Have you recovered the police sergeant's uniform from the hotel room?"

"Yes."

"Could we see the weapons used by the terrorists?"

"Yes, but you would have to write a note to the foreign ministry."

This was just a bone thrown his way, Chuck realized. He wouldn't bet a dime on Taroon and the regime making good on showing him the guns. Only one thing seemed certain as they stood to leave. Taroon just sat there, glaring at Ghafari in a particularly menacing way. Both he and Chuck got the message. The commandant was saying: "I'll be seeing you again, and soon."

By now, more and more foreign news correspondents were arriving in the Afghan capital. Taroon's boss, Amin, recognized an opportunity in this heightened international attention. His office announced the Vice-Premier would take their questions at a foreign ministry news conference on Monday, February 19. News of the event would appear locally on Tuesday, when Spike's funeral was scheduled to take place, with international coverage extending into Wednesday the 21st, one week after the armed assault on room 117.

Embassy Kabul officers heard all about Amin's news conference soon after it took place. The reporters who attended the bizarre session came looking for reaction and comments from the Americans. Amin had insisted on using a Pashto language interpreter, the journalists said. This, despite Amin using his own fluent English to correct the translator's words, where necessary, to craft carefully phrased replies. Still more peculiar was Amin's insistence that none of the correspondents should use any kind of recording device. Limited to pen and paper, the journalists were able to document only a fraction of the great man's statements.

At 10 p.m. that night, Radio Afghanistan carried the entire newser in Dari. It would be another full day, Wednesday, until the *Kabul Times* published a lengthy verbatim account of the questions and answers. Finally, the Americans could read the regime's evolving claims and obfuscations in plain, if at times strained, English. From the outset, Amin insisted the action taken one week earlier by Afghan forces at the Hotel Kabul was "a rescue effort." Sadly, this valiant attempt to save Ambassador Dubs became "a gunfight." Since the reporters hearing this had not been in the country at the time, much less anywhere near the hotel, none had yet learned there was no evidence of return fire from the men holding the ambassador. Only the attackers' guns had been blazing.

Then Amin went too far. He claimed, "We could not get hold of a single terrorist" before the entire gang, linked to Bahes, was killed. At this, Barry Schlacter of the Associated Press interjected: "Excuse me, but a few tourists had seen in the corridors of the Kabul Hotel that one of the terrorists was caught by a large number of the officers concerned. Was he investigated?"

Tripped up on the subject of the third man, Amin sat speechless for a moment. He replied: "The officers concerned had caught a few suspects but later on, it transpired that they had nothing to do with the terrorists. So they were immediately released." This was a bald lie. But here, too, Amin got away with the shameless invention, since none of the reporters had spoken to the American eye-witnesses who recognized the third man's corpse at the morgue.

The *Financial Times* correspondent, David Housego, asked why American diplomats could not track Amin down during the kidnapping, and felt he was indifferent to the abduction. Amin answered: "My offices are well known. Everybody knows that I am either at the House of the People or at the Prime Ministry, or at the Foreign Affairs Ministry or at the Defence Ministry. So my accessibility is meaningless. In case I was not available, my deputy was there. If somebody wanted to say something, he could say it to my deputy. And what was to be communicated to me or my deputy could be conveyed to the President of the Office of the Revolutionary Council, Comrade

Faqir, so that he would directly inform the Great Leader."

Amin took his deceptions to another level when *The Observer* correspondent asked about the Russians. "The U.S. State Department has said that at the time of the incident, some Soviet advisers were also present there. How do you comment on this?" Amin shot back: "The Kabul Hotel is one of the oldest hotels in Afghanistan. Also, from the viewpoint of size, it is second only to the Intercontinental. Right now, not only Soviets but also nationals from various countries are staying there as guests. Therefore, the presence of the Soviets on that particular day at the aforementioned hotel does not give rise to any question."

The reporter asked if the Soviet advisers were present specifically to help the Afghan forces. "I am annoyed by this remark of yours," Amin said, "because whatever we achieve by ourselves is not appreciated in certain parts of the world or is treated with skepticism. We accomplished the April Revolution so gloriously that not a single foreigner in the entire world had prior knowledge about it. Even countries that had spent millions of dollars for espionage purposes in Afghanistan could not get any information in this connection... Likewise, we ourselves took action to rescue Mr. Dubs but unfortunately the matter of Soviet "advice" was raised once again to distort the facts. This greatly angers us."

To their credit, the assembled journalists wouldn't let go. Amin was challenged: "Do you wish to say that there was no foreign adviser present at the place of the incident?" The Vice-Premier replied: "No foreign adviser including the Soviets was present there to give us advice." But Mark Tully of the BBC kept pressing. Who led the operation? Tully asked. Amin said: "The responsible person who reported to me was the Chief of the Security Forces, Sayed Daoud Taroon. It was he who led the rescue operations."

Taroon. Who did not leave his office until the shooting

ended, as Jim Taylor could attest. Amin was now visibly uncomfortable. The AP's Schlacter asked for his reaction to the Carter administration's protests over the incident. Amin replied: "We consider that protest to be entirely groundless because we undertook the operations to rescue the life of Mr. Dubs with a lofty humane spirit motivated by our friendship with the U.S. I see no action or moment in which we might have lapsed into negligence."

Claims by any government of being motivated by a "lofty humane spirit" do not sit easily with seasoned journalists. The reporters dug in, trying to crack Amin's facade. Did the regime have Bahruddin Bahes in custody? "No," said the Vice-Premier. "I am not in a position to locate him. He was jailed at Daoud's time and escaped in the beginning of the revolution."

What about the identities of the kidnappers? After all, one was seen captured alive. At this, Amin seemed to forget all about his claim, just minutes earlier, that the captured suspects had nothing to do with the incident and were released. "The terrorists usually use false names," he said. "Therefore, their real identities have not been disclosed yet." And never would be. Amin allowed at least one of the "terrorists" spoke with an accent consistent with Badakhshan, in northeastern Afghanistan. Asked what weapons the gang used, Amin claimed "they carried pistols, an unmarked machine-gun and a grenade but they used the pistols and the machine-gun."

Tom Lippman of the *Washington Post* asked why no effort was made to delay taking action. "I hope you will carefully listen to what I say," Amin fumed. "We made efforts to save time and consequently were able to delay the action for three and a half hours. But the terrorists at the expiration of the three and a half hours only gave us a 10-minute extension. They repeatedly warned that they wouldn't give another. Therefore, our efforts to get further extension were futile. I must say that there is no American in the whole world to have told us that we should not have taken any action even if the terrorists killed the aforesaid ambassador. We endeavored to rescue the late ambassador up to the last moments."

Hearing this, Schlachter wondered why the regime hadn't bought time by claiming they would turn over Bahes, but that he was being brought in from another part of the country. Amin refashioned his earlier response. "We had not told the terrorists that the person in question was not with us. We told them repeatedly that he was on his way and would arrive shortly. The Americans were also present there, witnessing this procedure. However, the terrorists did not accept this and did not extend the time."

In truth, the Americans had witnessed no such ploy. Amin ended the news conference by stooping still lower, by pointing the finger of blame at the U.S. ambassador himself. "Our security authorities had also suggested to the U.S. Embassy a few months ago that the police cars escort his automobile. However, unfortunately the ambassador did not accept this. Even the American escort was not assigned this duty." Another lie. But here, too, the reporters had insufficient background information to challenge the claim.

SPIKE'S FOREIGN SERVICE officers pored over the *Kabul Times* account of the news conference. At first, Mike Malinowski wanted to laugh out loud. Instead he threw the newspaper across the room. In summarizing the transcript for State in Washington, Embassy Kabul advised: "The journalists came away from the meeting feeling that Amin was basically cynical about the assassination of Ambassador Dubs. He paid lip service to maintaining friendly relations with the U.S. But, they felt, he really seemed indifferent on that point." Mike felt the same revulsion when the PDPA regime released its official account of the affair a few days later. "Their report was laughable in its brevity. For something as huge as this, it was something like a page and a half or two pages. It was virtually worthless."

This low watermark in official disinformation was notable in another way: now the Soviets were joining the campaign. Moscow instructed Ambassador Anatoly Dobrynin to relay to the Carter administration the Soviet Union's express denial of any responsibility in the handling of the siege at the Hotel Kabul. On the same day, Alexander Puzanov, Moscow's ambassador in Kabul, denied Soviet specialists had any role in the affair. The Soviets were now speaking, and posturing, in choreographed harmony with the Afghan Communist regime.

Confronted by this wall of disinformation, the Americans' anguished desire to get to the truth only intensified. The embassy staffers who had witnessed the events reviewed the salient details over and over among themselves, as if ensure their senses hadn't misled them all. To Chuck, the bottom line of the Soviets' and regime's joint responsibility for Spike's murder came down to that shadowy delivery of the pistol outside room 117. "Somehow the Afghan who took the weapon got into the room after the shooting started. Then the guns go silent, then the five pistol rounds. And then there he is, standing in the bathroom doorway when I went in. I think he executed the ambassador. He had time to do that and get back into the bathroom before we got there. But after I saw him, he stepped back and hid out of sight before the others came in."

Lloyd came to the same conclusion about where the fatal rounds came from. "I don't think there's any question. It was the same fellow who took the pistol, the same man I saw handed that weapon by the tall KGB operative."

But at least two of the Americans were not so sure. Doug thought it was the atmosphere of instability in the Afghan capital that forced the hands of both the regime and the Soviets. "We heard that word had gotten out to the marketplace, to the bazaars. And the Afghan people, particularly the business people were talking. They were closing up their shops, leaving to go home. And that was a sign that obviously troubled the Soviets, because they didn't know what they were in for. So, looking back to what the Russians did as far as ordering the Afghans to take the room, I don't believe the Russians had necessarily thought this thing through, or thought it would end up in the death of the ambassador. What they wanted was for the situation, the event, to be over. If they could do it and the ambassador came out all right, that'd be great. If they did it and the ambassador ended up dead at the hands of the police and whomever else, that's all right too."

Warren Marik shared that view. The Soviets were notorious for heavy handed responses to hostage takings. "Bottom line, the Russians who showed up were under orders to shut this incident down. Get it over with. Do what it takes. The welfare of the U.S. ambassador wasn't just secondary, it was thirdary." Yet even Warren had to admit the Soviets took a central role, one that only provoked suspicion. "Those three guys who knocked down the door and went into that room shooting? To me, they were Soviets, probably Muslim soldiers from the southern Soviet republics. The Soviets were the only force in town equipped to do that. None of the Afghans were capable of doing that. I saw them clear their weapons downstairs after the whole thing was over. They were professionals, not Afghan army regulars." Warren also noted the breach team's situational awareness once they got into the room. "When those three guys went through the door, they kept shooting but they never went all the way in. They knew where to be so they wouldn't be hit by the rifle fire coming in from the bank across the street. That takes experience."

To Mike Malinowski, Amin's claim about the gang being after Bahes' release only raised more questions than it answered. If there was any truth to the story, why execute the third kidnapper? And produce a fourth corpse out of thin air?

"That precluded any opportunity for these people to be questioned in depth by anyone. We wanted to talk to them to find out what they could tell us. So we had to wonder: what were the Soviets and regime trying to hide?"

Amstutz advised State that everything about the saga pointed to Amin having been "the decision maker" in the storming of the room. Embassy Kabul gave "greatest weight" to the regime "acting on the basis of a desire to crush immediately this dramatic evidence of opposition." But that conclusion would shift and keep on shifting as unseen hands behind the bloodshed were revealed.

Chapter 11

A Tragic Homecoming

> Prospects have not been helped by a feeling that America is a kind of helpless giant, kicked around and insulted at will. That emotion was fed by the murder of an ambassador in Afghanistan...
>
> - *Walter Cronkite, CBS Radio Network, February 20, 1979 on attempts to reach an arms treaty with the Soviet Union*

AS THE MYSTERY deepened in Kabul, Washington was focused on the sad rituals of repatriating a fallen statesman. President Carter flew by helicopter from Camp David to Andrews Air Force Base on Sunday, February 18th to greet the official party on their return from Afghanistan. Lindsay was there, having insisted her mother Jane, Spike's first wife, be allowed to attend. "It was a really cold day. DC was getting ready to experience one of its largest snowstorms in history."

In the biting 11-degree chill, Cyrus Vance presented Mary Ann Dubs with the Secretary's Award. This was the State Department's highest honor, awarded to Spike "for inspiring leadership, outstanding courage, and devotion to duty for which he gave his life." President Carter put a comforting arm around Lindsay's shoulder as Vance spoke. "Courageous and selfless men of the Foreign Service like Spike Dubs have all too often in recent years sacrificed their lives for their country. We owe them a debt beyond price. I pledge to you we will spare no effort to protect our diplomats overseas, and we will fight terrorism with all our resolve and our resources."

Lindsay witnessed all of this. But still numb with shock, she had a hard time accepting it as real. "We were kind of holding on to one another. I think we were all still living in this kind of fog, you know. As if this is not really happening."

The shivering crowd looked on as Spike's flag-draped casket was carried by an honor guard to a waiting hearse. The White House and State announced the body would be taken from Andrews to the Memorial Chapel of Arlington National Cemetery, where Spike would lay in state until the funeral on Tuesday, February 20. This is where the official version of events goes dark on the single most important element of the investigation into Spike's murder: the formal postmortem; the complete and proper autopsy performed on his remains.

The timeline between the body's Sunday arrival at Andrews and the interment at Arlington on Tuesday points to only one real possibility, particularly since the lying in state did, in fact, take place on Monday. Spike's body found its way to the Memorial Chapel at Arlington, but did so by way of Walter Reed hospital, better known as the National Naval Medical Center in Bethesda, Maryland. There, a thorough autopsy took place, including analysis of all the evidence and records assembled in Kabul by Dr. Rotz and his team.

On these procedures, however, the record goes blank. No detailed account of the autopsy was released. There was no indication who performed the procedure or how long it took. Given Lloyd Rotz's initial findings some four days earlier, technicians from the FBI's crime lab would have taken part, since they were then, as now, the country's leading forensics experts on firearms and ballistics. But for reasons that have never been disclosed to the American public, nearly all aspects of the Dubs autopsy were treated as state secrets. Instead of hard facts, the Carter administration placed an emphasis on ceremony.

Spike's funeral service was held at Fort Myer on the morning of Tuesday, February 20. The first lady, Rosalynn Carter, led the administration's attendees, including Vice-President Walter Mondale and Secretary and Mrs. Vance. After the service, the cortege proceeded to Arlington National Cemetery, where Section 5 had been cleared of the 24-inch snowfall from DC's worst snowstorm in 57 years. An honor guard fired a 19-gun salute and a bugler sounded taps. After 29 years in the foreign service, Spike Dubs was buried not far from the Kennedy family gravesite with its eternal flame.

Although Spike's remains had been interred with highest honors, little else was laid to rest. An American ambassador had been slain, yet the odds of anyone being held to account seemed remote. The Afghan regime's message to Vance on the day of the funeral only emphasized the unlikelihood of any measure of justice being realized. Amin wrote: "I assure Your Excellency that no efforts were spared by the Afghan security authorities to save the life of the late Ambassador Dubs from the cowardly act of armed terrorists who took him hostage and inflicted on him wounds resulting in his subsequent death." Case closed, the regime was saying. Any and all blame would be forever consigned to the four nameless corpses placed on display one week earlier.

Jim Taylor, for one, didn't buy it. An honorary pallbearer at the funeral, he told his colleagues at Foggy Bottom everything the Embassy Kabul team had witnessed. He would later write: "In my personal view, the individual shots the embassy team heard as they were detained in the hallway provide compelling evidence that the regime's forces had been instructed to eliminate any possible opponents of Amin and all witnesses to what had happened in that room, including (Spike) Dubs."

Lloyd Rotz, too, dismissed the regime's posturing. The physical evidence he and the others had carried from the hotel room–the body of their colleague and friend–proved Spike had been murdered. But the only real indications as to who fired the fatal gunshots, and how and when, conflicted with the Afghan government's account. And soon another revelation would come Lloyd's way. It was the only feedback he obtained from the formal autopsy at Walter Reed in Washington. "When the ambassador's body was taken back to DC, they checked his sweater. It had made no sense to me that we should find him sitting up there in a chair after all that automatic gunfire had gone on all over the place. Why hadn't he hit the deck?"

The sweater, it turned out, told a different story. It wasn't only soaked with blood, as Lloyd assumed when he and Jeannene removed it from Spike's body. The pathologists in DC detected an oily liquid and gunshot residue also present in the garment. This was consistent with the water from the shattered radiator, laced with microscopic particles of metal compounds left behind by discharged firearms. "Apparently, the sweater had absorbed some of the water on the floor. So the ambassador did end up on the floor, and somebody put him back up in that chair."

Where five bullets were fired into his brain.

"Who would have the presence of mind to shoot him twice on one side of the head, and then three times on the other? After all that machine-gun fire. The automatic weapons had to have killed those two kidnappers we found on the floor. Then those pop-pop-popping sounds we heard—those were the shots that killed the ambassador. Pistol shots. The rounds we found in his head."

This evidence was credible. And it was corroborated by multiple sources and supported by what little physical evidence had been collected and analyzed. But it was largely circumstantial. Solving the mystery wouldn't be easy. The perpetrators couldn't simply be rounded up and made to talk. After all, governments were emerging as prime suspects in this case. One was a weak, faction ridden, Third World band of hoodlums.

The other was a nuclear superpower: the Union of Soviet Socialist Republics.

Confronted by these obstacles, the investigators at Embassy Kabul wondered if they might ever get anything like a watertight case against Spike's killers. Soon another factor, an unexpected variable, would weigh in against them. The Carter administration's determination to secure a just resolution of the ambassador's murder quickly waned. Other geopolitical priorities began to constrict and complicate the U.S. government's response to the bloodshed in Kabul.

As the Soviet and Afghan governments continued to stubbornly obstruct the Dubs investigation, there were growing demands in Washington to punish the regime and the Russians, and get on with other business. Finally, a dismayed Jimmy Carter and his team came to the decision to change course in Afghanistan. The policies that followed would have dramatic and lasting consequences; some constructive, but many unintended—and catastrophic.

Chapter 12

The Show Goes On

EARLY IN HIS INVESTIGATION, Chuck Boles received a tantalizing tip. An American woman named Jessie Schilling called him, wondering if she could come by the embassy. She was a Peace Corps volunteer based in Kandahar; she had been working there for more than a year. On a recent visit to Kabul, she stumbled onto some information relevant to Ambassador Dubs' death. Chuck thanked her and told her to come on by. After all, Jessie had picked up the lead in a place well known for inside knowledge and hidden facts: Kabul's bazaars.

Five days after the storming of the hotel room, Jessie dropped into a needlework shop she visited whenever she was in the capital. Named after Afghanistan's nomadic tribes, the Kuchi people, the proprietor of Kuchi Kabul, Sher Ahmad, seemed surprised when one of his favorite American customers walked through the door. Why was she was still in Afghanistan? Why hadn't she left the country? Jessie replied she had no reason to leave. Why should she? Sher Ahmad leaned closer. Because the ambassador's kidnappers were "government men," he whispered. The gunmen in room 117 had been placed there by the regime.

Like any good investigator, Chuck had to wonder. Was this based on anything of substance? Or was it simply the kind of lurid teahouse gossip that runs hot through Afghanistan's bazaars? Sure, a setup, a fake kidnapping and rescue operation seemed more than plausible, given the conduct of Amin, Taroon and even the Russians. But the tip proved impossible to verify in any conclusive way. Chuck and his supervisor,

Ron Kelly, were forced to hold the information to one side. Irritatingly, though, they could not discount it entirely. Not in light of the continuing obstruction they were encountering from the PDPA regime, not to mention the fact that no group, faction or terrorist front had claimed responsibility for abducting and killing the U.S. ambassador. This was highly unusual in light of previous experience. One of terrorism's goals is to generate publicity, not least for the perpetrators themselves. So why did Spike's kidnappers commit themselves to such an empty, anonymous end? Their deaths had failed to accomplish even a suicidal expression of their cause.

At the same time, Amin and his cohorts were acting as though they had plenty to hide. After his leaden interview with Chuck on February 17, Taroon twice refused the American's request for a follow up meeting. When Chuck persisted, the commandant insisted that "future requests had to be submitted through the foreign ministry for prior approval." In the PDPA's Kabul, this was the kiss of administrative death. Bruce Amstutz tried to force the issue with the secret police chief's boss. The chargé sent formal diplomatic notes to Amin setting out the many details missing from the regime's official report. Getting no response, Amstutz met with his deputy, Dost, and amped up the requests by demanding a detailed account of the Russians' role. "It would be a grave mistake to continue to deny the presence of the Soviets when the Embassy knew for a fact that they were directly involved."

This, too, met only with silence. As a result, Embassy Kabul was at a loss to temper the prevailing mood in Washington, where the urge to punish the Afghan Communist leadership had reached a breaking point. Sadly, the steps being considered by the U.S. administration could not avoid injuring the innocent beneficiaries of U.S. aid: the citizens of Afghanistan; the very families living in greatest fear of the Soviet-backed regime. Nevertheless, President Carter ordered the American aid program to be slashed. No dollar amounts were made public, but Amstutz and his team were informed the $15 million economic aid program would immediately be cut by one-fifth, and up to a third the following year. The president's aides indicated the money saved would finance "humanitarian development assistance" in the country, but an unmistakable message was being sent. The United States, shaken by the murder of its ambassador, was reducing its profile inside Afghanistan. As well, the limited U.S. military training program for the Afghan military would be terminated. This was the same initiative Spike Dubs had sought to develop and prolong.

Within Embassy Kabul and the American community in Afghanistan as a whole, a traumatic present was giving way to an uncertain future. It was clear everything was on the table in terms of Washington's repositioning. The Peace Corps, USAID's programs—even the cultural center, with its committed Afghan following—all these could soon face cutbacks or complete elimination. For those closest to Spike, the grief of loss was compounded by an awareness that the policies he championed were now in the crosshairs of Cold War geopolitics. Lindsay knew exactly how her father would have felt about this. "He would have been deeply saddened. He really felt he had started making some inroads, that he had started to get some work done. It felt like all of came to naught."

Doug Wankel shared that view, as did many of his embassy colleagues. Reducing American aid undermined the goals Spike Dubs had strived to achieve. "He would have wanted obviously to find out what really happened, and do what was necessary to bring judgment and punishment, if that was necessary. But as far as Afghanistan and the Afghan people, then probably they needed even more in the way of aid and assistance, and to continue the US presence in a positive way. So, the people that knew him well argued against many of the things that transpired at that point."

For Chuck, Ron and Abdul Ghafari, the clouds of uncertainty gathering over Embassy Kabul added even more urgency to their investigation. Chuck realized the team needed to raise their game. At his request, State ordered Embassy Delhi's security officer, Al Bigler, to fly to Chuck's aid. Still, only if the beefed-up team achieved demonstrable results could they hope to convince State and the White House that the U.S. mission to Afghanistan might be down, but it was not out. One early embarrassment might have seen them thrown out of the ring entirely. Somehow the clothing Spike had been wearing when he was killed had not made it onto the official party's return flight to Washington. The error was revealed only when Vance's office relayed a request from the pathologists at Walter Reed. "If the clothing has not been destroyed, it should be treated as evidence and appropriately handled." Mike Malinowski found the items, safe and secure in the bag delivered after the autopsy by Jeannene. Inside was the telltale sweater with its trace evidence, as well as Spike's slacks, underwear, socks and shoes, and his hat. Mike pouched the clothes to DC along with the two Kalashnikov rounds recovered at the hotel by Bruce Flatin.

The episode left Chuck and Ron feeling they needed to get even more evidence to the scientists in DC. At their insistence, Bruce Amstutz once again pressed the PDPA foreign ministry to permit a team of U.S. investigators to inspect and photograph the interior and exterior of the Hotel Kabul, "including the room where the Ambassador was held." Only on March 6, some 20 days after Spike's murder, did the regime finally agree. As soon as the Americans saw the patched-up exterior surfaces of the hotel, their hearts sank. Inside, they found room 117 had been completely repaired. The broken doors were gone, replaced by spanking new ones. The floor had been scoured and painted and overlaid with carpet. The walls and ceiling wore fresh coats of paint. Not a single bullet hole was visible. The windows, the radiator, the furniture–everything was newly installed. Not a trace of the assault remained.

As a result, the FBI in Washington was left with only the most basic visual aids to help their investigation. In the immediate aftermath of the events on Valentine's Day, Mike and Chuck and the other witnesses helped record six rough pencil sketches of the room and the layout of the hotel, all from memory. These drawings would have been the only representations of the aftermath of the attack, had it not been for a chance intervention by an analyst at the U.S. Defence Intelligence Agency in Washington. The imagery specialist had spent a good deal of time poring over photographs of the latest Soviet-made military hardware deployed with regime forces in Afghanistan. The pictures were the product of Embassy Kabul's Defence Attaché Office.

So, in the early hours of February 15, the DIA analyst sent a cable to Kabul, seeking confirmation that pictures had been taken of the murder scene. Within minutes, one of the attaché office's staffers, Sgt. Dennis Wilkins, was on his way to the hotel. Slung over his shoulder was a government-issued 35 mm Leica, and his own Nikon. "I worked the intel side at the embassy. We took a good many pictures and had a darkroom in our section. So I guess DC thought we were the best bet for some quick shots of the scene." Dennis went to the front desk of the hotel and talked his way upstairs and into room 117. "I took two rolls of 36 exposures each. The room was a total mess. There were blood stains on the floor and all over the place. I remember the bed. There was blood splashed across it and onto the wall behind."

Returning to the embassy, Dennis developed the rolls and made prints in the enlarger. "I handed everything over to the colonel. I don't remember doing an intel report or a written record." Somehow, the photographs found their way to Washington. Oddly, however, no mention of them was made in the final State Department report on Spike's murder. This would be one of several perplexing omissions in that document.

IF THERE WAS one individual for whom the Dubs investigation was much, much more than simply frustrating, it was Gul Mohammed. As the man behind the wheel of the hijacked Oldsmobile sedan, Spike's loyal driver was forced to endure several weeks of questioning. He was grilled on one occasion by Commandant Taroon, then repeatedly by U.S. officials. For a time, the Americans treated Gul as a suspect in the kidnapping. Minor coincidences and inconsistencies led to doubts over his version of events. Embassy staffers who knew the man well leapt to his defense, dismissing suspicions described in cables to and from Washington. Still, Chuck realized all leads had to be followed and resolved.

For instance, why was the security communications radio in the ambassador's car only partially functional on February 14? An encoder mounted under the passenger side front seat was disconnected from the alarm system. Was it disconnected during the vehicle's routine servicing? Or could a saboteur be responsible? The residence's garage, it emerged, was not always locked. In the end, the answer proved anything but sinister. Gul Mohammed himself reported the system wasn't working three days before the kidnapping. But the security communications specialist responsible for addressing the problem was off sick until Valentine's Day. She simply hadn't gotten around to fixing it.

Equally troubling were the clashes of testimony among the eyewitnesses. Nancy Sandrock's version of Spike being led into the hotel varied slightly with Gul Mohammed's. Reasonably, this might be expected with one of the witnesses relying on what he had heard, rather than seen. After all, when the first gang members took Spike into the building, Gul Mohammed's head was bowed forward by the gun pressing into the back of his neck. Another question mark was posed by what a United

Nation's employee told Chuck he had seen of the carjacking. This witness was convinced that the uniformed gunman who got into the back of the Oldsmobile was wearing an Afghan army jacket, not the clothing of a police sergeant. But if that was the case, why did Taroon acknowledge, during Chuck's interview, that his men found the sergeant's police tunic in room 117?

For more than two weeks, Gul Mohammed patiently answered these and all other questions put to him. He never once diverged from his original account. Nevertheless, one cable sent to State by the embassy wondered: "If the chauffeur was involved, which is still not a certainty, the important question is, who was he working for? And how was the kidnapping set up and executed in an area well policed, congested and almost under continual surveillance by host government security forces?"

Finally, on March 2, 1979, a beleaguered Gul Mohammed was led into a windowless room at Embassy Kabul. There, Chuck and the embassy's CIA station chief introduced him to another American officer, a man Gul had never seen before. In the vernacular of the Central Intelligence Agency's field operatives, the "box guy" had arrived from Washington. He was a polygrapher, a specialist in lie detection. It soon became clear the expert had travelled a long way for a very brief examination. Minutes after seating his subject at the conference table and connecting him to the polygraph, the man from Langley reached his conclusion. This came as no surprise to Chuck, nor to Embassy Kabul's CIA station chief. "We had already questioned the driver, hard and often. We felt he was clean. Same with the box guy. It's pretty clear when the first question the driver was asked was 'Do you ever lie?' and he answered right away 'no,' and the polygraph said he was being truthful. From there he told the same story, consistent with his earlier version."

At last Spike's driver and friend was in the clear. Chuck's investigation was able to move on, and with a sharper focus. As for the station chief, the episode with Gul Mohammed helped persuade Langley there was no real value in pursuing a separate CIA probe. "There was no demand for an investigation. The administration was swamped by Iran. The agency had other priorities." Still, he and his case officers did what they could. "I worked on it for a long time. Eventually I got a look into the police file." This was something of an espionage coup. An Afghan officer, covertly working for the CIA, accessed the regime's secret file on the Dubs case. "He was someone I trusted a lot." But the intelligence uncovered was nil. "The file was empty. Completely empty. I didn't know exactly what we might have expected to be in it, but I was hoping for their best guess as to what was behind it all. Who the kidnappers were, why they did what they did. But there was nothing. It was picked clean."

This was more than merely suspicious; it was damning in the extreme. In Afghanistan, the late 1970s was an era of paper records, often manually written. Afghan officialdom was notorious for its paper burden. Even before the PDPA's doctrinaire bureaucrats, the country's governments had thrived on creating permits and licenses and documents of every description. The police, especially the maniacally severe Interior police, excelled at filling desks and filing cabinets and storage rooms with paper documents, adorned with elaborate wax seals and hopelessly flamboyant official signatures, all tied up in neat bundles. Yet the slaughter in room 117 yielded nothing but empty drawers. Every trace of paperwork had vanished. There were no statements, no transcripts. No event logs, no dates, names or descriptions. No photographs or drawings, no lists of guns, cartridge shells, bullets or unexpended rounds.

Where were the boxes stuffed with physical evidence? There were none. And for each of the four alleged gang members, there was not a single fingerprint pad nor any kind of certificate. Nothing showing even one man's date or place of birth, his father's identity and where the family lived. There was nothing but a big, black void. It was as though the men had never existed.

Making matters worse, the regime sought to impair Chuck's investigation in an even uglier way. As Abdul Ghafari left the embassy one evening, Taroon's men were waiting for him. They told him he was under arrest and forced him into the back of a car. He was taken directly to their commandant's basement dungeon at the interior ministry. There, Abdul Ghafari endured two days of questioning by the secret police. He was beaten repeatedly and tortured with the Communist regime's notorious "telephone." This device consisted of a small black generator, manually charged by spinning a hand crank in the manner of an antique box telephone. Wire leads attached to the victim's body delivered electric shocks, at times with enough force to burn skin. In Ghafari's case, the torturers connected his fingertips to the machine, then spun the generator fast and hard. It was an agonizing ordeal, but the prisoner refused to talk.

What happened next probably speaks to Taroon's purpose in arresting Chuck's cherished Afghan colleague: they let him go, almost as if they hoped Abdul Ghafari would spread word of the treatment awaiting anyone suspected of crossing the Taraki/Amin regime. Indeed, Ghafari did just that. He went directly to the U.S. embassy and told the security team everything that had been done to him. The impact was understandable. The Americans were made to wonder where the regime's terror tactics would end. How many more of their foreign service nationals would be subject to arbitrary arrest and torture? And would the threats end there, or would Americans find themselves locked up in Taroon's jails?

The answer wasn't long in coming. On March 8, Bruce

Amstutz's secretary, Soroya Massoud, was picked up and taken to the interior ministry. Under questioning, she was threatened with torture and death. Taroon's men forced her to sign a statement that she would become an informant for the regime. Soroya was released, but she related every detail of her ordeal to Amstutz and Chuck. The Americans welcomed her back to her post, refusing to be intimidated. But four days later, it happened again. A Peace Corps language instructor, Abaidullah Popal, was arrested and made to sign a document, a confession that he and a "certain Peace Corps volunteer" were CIA agents. Amstutz cabled Washington, stressing the obvious: "The embassy appreciated the increased risks assumed by these local employees who came forth and discussed their harassment with embassy officers. This required commendable courage on their parts." He concluded the message with a request. Should Abdul Ghafari and Soroya Massoud be forced to flee to Pakistan, Embassy Islamabad should "assist in processing them to enter the U.S. under conditional entry..."

NONE OF THESE EVENTS were going unnoticed in Washington, despite other world crises dominating the agenda. Emotions were still raw in the aftermath of Spike's funeral. Word of the Afghan authorities' increasingly aggressive and belligerent stance finally forced the Carter administration's hand. An active response was needed, not only over the ambassador's murder but to the growing influence of the Soviet Union over its client regime in Kabul. With encouragement from his hawkish national security advisor, Zbigniew Brzezinski, Jimmy Carter and his team began choosing from a selection of covert action options laid out by the CIA. These ranged from the soft approach of simply publicizing the Soviet role in Afghanistan, to full blooded support for the anti-Communist insurgency against the PDPA regime. Put another way, the president's choices ranged from "harassment to the actual overthrow of the present Communist government."

U.S. aid could be lethal or non-lethal in nature, the CIA advised in a memo dated February 28, 1979. "The easiest way to support the insurgents is to furnish them with money on a unilateral basis. We have identified a number of Afghan exile leaders through whom such funds could be channelled, although our ability to monitor how the money actually is spent would be limited." Then the memo turned to lethal options. Viewed now with the benefit of hindsight, the agency's rather bland phrases take on a haunting resonance:

Funds could be provided to the insurgents to purchase lethal military equipment:

> The Saudis could be asked to front for us on this...
> Equipment which could upgrade the insurgents' combat capabilities might include small arms, sniper equipment, light to medium crew-served weapons, unconventional demolitions, and anti-aircraft weapons such as the Soviet SA-7 missiles.
> Training also would be required, and with full GOP (Government of Pakistan) cooperation, a small CIA team could handle this in NWFP.

Most eerily, the memo described a possible consequence of U.S. support for the Afghan insurgents: escalation. American aid, the memo said, "could lead to increased Soviet involvement in Afghanistan, as we believe they will take strong measures to ensure that the communist regime is not displaced. A long drawn-out insurgency would result in great suffering for the people involved, with no guarantee that a satisfactory outcome would be achieved."

The CIA memo also struck a note of caution, a warning which arguably no United States president has ever come to comprehend:

> Because of geographical considerations, the cooperation—or at least tacit endorsement—of the Government of Pakistan (GOP) would be almost mandatory if we were to provide significant material support to the insurgents. Such cooperation is by no means assured; the GOP would be likely to demand a high price in return for its cooperation—viz. greatly increased military and economic assistance. This would involve us in supporting the political status quo in Pakistan.

Decades later, that "high price" continues to be paid by the United States. Pakistan's military establishment imposed its own objectives on the CIA program, and did so from the start. Extremist Afghan opposition figures were favored over moderate nationalists. By the mid-1990s, Pakistan was nurturing the Afghan Taliban, paving the radicals' road to power. Even today, the Afghan Taliban's return to Kabul is supported by the movement's patrons within Pakistan's military.

AS MARCH turned to April, Chuck Boles and his team encountered increasing hostility from the regime. Still they continued approaching contacts in the Afghan ministries, junior office holders and functionaries who previously had been helpful sources. Many refused to speak with the investigators. To the small number still willing to risk meeting Chuck or taking his calls, he asked for their thoughts on the nagging issues left hanging by the events of February 14. Why was the ambassador's car stopped so near the Prime Ministry and the USICA American Center? The place was within sight of no fewer than three Afghan police sentry posts. And the three men who joined the first gunman: one source claimed they were seen getting out of a police vehicle before approaching the Oldsmobile. Could anyone verify that? And what about the

Hotel Kabul? Why choose a room exposed to the street to make a final stand? Were the kidnappers somehow given assurances they would make a clean getaway?

The Americans made little headway with these lines of inquiry. Then, one afternoon at a regime gathering for foreign diplomats, Chuck spotted a familiar face in the crowd: Lt. Col. Sergei Bakhturin. The Soviets had been stonewalling Chuck's attempts to question their personnel. Now here was the lead KGB officer himself, striding across the room towards him, extending an open hand, greeting the American as one would an old comrade. "He said to me: 'You know, Chuck, I didn't have any control over the Afghans. It was beyond my control.' So I flat out asked him. Did he expect us to believe we had just been seeing things? That our eyes played tricks on us? He didn't much care for my questions after that. He just kind of slunk away. We had no way to compel the Russians to cooperate with us. And so they didn't, not in any way."

Similarly, Bruce Flatin managed to buttonhole the elusive Afghan Foreign Minister at an official gathering. But the political counsellor's queries about the Valentine's Day bloodbath drew only "slippery answers" from Hafizullah Amin. As to the firearms the Americans were seeking, Amin claimed, "We have all kinds of weapons we pick up here throughout the city for various crimes all the time." In other words, it was hard to tell which weapons were which anymore.

Through the gloom and despair of this time, the broader American community in Kabul continued to go about daily life. At the American Center, a gradual realization came over Louise Taylor and her colleagues: the show must go on. "Shortly after we began recovering from Spike's death, our embassy went ahead with the production of *Oklahoma!* I did the direction and the choreography." The production's 60 to 70 cast members and crew had taken a hiatus after Spike's death. "We finally decided that he would have wanted us to go on with this and we resumed it. My husband took over Spike's role. By April or so, when we put the production on for a week, Kabul had more or less come back to its normal, fairly vibrant self, except the Russians were really not part of this." It took 16 different nationalities to mount the show. David Litt played the role of Curly, and several of the embassy's Marines sang and danced.

For Louise's husband, Jim, the staging of *Oklahoma!* was a way to "move beyond the tragedy." Younger members of the American community, too, sensed tensions easing somewhat. Steve Rotz and his schoolmates continued to ride the bus to class. "There were certainly increased levels of security and awareness. We still had free range–I'd walk out onto Darulaman Road and flag down a taxi, and go drink chai and eat nan with the street dealers. And we'd talk politics. Many Afghans openly said they hoped we'd help them fight against the Soviet Union. They would always welcome you and encourage you in that conversation."

The school even continued road trips. The annual basketball tournament in Islamabad came off on schedule, with the American school teams from Pakistan, Afghanistan and India. "We loaded up one of those Blue Bird buses and drove over the Khyber Pass, down through Peshawar and into Islamabad. And that was harrowing. Those roads are narrow, and we saw guys walking around with Kalashnikovs. A lot of the parents followed in their personal cars, we were kind of a convoy."

The American families had no inkling they would be among the last travellers to pass freely over the Khyber Pass. Within months, this ancient Silk Road passage through the Spin Gar mountains between Pakistan and Afghanistan would become a forbidding geopolitical demarcation, a chokepoint in one of the Cold War's bloodiest standoffs. Soviet tanks would roll past the teahouses of Kabul. And talk of conflict would give way to the sounds of war; continuous warfare that rages to this day.

Chapter 13

Spies, Guns and Money

Soon after President Carter received the CIA's list of possible actions in Afghanistan, an event occurred that proved to be a catalyst for covert U.S. aid to the anti-Soviet mujahideen: a popular uprising in the northern Afghan city of Herat. In mid-March, Afghan National Army troops stationed in the city mutinied in support of a citizen insurrection against the PDPA regime's radical reforms for agricultural landholdings. Soviet advisers and citizens were killed in the initial stages by mutineers and anti-government fighters. When Amin and Taraki ordered Communist forces to recapture of the city, thousands of Herati civilians lost their lives.

To get a clearer picture of the losses, CIA case officer Warren Marik touched base with friendly East Bloc sources in Kabul's diplomatic community. "Because my family's background is Czech, the guys at the Czechoslovak embassy would whisper in my car. They told me about the Herat massacre because so many of their citizens died there." To the CIA and the president's National Security Council advisers, the bloodletting in Herat emphasized the weakness of the Kabul government—and the Afghan people's hatred of the regime's Soviet patrons. The agency talked up the armed opposition forces based in Pakistan and their backers in Saudi Arabia, providing Carter with further encouragement to aid the guerrillas.

"Senior members of the Saudi Government are very much

impressed with the recent military successes of Afghanistan rebel units," the CIA reported on March 27, 1979. "They believe that these units have accomplished major victories in spite of a lack of weapons, money and logistical support." The report detailed negotiations between the Saudis and Pakistani President Zia-ul-Huq to finance the Afghan National Liberation Front, the ANLF. "At the moment, Saudi and Pakistan Governments are in continuous contact on this issue. In mid-March Zia informed Crown Prince Fahd that he believed that any kind of Pakistani aid to the ANLF would cause him problems with the Soviet Union, which, at the moment, he perceives to be almost insurmountable. Because of their promise not to aid the ANLF without Zia's approval, senior members of the Saudi Government are considering making a discreet approach to the United States Government (USG) with regard to providing support to the ANLF."

The following day, the CIA reported Pakistan had been subjected to an implied threat by the Kremlin by way of a strongly worded diplomatic cable, or démarche, sent to President Zia. "In the démarche, the Soviets accuse the Government of Pakistan of 'connivance' in the activities of the Afghan dissidents against the Kabul regime, and say that they 'cannot remain indifferent' to armed attacks on a country with which they are allied by treaty." At the same time, the Soviet leadership was beefing up PDPA forces in Afghanistan. Although rejecting the Taraki government's pleas for Soviet troops to help put down the Herat rebellion, the Kremlin increased its shipments of military hardware to the regime. The PDPA's firepower was bolstered with Mi-24 helicopter gunships and T-62 tanks, as well as MiG-21 warplanes configured for ground attacks against opposition targets.

All of this made clear that the Communist regime's second year in power was certain to be even more violent and unpredictable than its first. In numerous cables to Embassy Kabul,

Secretary Vance's office wondered if a breaking point was at hand. Would American foreign service officers and their families no longer be safe in Afghanistan? In particular, was Chuck Boles placing himself in the regime's crosshairs by so doggedly pursuing the Dubs probe? On this issue, Bruce Amstutz found it impossible to disagree. He replied on April 2 that Chuck should be reassigned out of Afghanistan due to "his now awkward relationship with the interior ministry." It was a recommendation Amstutz did not make lightly. "For selfish reasons, I will be sad to see Boles leave. In my 22 years in the foreign service, I have never served with an RSO as competent and steady as he. He is unquestionably one of the very best."

Vance's office agreed to have a replacement in Kabul by May 16. Chuck would be given a week to get the new officer up to speed, then leave for Washington on May 23. Immediately upon his arrival in DC, he would present the final findings of his investigation. In the meantime, the pathologists and ballistics experts in Washington continued their work. Amstutz was advised by cable: "The report on forensic examination of Ambassador's clothing not yet finalized. Our review and analysis of all available data is continuing. We will advise you of results of forensic examination and will provide any additional significant data that might be contained in complete autopsy report upon receipt."

CHUCK BOLE'S SUPERIORS at the U.S. State Department's Diplomatic Security Service thought they knew what to expect from his final report on the murder of Ambassador Dubs. But when Chuck arrived at Foggy Bottom in the last week of May, 1979, the office was shaken by his findings. "State sponsored terrorism," the report declared. Spike's abduction was planned and executed by the Afghan Communist regime. The kidnappers were patsies; mere pawns. Once the ambassador's captivity was secured, nobody in room 117 was meant to come out alive.

Ron Kelly, the supervising security officer, concurred with these conclusions–which only made Chuck's other central finding that much more chilling. "That section was about the Soviets' role. We couldn't be sure they were in on the planning, but they certainly took part in Spike's murder."

The fatal gunshots were the pistol rounds heard after the automatic fire ended. The shooter was the plainclothes regime cop, armed by the KGB. The cover-up afterward further evidenced the premeditated nature of the crime: the murder of the third gang member; ditto the fourth man, the mystery corpse. The sweeping up and disappearance of all the physical evidence. And, of course, the coordinated, unyielding obstruction by the regime and the Soviets. All of this spoke to a purposeful attempt to bury the truth about the assassination of the United States Ambassador in doubt and disinformation.

Vance and his aides realized the first thing they must do with the report: put it under wraps. Only with the utmost discretion would the document be shared with the president and his top security officials. Without question, no aspect of the investigators' findings would be made public. Only when the State Department was ready to compile a complete report, including the final autopsy and forensics results, would the government provide a carefully drafted summary to the American people.

It is impossible to measure the degree to which Chuck's report influenced the Carter administration's next steps on Afghanistan. But the secret, limited distribution of his findings coincided with a tougher, more determined stance against the PDPA and the Soviet Union. On April 6, Vice-President Walter Mondale convened an intelligence meeting on Afghanistan at the White House. The list of attendees spoke to the substantially increased profile the issue was commanding on the administration's foreign policy agenda. In the chair was Zbigniew Brzezinski, flanked by senior officers of the National

Security Council, together with CIA Director Stansfield Turner and his deputy Frank Carlucci. Attorney General Griffin Bell was there, as were officers of the Joint Chiefs of Staff and the Office of Management and Budget. Noticeably missing was anyone from the State Department. Neither Cyrus Vance was there, nor his deputy Warren Christopher. And most certainly the room was devoid of a single American foreign service veteran steeped in Spike Dubs' beliefs in a constructive, conflict-averse approach to international affairs.

Mondale opened the session at full throttle. "It seems to me that this Afghanistan issue provides a good opportunity for us here. We have the Russians deeply involved in the internal affairs of another country and they are obviously trying to mask it with counterattacks to put us on the defensive. They are supporting a highly unpopular government in Afghanistan; secondly, they are fighting the world of Islam. It is embarrassing to them. It would be nice for us to be seen on the other side... I think we ought to keep the heat on this. The Russians are jumpy as hell about this."

Right away, the discussion turned to Pakistan and its hosting of Afghan opposition forces. The Pakistanis were reluctant to become too involved for fear of Soviet retaliation. Mondale interjected: "The Russians are getting away with murder and we should not take it." Spike's name was not expressly mentioned. It didn't need to be. Brzezinski took Mondale's outburst as his cue. "We have a few modest proposals for assisting the Afghans and the Pakistanis. In view of the Vice President's comments—which are shared by the President—let us go first to the action proposals for Afghanistan. We have all read Stan's paper—the proposals all involve either some assistance to the Pakistanis or direct financial aid to the insurgents." After going through the CIA Director's proposals, Brzezinski said, "We are aware that a major insurgency is in progress. It is in our national interest that this insurgency continue even if it does not succeed."

Stansfield Turner stressed, "I want to make the point that covert actions will not turn the tide but they could help sustain insurgency there. Whether we are going to overturn the government or not should not be the main question. This program has to be accompanied by a strong policy of support for Pakistan."

In those early days, no one in the room could have foretold the CIA Director voicing what was destined to become the Achilles heel of America's involvement in Afghanistan: "A strong policy of support for Pakistan." Instead, Brzezinski picked up where Turner left off. "My inclination would be to pick from this list those actions that we would only undertake with Pakistan if they are willing to cooperate. If they are not willing to cooperate, we do not do it." He took the group through the CIA's options, starting with non-military measures, beginning with propaganda broadcasts into Afghanistan from stations in Pakistan. "Then we could consider some financial aid and send in a survey team to examine on-site possibilities for other forms of support—all of these actions would require cooperation with the Pakistani intelligence services."

There was no discussion of the espionage entity central to Pakistan's support for the Afghan resistance, the Inter-Services Intelligence agency. Staffed by serving officers of the country's military, the ISI in 1979 was growing rapidly in size, capability and political power. This was hardly surprising, given that Pakistan's president, Zia-ul-Haq, was a four-star general who seized power in a coup two years earlier. Yet not the slightest concern was raised, during that meeting at the White House, over the many ways the Zia regime resembled Afghanistan's PDPA. No one voiced a warning that channeling military aid through the spying apparatus of a third world Islamic dictatorship might backfire. The ISI was already favoring Afghan resistance groups from only one of the country's ethnic groups, the dominant Pashtuns. Equally viable opposition fronts from the Tajik, Uzbek and Hazara communities were tolerated by the Pakistanis, but severely rationed, if not starved, of material aid.

No one suggested an alternate strategy. For instance, why couldn't the United States devise the means to side-step both the Communist regime and the opposition guerrillas, boosting humanitarian assistance directly to rural Afghan communities? Why not try a bold, non-military scheme before getting involved in an escalating civil war on the other side of the globe? Sadly, there were no submissions of this kind from anyone seated at that conference table, or for that matter from anywhere within the administration. Arguably the only American foreign service professional who would have dared press such an unconventional initiative was now lying in Section 5, Site 149 of Arlington National Cemetery.

Three weeks later, Turner reported the CIA's progress to Brzezinski. "You should be aware that Islamabad Station is in unilateral contact with a fairly prominent Afghan dissident leader, who, on 24 April requested $1,000,000 from us to purchase ammunition from unidentified sources in Pakistan. We advised him that we had no policy authority to grant his request." The agency was focusing on propaganda as instructed, Turner wrote. "We are readying a senior covert action officer to visit Islamabad and Kabul, to assess and, where appropriate, to initiate psychological operations against the Soviet presence in Afghanistan. The activities which this officer will discuss in the field include: distribution of anti-Soviet propaganda leaflets; production and distribution of cassette tapes; development of spokesmen to project the dissident message effectively; means of getting that message to the foreign press; and black operations."

Though Congress, at that time, was withholding approval of aiding the mujahideen by way of "black operations," the United States had now entered the darker regions of the armed

...

conflict in Afghanistan. Exactly as Spike Dubs would not have wished.

AT EMBASSY KABUL, Spike's former staffers realized their mission's future was in doubt. While not in the loop about plans for aiding the mujahideen, they could sense Washington was poised to take much more drastic steps than the aid reductions announced thus far. Bruce Amstutz realized he needed to advocate his team's interests more forcefully—and in the spirit of their fallen ambassador's principles. In early June, the chargé pleaded his officers' case in a lengthy cable to State in DC. "We are very mindful of Ambassador Dubs' own views on Afghanistan. He recognized that the U.S. has few interests in Afghanistan, per se. Accordingly, he felt that the U.S. should look on Afghanistan primarily in terms of regional stability. He strongly believed that Afghanistan should not become a destabilizing factor and that we should cooperate with other nations, including the free nations of this area, in seeking to offer the Afghans an alternative presence to that of the Soviet Union."

Amstutz argued that the people of Afghanistan wanted and needed U.S. aid to continue. "Our modest aid projects have been directed at meeting basic human needs and serve to demonstrate that the U.S. continues to have humanitarian concerns about impoverished Afghanistan and its people, notwithstanding the leadership's sometimes hostile stance. We would also note that, to the best of our knowledge, none of the countries of the area have suggested that the U.S. cut off all aid to Afghanistan. The maintenance of such a presence would, moreover, enable the U.S. to respond more rapidly to any favorable developments on the domestic Afghan political scene."

It is unlikely these words or sentiments ever reached the White House. There, the only telescope now looking at Afghanistan was focused on a far different kind of intervention.

On July 3, 1979, Jimmy Carter signed a secret finding authorizing the CIA to provide some $695,000 in cash or non-military supplies to Afghanistan's "insurgents." Everyone concerned with the top-secret measure must have realized this first modest stipend of support could prove to be the thin edge of a dangerously swelling wedge. But no one could have predicted that within just one year's time, a covert aid program launched with barely enough cash to fill a large briefcase would balloon to some $20 million and more—and in the form of cold, hard gunmetal; weapons to be used against Soviet troops.

In that early summer of 1979, U.S. policy makers were beginning to appreciate the Soviets' own frustrations with the Afghan regime. On July 16, the NSC convened a meeting with State and the CIA to consider a leak provided to Bruce Amstutz by none other than the Ambassador of Communist East Germany. The Soviets, the envoy disclosed, were fed up with the PDPA's Khalqi leadership. They would be ousted in August to "protect the Afghan revolution." The NSC puzzled over the reasons why a Soviet bloc official had forwarded the signal to the Americans. "Perhaps just to alert us to protect our people since we have been hitting them hard in the aftermath of the Dubs killing, or perhaps they want us to acquiesce in Soviet establishment of a new government." Still, the East German had expressed a good deal of urgency to his American counterpart: for his own family's safety, he was sending them home.

Embassy Kabul's own network of sources was indicating the PDPA government was wobbling out of control. In response, State gave Amstutz two days to decide whether the mission's dependents should be evacuated. As well, he should make direct contact with the Soviet political counsellor who had been tipped as the point man in Kabul for the "dump Amin" plot. Amstutz was to convey the administration's position that "we do not believe that any cosmetic changes in the Afghan Government will solve the Soviets' problem; we will not give our blessing to any such government; we believe that a restoration of a truly neutral Afghan Government would be in our mutual interests; and we have no interest in seeing a government in Afghanistan that would pose a threat to legitimate Soviet interests." As well, the CIA station in Kabul was to seek additional intelligence either confirming or discounting the East German leak.

As July wore on, the pace of events accelerated. All the parties–Afghan, American, Soviet–seemed at a loss to control their respective agendas. Kabul was wracked by uncertainly and fear. Such was the chaos within the PDPA leadership that nobody dared predict what turmoil the coming weeks might bring. For their part, many of the American families in Afghanistan had already begun their contingency planning. The decision had been taken to close the American School. Should parents now enroll their children at another, more stable American outpost in Asia, or return home to the States?

On July 23, the matter was taken out of their hands. The State Department issued an order for the mission's dependents to leave Afghanistan as soon as possible. The logistics of the withdrawal meant this would take weeks, not days, especially because the embassy's staff was also being drawn down. From a peak of 160 employees, Amstutz would be left with only 48 officers. Mike, Doug and Warren were staying on, as was Jim Taylor. With her Russian language skills, Louise was able to remain as an assistant in the CIA station.

For the officers who would continue working in Kabul, even the summer's heat couldn't relieve the unsettling chill that had come over the embassy. The departure of so many fellow Americans became yet another sad epilogue to the loss of Ambassador Dubs. Their leader had been stolen from them, savagely. Now entire families were ferried from their homes to Kabul Airport for a flight out of Afghanistan. August saw a succession of tearful goodbyes. Steve Rotz, for one, did not want to leave. "I really liked it there and I felt it was too short of a stay. I think my sister Christie was happy to go back home. She was happy to see her friends. But I was sad about leaving." So too was his teacher, Jim Gurnett. "My visa depended on working at the school, and there were really no other possibilities at that time. Leaving wasn't something we wanted to do but there was no real choice."

Like Steve, Mark Flatin was heading home with a copy of the American School's yearbook under his arm. A lot of work went into assembling the volume, with pictures supplied by photo instructor Jim Gurnett and his students. Tensions in Kabul led to a road trip to Peshawar to have the yearbooks printed. A dedication page for Spike took pride of place in the volume. The students wrote:

> Adolph Dubs cared very much for our school and for the children here. He showed this by telling us during a visit to our school that his door would always be open to us. He called this school "tops".
> He came to many of our sports and drama events and cheered us on like not many ambassadors care to do. He was, in short, our biggest booster. He sat in on parent-teacher meetings and offered many ideas and suggestions to involve the community in the workings of this school.
> A wise man, kind to us beyond the call of duty. He truly represented (us) and is our inspiration.
> Each of us at AISK offers our condolences to Mrs. Dubs, and all of his other relatives. Each of us will remember his death as a personal loss.

A number of the family members leaving Kabul behind were startled by the reception awaiting them at their next destination. The wife of one senior Embassy Kabul professional was met at the arrivals gate in Frankfurt by two American officials. There was no greeting, no 'Welcome to Germany.' Instead, the men told her: "Say nothing. Don't talk to reporters. Don't tell anybody about anything that happened in Kabul."

CLOUDS CONTINUED to gather over the mission left behind. On the evening of August 12, Abdul Ghafari answered a knock at his front door. Before him were two plainclothes operatives from the interior ministry. Bruce Amstutz cabled State that the secret policemen put his Afghan security officer in the back seat of a Volga sedan, outfitted with blinds over the windows "to screen its occupants from outside view." Taking a "circuitous and confusing route" to a safe-house, the men hustled their prisoner inside and down to the basement. There, Abdul Ghafari was questioned by "Dari-speaking men." The interrogators "concealed their identity by staying behind a heavy drape," about which Amstutz added, "NOTE: A usual procedure reportedly when Russians are present at an interrogation." In the end, Ghafari was verbally assaulted and threatened, but not beaten. "He was warned if he informed the Americans of his questioning, he would be killed." Then he was driven home. As before, Abdul ignored the warning and immediately reported the incident to the Americans.

Meantime, the CIA was acting on President Carter's approval of the agency's covert operations plan. On August 22, Langley informed the NSC, "A special team of propaganda and linguistic experts has been assembled and is producing both broadcast and printed material for distribution inside Afghanistan. Six leaflets have been produced and two of these have been circulated in Afghanistan, including Kabul. Four tape cassettes have been recorded with two of these distributed in Afghanistan. Radio material is being produced regularly for a low-power insurgent radio now operating near the Afghan-Pakistan border."

As for the cash and non-lethal aid, a disbursement had been made to an "asset" in Nuristan province "in support of that tribe's unique insurgency effort." As well, one of the agency's own Afghan agents "with excellent ties to the Peshawar insurgent leadership is enroute to Pakistan" to provide funds to "a coalition of dissident Afghan leaders." Separately, an entity described as "Pakistan liaison"–the ISI–agreed to serve as a channel for CIA aid to the Afghan guerrilla groups. A powerful shortwave radio transmitter capable of broadcasting to "nearly one-half of Afghanistan" would soon be ready for shipment to the mujahideen, via the ISI. The agency also advised that "Action is being taken to assemble up to 50 medical kits for the insurgents, one kit serving 50 men."

On August 25, the State Department received an alarming cable from its chargé in Kabul. Amstutz wrote: "I send this because I am worried about our presence here." His concern was not only for the safety of his remaining American staff, "but for the honor of the U.S. Government" in the face of the Afghan Foreign Minister's hostility. Amin was continuing to mistreat and intimidate Embassy Kabul's Afghan employees. "Not only does it confirm the enmity which Amin has for the United States (the secret police are under his direct control), but it raises a real concern about the safety of our American personnel."

Amstutz referred to the regime's "all-out effort to plant listening devices in our residences." More aggressive action was taken against the Pakistan embassy: one of its officers had been abducted by Amin's men. He was still missing. The PDPA regime, the chargé cautioned, "is not above ignoring diplomatic immunities and international standards of decency." At some point, "Amin may arrest one of our American employees, on doctored or circumstantial evidence, in order to 'prove' some point of his or hold us hostage." He cited "Amin's semi-psychopathic desire to humiliate and revenge himself" against the

U.S., and "the still unfinished business of who was responsible for Ambassador Dubs's death." About this, he wrote, "we continue to get disturbing reports about Amin's role in the affair."

THE AIR OF CHAOS hanging over Kabul was reaching a breaking point. But it was Amin himself, and his rivals, who would be caught in the next tremor of violence. On September 12, 1979, President Taraki invited Amin to meet him for talks at the presidential palace. Amin's staunchest Khalqi opponents, known as the "gang of four," would also be there. Amin refused the invitation. He'd been tipped off: he knew the Soviets had made him a marked man. And although Taraki had promoted Amin to Prime Minister some months earlier, his powers were actually reduced. As well, his ally Taroon had been replaced as Commandant of Police. Still, the Soviets put on a show of wishing to end to the regime's infighting. On orders from Foreign Minister Andrei Gromyko, Puzanov spent two days cajoling a gloomy, truculent Amin. He should meet and talk with Taraki, with Puzanov as mediator. Finally, the Soviet envoy managed to reschedule the meeting.

On September 14, Amin arrived at the palace, accompanied by Taroon and one of his subordinates. Puzanov was waiting upstairs in the president's residence with Taraki. As Amin and his men entered the stairway, Taraki's bodyguards opened fire. Taroon was gunned down and died on the spot. Amin barely escaped with his life. Desperate to survive, he sped across town, directly to the Afghan National Army garrison. There, he convinced his Khalqi confederates among the command to do his bidding.

Within the hour, troops entered the palace and placed Taraki under arrest. Tanks and other armored vehicles took up positions at strategic points in the capital. Amin's power grab succeeded. The public at large, and the foreign diplomatic community, were left completely in the dark. On the evening of September 16, Kabul Television announced that Nur Mohammed Taraki had informed the PDPA's politburo that he was "sick" and could no longer carry out his duties. Hafizullah Amin had been named President of the Revolutionary Council and Secretary-General of the PDPA. He would also retain his title as Prime Minister.

Amstutz cabled Washington with the news. Taraki, it was rumored, had been wounded in a shootout. Word of a violent confrontation had been confirmed when Amin ordered flags to fly at half-mast in the city for the "martyr" Taroon. The chargé concluded his cable on September 16 with a note of searing contempt. "Taroon's passing will go largely unmourned. This brutal, psychopathic killer was second only to Amin in the amount of blood on his hands."

Soon enough, Amin burnished his own dark reputation. He ordered the wounded Taraki to be murdered in his hospital bed. The leader Amin once regaled as The Great Thinker was smothered with his own pillow by Amin's henchmen. Meantime, the new president's "gang of four" rivals had been forced to take sanctuary in the residence of a senior official from the Soviet embassy. From there, they heard Kabul Radio announce that Taraki had perished from a serious illness, after dedicating his life to the glorious revolution.

The Soviets were stunned by these events. Leonid Brezhnev, records later revealed, had expected Amin to move Taraki to one side, not butcher him. The episode steeled the Kremlin's resolve to finally deal with their mercurial Afghan underling. A decision was made to spirit Amin's four PDPA opponents out of Afghanistan to Moscow, where they could be held in reserve for the day Amin's removal might become an unavoidable necessity. Yuri Andropov, Chairman of the KGB, had just the officer in mind to orchestrate the extraction: Lt. Col. Sergei Bakhturin, assistant ambassador and security chief of the USSR Embassy in Afghanistan.

The colonel executed the mission with cool precision. Although one of Amin's rivals strayed into the city and was apprehended by Afghan police, Bakhturin spirited the three remaining fugitives to a safehouse within the walls of the Soviet embassy. This was the hideout of a top-secret, 38-man advance guard of KGB Special Troops. Their presence was concealed even from the embassy's officers and employees. Code named "Zenit," the unit had arrived in Kabul two months earlier. It had been Bakhturin's mission to move the men and their weapons undetected across the capital and into the embassy grounds. In the same way, he now devised a plan to move the three Afghans to Bagram Air Base, an hour's drive north of Kabul, in shipping containers, safe from the prying eyes of Amin's police. The caper came off without incident. An Ilyushin-76 cargo plane carried the fugitives out of the Afghan capital and north to Tashkent.

For his efforts, Bakhturin received a personal commendation from Andropov. Within weeks, the colonel had his next assignment. Another squad of specially-trained KGB troops, the Alpha Group, was dispatched to Kabul. Like the Zenit team, their presence was to be concealed from the Afghan regime. Bakhturin and his rezident, Viliov Osadchy, needed no further explanation: the Kremlin was laying the groundwork for a military incursion, an armed intervention in Afghanistan. The Zenit and Alpha groups were shock troops. Their insertion would give Soviet forces the potential for a powerful first thrust. In advance of what, exactly? A full-scale invasion? Doubtless that information would follow. For now, the KGB men had only their orders, which they were obligated to conceal not just from the Afghan regime, but from their own ambassador and his staff as well.

BY THE AUTUMN of 1979, all of Kabul was preoccupied with trying to foretell the future. The bazaars, the government's ministries, the city's foreign embassies—all were alive with rumor and conjecture. The 48 Americans left staffing Embassy Kabul were hungry for reliable clues as to what was really going on within Amin's leadership cadre. And how would the Soviets adapt their strategy in Afghanistan? The embassy's sources had managed to confirm Ambassador Puzanov's presence at the gunfight that ended Taraki's career. Just how secure could the USSR's colony in Afghanistan hope to be? It had swollen in size to nearly 7,000 Soviet citizens, almost all of them located in the capital and at Bagram Air Base. Would Moscow act to protect this major outpost?

Langley was showing only a passing interest in the matter. Not so their station chief in Kabul. He longed for answers, for reliable intelligence. Helpfully, he bumped into an acquaintance at a diplomatic function one evening in October: a military attaché from the Soviet embassy. As in their previous encounters, the Russian was at ease chatting with the American, whose intelligence role was known to the Soviets. The CIA man commented that the attaché and his comrades must be feeling exposed, in light of Amin's erratic behavior. "Yes," the Russian replied, "but soon we will solve that matter, and we won't be exposed any longer."

The next day, Langley received a report from its Kabul station on this and other clues regarding the Soviets' strategic mindset and possible intentions. The signal was ignored. No follow up action was requested. Washington's indifference was baffling to Embassy Kabul's staffers. Political counsellor Jim Taylor, for one, believed the Kremlin's impatience with their unstable Afghan client regime was nearing a breaking point. But getting this across to State and the Carter White House was next to impossible. "(We) eventually got to the point of addressing the issue of what would the Soviets do if things really got bad. Then, of course, you get into the bureaucratic problem of, 'Hey, we are the embassy in Kabul and are not supposed to be reporting on what the Soviets will or will not do, that is Embassy Moscow's job.'"

Still, Jim and his colleagues persevered. "Embassy Moscow, in this particular debate, constantly took the position that the Soviets would not send troops to Afghanistan. It was just outside their vital sphere of interest and they don't belong to the Warsaw Pact, and all of the reasons that it just made good sense for Soviet specialists. So, therefore, you had the two opposing positions. We could not say, "Yes, they will send troops," we said in effect, "Yes, the Afghans believe that the response will be a positive one when they request it [not if they request it]." Jim's counterparts at Embassy Moscow were unimpressed. "A couple of times they came back and in effect told us to mind our own business."

In Washington, the administration had no time for turf wars among its diplomats overseas, least of all on the subject of Afghanistan. More urgent global crises were going critical. On November 4, Embassy Tehran was stormed once again, this time with dire consequences: 52 Americans taken hostage. One of the U.S. foreign service officers held by the Iranian revolutionaries was Al Golacinski, the security specialist who had backed up Chuck Boles in Kabul in the early stages of the Dubs investigation. He and the other hostages would be held for some 444 days until January 20, 1981. Jimmy Carter denounced the action, declaring the American captives "victims of terrorism."

THE HOSTAGE CRISIS further distracted the administration from the storm gathering over Afghanistan. By mid-December, Col. Bakhturin was concealing what he described as "a ragged hive" of KGB special troops camped out in the basement rooms and hallways of villas inside the Soviet embassy's walls. Yet to the outside world, only the usual 100-man Border Guards company was visible, standing guard on the mission's

Secret U.S. cable on ambassador's slaying

Soviet signal started gunfire

(Times-Post news service)

WASHINGTON — "One Soviet adviser helped to arm an Afghan policeman. Two other Soviet police advisers and (Sergei) Bakhturin (Soviet embassy security officer) went out to the balcony. The tall, senior Soviet adviser then made hand signals from the balcony, presumably positioning the snipers across the st

Then, acc state depa police com gunfire int where U.S "Spike" Du tage. Horri helplessly barrage o the shatt dead.

Despit Afghanis advisers assault confider availab

asserts that at least three advisers played "operation roles" in the unsuccessful Afghan effort to rescue Dubs.

Written two hours after Dubs' killing, and before controversy began to swirl around the Soviet role, the cable and the eyewitness accounts it contains underpin the administration's publicly stated anger at the Soviet envoy.

headquarters on Feb. 14 shortly after Dubs was abducted by four men — include:

● Soviet advisers gave hand signals that began and halted the gunfire. After the 40-second volley, Afghan "police snipers across the street continued to fire until two Soviet advisers gave hand signals to cut it off."

● Throughout the siege, a Soviet civilian was in the office of Maj. Daoud Taroun, the commander of

ted fic- art- of ver- the im- rev- the

Flags at half mast today on US envoy demise

KABUL, Feb. 15, (Bakhtar).— On the demise of the United Kabul, e flags epublic fly

```
Z 140840Z FEB 79
FM AMEMBASSY KABUL
TO SECSTATE WASHDC FLASH 2170
AMEMBASSY ISLAMABAD FLASH
C O N F I D E N T I A L KABUL 1076
E.O. 12065: GDS 2-14-85 (AMSTUTZ J. BRUCE) OR-M
TAGS:
SUBJ: KIDNAPPING OF AMBASSADOR DUBS: SITREP NO. 11
1. I HAVE JUST PHONED DEPUTY FOREIGN MINISTER DOST AND TOLD
HIM THE FOLLOWING: I SAID THAT IN TOTAL DISREGARD OF OUR
REPEATED REQUESTS TO HIM AND HIS GOVERNMENT TO AVOID ANY FORCED
ACTION, THIS WASDONE AND AMB. DUBS IS NOW DEAD. I ASKED HIM
TO CONVEY THIS PROTEST IMMEDIATELY TO DEPUTY FOREIGN MINISTER
AMIN AND PRESIDENT TARAKI THAT I TOGETHER WITH THE AMERICAN
GOVERNMENT WAS HIGHLY UNHAPPY AND COULD NOT BE MORE DISTRESSED
WITH THE ACTION OF THE DRA. THAT AS DEPUTY MINISTER DOST KNEW
EVEN SECRETARY VANCE HAD PERSONALLY APPEALED THAT NO FORCED
ACTION BE TAKEN.
2. ACCORDING TO FLATIN AND BOLES, CALLS FROM THE HOTEL, THE
AMBASSADOR WAS STRUCK IN THE HEAD AND HEART. WHETHER THE
BULLETS WERE FIRED BY THE TERRORISTS OR BY THE POLICE COULD
NOT BE DETERMINED BY OUR PEOPLE. THE BODY HAS BEEN TAKEN TO
OUR DISPENSARY.
3. ACCORDING TO BOLES, THE TWO TERRORISTS WERE ASLO STRUCK
AND HE BELIEVES ONE IS ALSO DEAD.
4. PLEASE CONVEY MY PERSONAL AND THE EMBASSY'S DEEPEST
CONDOLENCES TO MARY ANN AND LINDSEY. AMSTUTZ
CONFIDENTIAL
```

Trouble in U.S. embassies

Ambassador to Afghanistan shot

The American ambassador to Afghanistan, Adolph Dubs, was fatally wounded yesterday when police firing automatic weapons stormed a hotel room where Moslem gunmen were holding him hostage in the Afghan capital of Kabul.

U.S. diplomats in Pakistan said that the kidnappers, who were not identified, sought the release of three Shi'ite Moslem clergymen who were recently arrested by the leftist Afghan government.

dispensary. The station also said that all four kidnappers were killed, but an American who witnessed the assault said one kidnapper was captured.

"He was brought down the stairs fighting and kept trying to raise a leg to kick one of his captors in the groin," said Sandy Stiebel of Highland Park, Ill., in an interview.

Mrs. Stiebel's husband, Mayer, said that police fired into the windows and through the door for a full minute before rushing in.

sympathy. Carter issued a statement saying, "The act of brutality which took his life has deprived our nation of one of its most able public servants."

Kabul Radio said that the kidnappers, disguised as traffic police, pulled Dubs' chauffeur-driven limousine over Wednesday morning, seized him and took him to the Kabul Hotel in the center of the Afghan capital. Once there they communicated their demands to authorities.

U.S. embassy in Iran stormed

The Carter administration plans to resume mass evacuation of Americans from Iran this weekend with the ultimate goal of airlifting 5,000 from the embattled country, it was learned yesterday.

U.S. officials said that 1,700 of the nearly 7,000 Americans still in Iran are prepared to leave immediately. The Tehran airport, kept shut by the new regime of the Ayatollah Ruhollah Khomeini as it tries to solidify its control, is expected to be reopened

the storming of the U.S. embassy in downtown Tehran by an armed band that took Ambassador William Sullivan and 101 other Americans hostage.

Hours after the Americans were freed yesterday, State Department spokesman Hodding Carter said that he did not know whether any of the attacking forces remained in the compound.

The spokesman credited the Khomeini regime for acting quickly to free the ambassador and the others and

There is no secure channel open for the passing of sensitive information.

Defense Department officials said that some airlift units in Europe have upgraded their readiness, but that no military forces have been placed on special alert.

By freeing Sullivan and the hostages who had been held by guerrillas in the U.S. Embassy in Tehran, the Khomeini regime spared U.S. officials from having to decide whether to take

Main: Bruce Amstutz's 11th cable on February 14, 1979.

Partially covered and arranged for the cameras, the corpses of the men alleged by the Communist regime to be the killers of the U.S. ambassador.

Chuck Boles with Mary Ann Dubs following her arrival at Kabul Airport, February 16, 1979, two days after her husband's murder.

Short biography of U.S. envoy

H. H. U.S. Ambassador to Kabul Adolph Dubs who was assassinated, regretfully, by a number of terrorists and enemies of people of Afghanistan, in Kabul on February 14, had presented his credentials to Noor Mohammad Taraki, President of the Revolutionary Council and Prime Minister on July 12, last year.

Following is a short biography of late Adolph Dubs:

He has served as resident officer in Frankfurt, W. Germany 1950—52, economic officer in Monrovia, Liberia 1952—54; political officer in Ottawa, Canada 1954—57, international relations officer, Department of State 1958—61; political officer, Moscow; USSR 1961-63.

He attended the National War College 1963—64 and served as counselor for political affairs in Belgrade, Yugoslavia 1964; and served

for Near Eastern and South Asian affairs, Department of State, 1975—78.

Dubs is survived by his wife and a daughter.

The cortege sets off for Kabul Airport, Saturday, February 17, 1979. Left to right: Sgt. J. Bowman; George Carner; Al Karian; Sgt. D. Wilkins; Denton Larsen; Arnie Long; Ray Fort; David Litt.

Spike was interred in Section 5, Site 149 of Arlington Cemetery on February 20, 1979, six days after his murder in Kabul.

Top: Michael Malinowski, U.S. Consul to Kabul 1978 to 1980.
Bottom: Lindsay Dubs McLaughlin, Spike Dubs' daughter.

Top: Harold "Doug" Wankel, Embassy Kabul's DEA attaché.
Bottom: Chuck Boles, the State Department's security officer at Embassy Kabul.

Top: Former KGB archivist Vasili Mitrokhin following his defection in 1992.
Bottom left: Statue of Felix Dzerzhinsky in front of the KGB's Lubyanka headquarters.
Bottom right: KGB Border Troops.

Left: Sergei G. Bakhturin in Moscow, January 2019.
Right: Col. Bakhturin in Kabul, 1980.

DEPARTMENT OF STATE
Washington, D.C. 20520
UNCLASSIFIED

THE KIDNAPPING AND DEATH OF AMBASSADOR ADOLPH D

FEBRUARY 14, 1979

KABUL, AFGHANISTAN

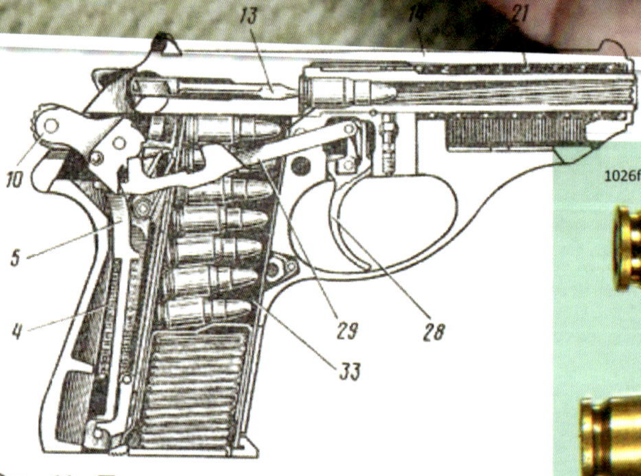

13 14 21

10

5

4

29 28

33

Рис. 20. Положение деталей и сборочных единиц перед выстрелом:

4 — боевая пружина; *5* — тяга курка; *10* — курок; *13* — ударник; *14* — затвор; *21* — возвратная пружина; *28* — спусковой крючок; *29* — спусковая тяга; *33* — магазин

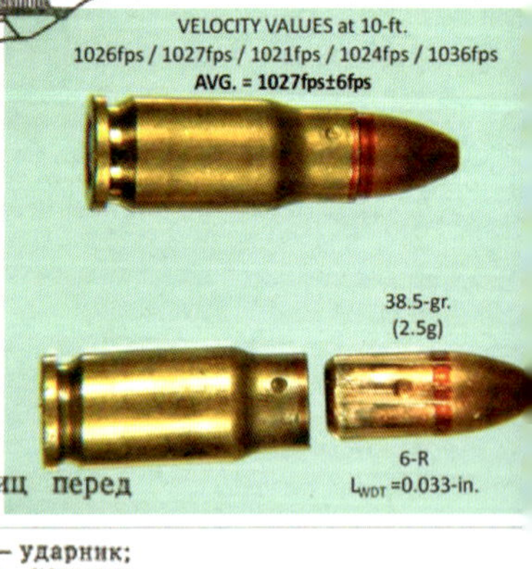

VELOCITY VALUES at 10-ft.
1026fps / 1027fps / 1021fps / 1024fps / 1036fps
AVG. = 1027fps±6fps

38.5-gr.
(2.5g)

6-R
L_{WDT} =0.033-in.

Top: The Soviet-made officer's pistol, PSM, in actual size and as pictured in the manufacturer's manual.
Bottom right: The PSM's 5.45 x 18 mm bottlenecked cartridges.

Afghan National Army defectors join the opposition mujahideen in Ghazni, March 1980.

Brother and sister of the 1980s Afghan refugee nation. Four decades later, the children of Afghanistan remain captives to war.

perimeter. On December 20, Bakhturin returned to Bagram Air Base to greet a distinguished visitor from Moscow. Smoothly and secretly, Bakhturin delivered Major General Yuri Drozdov to his shock troops, waiting in their subterranean haven beneath the embassy. The men greeted their new operational commander with great enthusiasm. At last their entombment was coming to an end. The leader of KGB Operation Storm-333 was on the ground and ready for action.

What happened next defied comprehension in Washington. On Christmas Day, more than 200 Soviet heavy transport aircraft flew into Kabul and Bagram, disgorging half an armored troop division into the capital. A full-scale invasion of Afghanistan by Soviet forces was underway. On December 26, President Carter was cautioned by Zbigniew Brzezinski that "the Soviet intervention in Afghanistan poses for us an extremely grave challenge, both internationally and domestically. While it could become a Soviet Vietnam, the initial effects of the intervention are likely to be adverse for us."

A number of the administration's top priorities were threatened, including the SALT II nuclear arms talks with the Russians. Brzezinski stressed the need to breathe life into the Afghan resistance. "This means more money as well as arms shipments to the rebels, and some technical advice." Only with Pakistan's help would the CIA's covert arming of the mujahideen succeed. "We must both reassure Pakistan and encourage it to help the rebels. This will require a review of our policy toward Pakistan, more guarantees to it, more arms aid, and, alas, a decision that our security policy toward Pakistan cannot be dictated by our non-proliferation policy." Not only was Pakistan set to become a favored U.S. ally. The goal of reigning in General Zia's nuclear weapons ambitions would have to be sidelined.

In Kabul, the Americans watched from the embassy rooftop as Soviet forces fired on loyalist holdouts among the Afghan

National Army. The situation was confusing, but soon took a decisive turn. On the evening of December 27, the Russians unleashed Operation Storm-333. Just after dark, Gen. Drozdov led 50 soldiers of the Zenit and Alpha groups out of the Soviet embassy and onto Darulaman Road. There, they were joined by more than 500 men of the 154th Spetsnaz Detachment, advancing from the airport. Known as the Muslim Battalion, the soldiers were highly trained conscripts from the mainly Islamic southern Soviet republics.

The combined assault group headed south on Darulaman, passing the shuttered American School. The force's objective was the Tajbeg Palace on Kabul's southern outskirts, the residence of President Amin and his family. Since Taraki's overthrow, it had become the headquarters of the Khalqi regime. The palace's Afghan Army defenders, though numbering more than one thousand men, had little chance against the attacking force storming towards them. Soviet troops poured off Darulaman road and up through the palace's approaches, opening fire on every guard post and gun emplacement in their path.

The battle was over in 43 minutes. Hafizullah Amin stumbled, badly wounded, from the rubble of his living quarters. He was slaughtered on the spot by Drozdov's men. A daughter survived; Amin's son did not. Some 350 Afghan soldiers also lost their lives. The year 1979, one that began in bloodshed at the Hotel Kabul, now ended in mass murder. The difference this time: the perpetrators exposed themselves in full. The Kremlin was showing the world what enforcement of the Brezhnev doctrine looked like. No state won over by Soviet Communism would ever be allowed out of Russia's grasp.

Within hours, a radio signal was transmitted from Soviet territory announcing the new President of the Revolutionary Council of Afghanistan. He was Babrak Karmal, a longtime Parchami challenger of the PDPA's Khalqi leadership. The new

Afghan president had been flown into Kabul by the Soviets, along with the surviving members of the "gang of four." This was the nucleus of Afghanistan's restructured Communist government. The PDPA was now undeniably a puppet of its Soviet masters.

It was everything Spike Dubs had strived to prevent. The people of Afghanistan were now captives, trapped between the forces of an alien superpower and a rag tag array of Muslim guerrilla fighters. Worse, the United States was about to pour vast quantities of fuel on the fires of war. In January 1980 alone, the CIA shipped some 16 tons of weapons to the mujahideen by way of the ISI. The arming of the Afghan resistance would become the largest covert support operation in the CIA's history—misshapen by the Pakistani military establishment's determination to prevent Afghanistan becoming a stable, responsibly governed nation. The ISI fancied having its own client state in Kabul, not a worthy regional competitor to Pakistan.

In turn, the Kremlin escalated its own Afghan campaign in cash, weaponry—and violence on a truly horrific scale. By the time I entered Afghanistan with mujahideen groups in March and April of 1980, entire regions, such as the Kunar Valley, had been bombed and rocketed by Soviet aircraft and helicopter gunships. The upper reaches of the Kunar were entirely depopulated. For a 26-year-old reporter, it was a lot to take in. The beauty of the landscape, the wonder of the people. Yet their villages had been reduced to rubble. This was no mere military incursion. It was criminality. Unrestrained aggression, on a massive scale.

By the end of 1980, the number of Afghan women, children and men taking refuge in Pakistan and Iran had tripled to more than two million. This refugee nation would grow to six million by the time the Soviets withdrew from Afghanistan in February 1989.

One U.S. objective was achieved. The "bleeding wound" of the Afghan war indeed did become the Soviets' Vietnam. Mikhail Gorbachev ordered the Red Army's disengagement, but the conflict had by that time inflicted irreparable harm on the Soviet state. It was a major contributing factor in the Soviet Union's downfall in 1991. The Communist regime in Kabul collapsed one year later in the face of unyielding pressure from the U.S. backed mujahideen.

In the long term, however, it is the United States, not Russia, that has suffered the direst consequences of the superpowers' proxy war in Afghanistan. From those dark months in 1979 until today, there has been something missing in Washington's calculations in Afghanistan. A voice of caution, of reason; a voice advocating purposeful, yet restrained, constructive engagement. Exactly the voice that was silenced forever in room 117 of the Hotel Kabul.

PART FIVE

CHAPTER 14

FROM RUSSIA WITH CLUES

FOR THE UNITED STATES, January 1, 1980 marked the dawn of a troubled New Year. The hostage crisis in Iran showed no prospect of resolution. The Kremlin, meanwhile, was sending still more Soviet troops and armor into Afghanistan. The Carter administration appeared at a loss to project any effective measure of global influence. It was onto this bleak landscape that the State Department finally declassified a version of its findings on the murder of Spike Dubs. Not surprisingly, the report went virtually unnoticed. Even journalists covering the Red Army's tightening grip on Kabul paid scant attention to the document's release.

The title page speaks to the restraint exercised in creating the 18-page document. For some reason, the "Summary of Report of Investigation" mentioned nothing about the conclusions of state sponsored terrorism and premeditated murder found by the department's security team at Embassy Kabul. Instead, the report was benignly titled: *The Kidnapping and Death of Ambassador Adolph Dubs.*

Early on, the report stresses the investigation was "severely hampered" by the Afghan regime's refusal "to provide even basic investigative data." During the crisis, Embassy Kabul was "unable to determine the terrorists' demands, the Afghan government's plan of action and other relevant information." Americans on the scene "made it clear to the Soviets present that the US Government desired no precipitous action be taken which might endanger the life of Ambassador Dubs." While the Soviets did not take part in the actual assault on room 117, they engaged in "an operational role" just before it took place. "One Soviet was observed assisting an Afghan security official with the loading of a weapon," while others positioned snipers across the street.

The report noted disparities between the Soviet Union's official pronouncements and the actions Spike's officers saw with their own eyes. "The Soviet Union acknowledged the presence of Soviet representatives at the hotel but alleged that their presence there was to protect the lives of Soviet citizens residing at the hotel." Similarly, the document recounts Amin's contradictory claims about the kidnappers seeking the release of Bahruddin Bahes. But it does so in an inconclusive way, noting: "To date, no terrorist organization or dissident group has come forward to claim responsibility for the kidnapping and killing of Ambassador Dubs." This fact was at the heart of Chuck Boles' findings, but expressed with real significance: the reason no terrorist group had "come forward" was because responsibility for Spike's murder lay with the Afghan regime and the Soviet Union.

Only a truncated account of the autopsies was included in the report. There was very little mention of forensics analysis; what little there was turned solely on the regime's claims about the number and kind of firearms found in the dead kidnappers' possession. "Autopsy and forensic examinations performed by agencies of the U.S. Government point to a discrepancy. The Ambassador died as a result of at least 10 wounds inflicted by small caliber weapons. Two of the chest wounds were the result of bullets fired from the same .25 caliber weapon. One wound to the right side of the head, three wounds to the left side of the head and one wound to the left hand were the result of bullets fired from a .22 caliber weapon. At least some, if not all, of the

.22 caliber wounds were fired by the same weapon, and associated powder burns reveal the weapon was fired from point blank to three inches in range."

Despite the U.S. government challenging the regime over the disappearance of nearly all the physical evidence, the PDPA persisted with the positions taken in its own scant report, the document deemed "laughable" by the American witnesses. "The (regime's) report provided no ballistics information, no autopsy reports, no forensic information nor any identification of the terrorists." Summing up, the State report condemned the Afghan government's account as "incomplete, misleading, and inaccurate," amounting to a "serious misrepresentation or suppression of the truth."

However, in contrast to Chuck's damning findings, the State account for public consumption concludes not with answers, but only with questions. Why was the ambassador kidnapped? Who were his abductors and what were they after? Why was the room stormed, and who fired the small-caliber weapon that killed Spike? Why was the third man killed "while in captivity," and who was the fourth dead man? Why was the regime uncooperative, providing Washington only misleading information? Most troubling of all: "What was the involvement of the Soviets in the decision making process in the operation directed against the terrorists?"

For Lindsay Dubs, still mourning her father's death, the lack of clarity was impossible to come to terms with. "The reports done by the State Department and news media—basically they all said 'inconclusive.' We don't know exactly what happened. And it struck me, with the Soviets on the scene, and the Americans being there, it seems there should have been an answer.

"So on one level, I think, we should be able to figure this out. On another level, part of my attitude was, when I came out of this, sometimes violence doesn't have an answer. And if you want to work through the grief, perhaps it's more healing not necessarily to go searching for answers of specifics, but to work on the sense that a lot of times the world does not make sense. It doesn't make sense."

Chuck Boles found it even harder to accept the administration's waffling. The only senior official who expressed even a partial, hesitant conclusion was Zbigniew Brzezinski. He blamed Spike's death on "either Soviet ineptitude or collusion"—as if not knowing was an option. To this day, Chuck can't shake off his belief the United States needed to respond much more forcefully. "I never understood Washington's reaction. The American ambassador was killed by an Afghan with Soviet support, and yet we didn't do anything. My reports were going in to the State Department and the Secretary of State was reading them, and sharing them with the White House. And why they didn't act, why President Carter didn't take some stronger action, is beyond me, I've never understood that. We lost an American ambassador and didn't do anything."

THE TRUTH LAY HIDDEN for years. Hidden throughout the Soviet occupation, hidden after the Red Army's withdrawal from Afghanistan in February 1989. Hidden beyond the collapse of Soviet Communism in 1991 and the PDPA regime the following year, and throughout the savage Afghan civil war that followed. Hidden even after the capture of Kabul in 1996 by the Taliban, armed and advised by Washington's duplicitous ally, Pakistan's ISI.

One glimmer of a clue emerged in the months prior to the Soviet Union's abandonment of its Afghan campaign. At the time, Tom Gouttierre was an adviser to the U.S. negotiating team working with Kremlin officials to secure the withdrawal. He spent a good deal of time with his Russian counterparts, members of the USSR's Institute of Oriental Studies. During a break in the talks, a discussion over drinks turned to the late

U.S. Ambassador, Spike Dubs. "They brought it up. These academics were pretty clear about it. They believed the ambassador's death was the result of a Kremlin and KGB guided policy. They wanted rid of Spike because he was getting too close to Amin. The Soviets were despairing of the Khalq-Parcham split in the Afghan Communist party, and the unrest in the countryside made them even edgier."

This was a credible piece of analysis, but no sources or source materials came out of the exchange. It would take another decade, until the late 1990s, before the *substantiated* truth was finally revealed about the Soviet leadership's enmity for Spike Dubs. To the Russians, he was an enemy to be feared—and eliminated, if possible:

> (The KGB) was anxious about the appointment of Dubs as ambassador to Afghanistan. When he had been in Moscow as a First Secretary at the embassy he had been closely covered. The KGB considered that Dubs knew the region well and that he was connected to the CIA and trusted by them. His accreditation was therefore viewed as part of the USA's desire to influence the new Afghan government and to make sure that Afghanistan did not become too close to the USSR. Dubs had been [instrumental] in strengthening American positions and influence in the Middle East and the region of the Persian Gulf and was one of the people behind the idea of the Afghanistan-Pakistan-Iran triangle.

Unknown to the Carter administration, Moscow Center ordered its intelligence officers to regard Spike Dubs as a singular threat to the Kremlin's designs on Afghanistan:

> On August 3rd, 1978, the KGB Resident in Kabul, Viliov Osadchy, received a telegram about Dubs which

> expressed the fear that: "it cannot be ruled out that in his contacts with the Afghan leadership, Dubs will take advantage of his 'deep' understanding and knowledge of the situation in the USSR and Soviet foreign policy. This, in our view, is one of the most dangerous aspects of his activities.

This chilling assessment was not unearthed by American investigators. Instead, the truth about the Russians' hostility towards Spike Dubs had to wait for a messenger to walk out of the ashes of the Soviet Union. Vasili Mitrokhin served as an officer of the KGB for more than three decades. Early in his career, he was stripped of operational duties and assigned to the service's archives, retrieving records on request. Rising to the rank of major, he had access to highly classified papers dating back to 1918, the earliest days of Soviet Communism.

It was like leafing through a vast diary of the KGB and all the agencies of state repression that preceded it. Mitrokhin was horrified by what he found. Violence and terror were institutionalized. "The nation's wealth was plundered. Groundless slander and denunciations flourished. Respectable and honest people were subjected to repression by the police. The country turned into a mass torture-chamber. People were executed without any investigation or trial. A vast chasm formed between the people and the regime which relied on force and the support of the security organs, the army and the police. It demanded absolute submission from everyone and everything."

Determined to resist the state's tyranny, Mitrokhin secretly made handwritten copies of cables, files and other records. He smuggled the notes home in his shoes after each workday, typing them up on weekends at his dacha outside Moscow. Gradually, he amassed his own archive of top secret documents, buried in aluminum cases beneath his country home. After the Soviet government collapsed in 1991, the old spy decided to defect. He travelled to Riga, Latvia with samples of his collection. At the U.S. embassy, Mitrokhin received a chilly reception from the local CIA station. Here was a haggard, greying, 70-year-old Russian, eager to reach the West. The men from Langley sent him packing.

Mitrokhin received a far different reception from the British, sparking a relationship with officers of the United Kingdom's foreign intelligence service, MI6. London was convinced his archive had merit. In November 1992, Mitrokhin was exfiltrated to London. With him came an intelligence windfall: a 2,000-page library documenting the Soviet Union's darkest secrets. In time, the old spy and his records were provided by British intelligence to a trusted historian, Christopher Andrew. Together, they co-authored the seminal 1999 publication, *The Sword and the Shield: The Mitrokhin Archive and the Secret History of the KGB*. Having been dismissed by the CIA, Mitrokhin and his works were now hailed by the FBI as "The most extensive intelligence ever received from any source."

In 2002, nearing 80, Mitrokhin finally fulfilled his goal to expose the secrets behind the disastrous Soviet military incursion into Southwest Asia. Written for the Woodrow Wilson International Center in Washington, DC, *The KGB in Afghanistan* is his gripping chronicle of the organization's Afghan exploits between 1978 and 1983. In this final work, Mitrokhin stressed that the murder of Spike Dubs deserved "special mention." The KGB's spies in Afghanistan, he wrote, had fervently stoked Moscow's fears about the new U.S. ambassador:

> The Residency in Kabul wrote to Moscow in the same vein: that the American embassy in Kabul under Dubs was actively engaged in spreading propaganda amongst the people and the intelligentsia, and was trying to make them believe that the USSR was occupying the country with a view to using it as a bridgehead for spreading its

influence to India, Pakistan and Southeast Asia.

This paranoia was spread like "leaden clouds" by the KGB, and would ultimately be followed by "automatic hail." Mitrokhin stops short of concluding Moscow targeted Spike for assassination prior to the kidnapping. But once Spike was known to be held captive, entirely at the mercy of his abductors and the troops surrounding them, a cold-blooded Soviet complicity with the Kabul regime emerges in the cable exchanges between the Center and its Kabul residency. Nowhere is this more obvious than the urgency with which Moscow conspired with the Afghan Communists to deceive the Americans, and the world, about what really happened at the Hotel Kabul on Valentine's Day, 1979.

Osadchy was given the assignment to contrive a cover story with the Afghan regime's point man on the Dubs affair: Hafizullah Amin. The KGB *rezident* was scrambled to the foreign ministry soon after Spike's murder. "Osadchy visited Amin, on instructions from the Center in Moscow, to agree on how to justify the affair to the Americans. They agreed to express their condolences to the Americans, to lower flags on government buildings and to print photographs of the four terrorists in the newspapers. In order to frustrate requests from the Americans to question the detained terrorist and hunt down the one who escaped, it was decided to shoot the one who had been detained and to shoot another prisoner pretending that he was the fourth terrorist. The story that all four kidnappers had been killed during the assault would be fed to the newspapers."

Thus two additional premeditated, cold-blooded murders were committed to confuse and conceal the truth about the carnage in room 117. "If the Americans were to ask for an explanation for the involvement of Soviet advisers in the operation to capture the terrorists, Amin, (intelligence chief) Sarwari and

Taroon were to say that the Afghan side had independently and without consultation decided to take radical action to deal with the terrorists and that there had been no Soviet advisers present at all."

By mutual agreement, Amin and the Russians repeated this lie again and again: no Soviet advisers had been present at the scene. Even by KGB standards, this was breathtakingly shameless disinformation. Much more would follow. And with fateful irony, Amin would eventually wind up on the receiving end of the campaign.

"As soon as the Cheka (the KGB) got rid of Amin, in December of 1979," Mitrokhin wrote, "the disinformation service planted a new version of the death of Ambassador Dubs in the foreign press." Amin, the story went, was a covert agent of the CIA. The four kidnappers were Shia Muslims "reacting to Amin's unjustified mass repression." Amin was acting as "an imperialist agent" in killing the Muslim hostage takers and labelling them "terrorists." This revisionist history insisted the kidnappers had a creditable motive. "They had planned to kidnap the American ambassador and to force him under the threat of death to reveal his cards and acknowledge the ties between the embassy of the USA in Kabul and Amin."

By this point the KGB's propaganda machinery was in top gear. It had all been Amin's doing–the "otherwise needless assault" on the hotel room and the order "that no mercy should be shown." Amin acted "to eliminate all the members of the group and to save himself from exposure." For good measure, the Russians ensured blame also rested with Spike Dubs' masters. "The conduct of the Carter administration was shocking," the KGB account stated. "It found it easy to sacrifice the life of the American ambassador in order to keep secret Amin's connections with the CIA."

One year after Spike's murder, with the Red Army's occupation forces in complete control of Kabul, the KGB used one of their Afghan agents, a militia commander, to conduct a sham investigation. An article resulted, headlined: "On Whose Conscience is the Death of Ambassador Dubs?" Laying the blame squarely on the United States, the false account was cloaked by the KGB's Kabul residency as a genuine Afghan government finding, then disseminated to the local and foreign press.

The Russians didn't stop there. To support the fictional assertion that Amin had been a CIA agent, documentary evidence was created. The KGB then sought to legitimize it by way of the frontman of their new quisling regime in Afghanistan, Babrak Karmal. "A handwriting specialist was in one of the KGB operational groups sent to Afghanistan," Mitrokhin wrote. "After Amin's death, a note with a CIA telephone number in Amin's handwriting was found in (Amin's) notebook. On February 16th, 1980, a KGB adviser gave Babrak Karmal this notebook and showed him the entry. Babrak declared that this was yet further definite proof that Amin was connected with American intelligence."

The KGB suggested Babrak "ask the American administration to hand over the CIA and FBI files on Amin." Then, "notices should be put in the press through the embassies in Paris, London, Rome and Bonn asking anyone who had any information on Amin to send it to the authorities." The cascade of lies and false accusations was as relentless as it was preposterous. It was classic Soviet disinformation, a multi-layered campaign of character assassination and deceit, all to direct suspicion away from the KGB's involvement in Spike's murder. The Soviet spies at the hotel; the operative hovering over Taroon's shoulder; the arming of the plainclothes secret policeman; the signals to the breach team and rifle squad to open fire—all of it was concealed behind a billowing smokescreen of fraud and fabrication.

Mitrokhin's exposé confirms the presence of Bakhturin,

Klushnikov and Kutepov at the Hotel Kabul. But the records he copied evidently did not identify the other KGB officers observed there and in the police commandant's office. One new detail was disclosed: the planting of a submachine gun with the dead kidnappers. "In case the room was to be examined by experts, a gun of unknown origin similar to a Kalashnikov was planted in the room and registered as taken from the terrorists." This was likely the firearm claimed by the regime's perfunctory report to be a "CMH machinegun." If so, this would point to a Belgian-made 9 mm Vigneron submachine gun, a weapon virtually unseen in Afghanistan.

Overall, Mitrokhin's account invites a damning conclusion. Chairman Andropov's motives in using every trick in the KGB's book of deception is self-evident: to hide the KGB's guilt in the murder of Spike Dubs. Still, much of the evidence is circumstantial. If only questions could be put to the Russian spies central to the mystery. Particularly the ranking KGB officer who was seen by so many witnesses to be directly responsible. The affable, smooth-talking colonel in the black leather coat and faux fedora.

Chapter 15

Challenging the Colonel

FORTY YEARS AFTER the murder in room 117, Sergei Gavrilovitch Bakhturin is not an easy man to find. In 2019, he turned 86. But was he still alive? Moscow was the logical place to start looking for a retired veteran of Bakhturin's standing. However, given his years of service as a secret intelligence officer, it came as no surprise that his whereabouts were concealed not only by the mists of time, but also the shadows cast by his life's work.

To begin with, I made an indirect approach: enquiries by way of Russian news professionals said to be on good terms with survivors of the former Soviet intelligence world. The response came back slugged "bad news from Moscow." Bakhturin had "unfortunately passed away." Word of his alleged death came from "someone who knew him personally for many years."

On a hunch, a second approach was made through different sources. Almost immediately, they confirmed Bakhturin was alive and living in Moscow. There was just one problem: he had no interest in meeting with a foreign journalist. That simply was not going to happen. Next, a trusted colleague, a specialist on Russia and the Russian people, introduced me to the country's new generation of investigative reporters. These young journalists are hard-driving and inquisitive, and work not only in Russia but from adoptive homelands to all over the world. It is a truly international network, bound together by a fierce devotion to their country—and opposition to President Vladimir Putin's dictatorial rule.

Soon, the Bakhturin inquiry was in the hands of one of these enterprising newshounds. For the purposes of this book, he will go by the name of Pyotr. He made a third approach to Sergei Bakhturin. If he did not want to speak to a foreigner, maybe he would answer questions put to him by a fellow Russian. At the very least, wouldn't the octogenarian former spy wish to satisfy his curiosity? Why were all these feelers being put out to him, dredging up the name of Dubs after so many years? The whole affair had lain dormant for decades. What kind of questions did these people want to put to him; first a Canadian, and now a Russian sounding barely out of his 20s? Bakhturin was clearly intrigued: he asked Pyotr to leave the request with him for a while. Finally, after repeated calls and weeks of excuses about his health, Bakhturin agreed to meet.

It had the look and feel of a scouting mission in reverse, a rendezvous designed in the netherworld of espionage. Bakhturin's plan placed Pyotr at an instant disadvantage: the cagey old KGB hand insisted the meeting take place in a busy Moscow Metro station. It was a loud and public place, one where Sergei would get a good look at Pyotr before Pyotr could spot Sergei. The old man could check to see if the young reporter was alone, if he carried a camera; if something about him wasn't right somehow.

As things turned out, Bakhturin could see nothing out of the ordinary. Not a single foreigner was in sight, nor any watchers or photographers. Everything about Pyotr would put him at ease. Here was a bright looking young man, walking along the station platform, searching into the windows of the approaching train. Being Russian, he must possess some degree of national pride, of patriotism. The colonel could play to that. He could impress the young man with his stories about the KGB's praiseworthy missions at home and abroad.

We cannot know for certain, but these were likely the thoughts, the calculations, that led to what Sergei Bakhturin did next. Slowly, leaning heavily on a cane, he stepped from behind his hide, a kiosk midway down the platform. Now he was in the open. Pyotr picked him out of the thinning crowd. A moment later they stood together, clasping hands and exchanging greetings, their voices barely audible beneath the roar of a departing train.

Now it was time for the old spy to dictate the terms of their discussion. It must take place over tea, and nearby. He had a favorite spot in mind. So it was that a stalwart veteran of the KGB shuffled up the stairs and onto the street, accompanied by a reporter digging into the murder of a prominent American diplomat. A short walk led them beneath a red and white sign announcing the venue for their discussion. Here they would revisit one of the Cold War's darkest episodes. "Бургер Кинг," the sign read: Burger King.

SERGEI BAKHTURIN retired from the KGB in 1991. His career wound down much as it began during his postings to Iran, Pakistan and Afghanistan. The colonel spent his days searching for traitors within. Then came the Soviet empire's demise. He despaired over Russia's new leaders, clamoring for democratic freedoms. Still loyal to the old cause, he realized things would never be the same at the Lubyanka. So Bakhturin turned to his old friends at NIIMash, the mechanical engineering firm that had provided his cover some 30 years earlier. They welcomed him back with a desk job in Moscow.

These days, the retired intelligence officer has only scorn for Gorbachev's decision to withdraw Soviet forces from Afghanistan. "I consider that we left things in a very untidy way. We did not solve problems there, we left the situation unresolved, ugly even." Pyotr brings the discussion around to Valentine's Day 1979. He mentions a few of the most notable events at the Hotel Kabul. Bakhturin reflects for a long moment. He's taken aback by the young journalist's knowledge of the affair. Finally, he says: "There was a strategy. It was the work of our adviser to the Ministry of Internal Affairs, Klushnikov, and our security adviser. Kutepov is his last name."

The Burger King is busy and alive with background noise. Voices peak and mingle with clatter from the kitchen and the sound of chairs scraping the floor. Still, the old man's words reach Pyotr's microphone. "This is important," he says. "The whole thing was controlled by Amin personally. Everything was under his control, and he controlled the operation. It began prematurely, in general, they were not quite ready when they began to act. But they were no longer listening to us. They listened to their own orders." Bakhturin sticks to this theme. The Afghan regime's Foreign Minister was giving all the orders. They were carried out by his police commandant, Taroon.

As for the Americans, they were completely wrong about Sergei Bakhturin signaling the shooting to start. "Understand," he says, leaning over the table towards Pyotr: "the order to shoot was given by the Afghans. The Afghans acted on their plan. In the same way, the terrorists acted after being kept waiting for a long time. It was not the result of cowardly, wrong actions on our part." He relaxes back into his chair, sips his tea. "We silent observers were also there at the same time. But the final word was the Afghans'. Their security service. They determined it."

Silent observers? Pyotr asks about the eyewitness testimony to the contrary. At this, Bakhturin amends his story. Yes, he and his KGB comrades had a limited role in the planning of the operation. "The Ministry of Internal Affairs planned the operation with help from Alexander Klushnikov. And since our people were staying in the hotel, we had to go there."

This is in reference to the Soviet citizens Bakhturin and his men ushered out of the line of fire. But he insists his actions were nothing like the operational role found by the Boles investigation, and later cited in the State Department report. Instead, the "unfortunate outcome" of Ambassador Dubs' death was due only to the impatience and inexperience of the Afghan regime. "We have to take experience into account. The Afghans had not often dealt with a case like this. They somehow wanted us to present them a solution on a blue platter. That would be splendid, of course. But this is the problem. When the process has already begun, it is tough going."

Things would have been different, Bakhturin claims, had Soviet special forces troops, such as the Alpha Group, carried out the "rescue mission." Amid this bluster, there is one operational task he not only admits to, but takes credit for. This has to do with the ammunition used in the assault on room 117. All of it was provided to the Afghans by the KGB, Bakhturin says; by he and his fellow spies. This is an important admission, a helpful clue that might well contribute to solving this cold case. Because it begs the question: why on earth did both the breach team, and the rifle squad on the bank balcony, fire rounds provided by the KGB? The answer will have to wait for further forensics investigation—because Bakhturin, when asked, changes the subject.

"I can confirm there was a man standing near Dubs who held a pistol at his temple." How he came to know this he will not say. Nor does he explain why an assault was launched when the hostage was known to have a gun at his head. Instead, Bakhturin cuts to a different part of the chase—and blows smoke. "Yes, we provided the ammunition which was fired from the machineguns. But, when the door was forced, well, a German Schmeisser was not our weapon. This means that the Americans supplied the weapon from which the shots were fired."

This claim is contradicted by the evidence. No German-made

Schmeisser submachine gun, or MP40, was found at the scene. The Americans at the Hotel Kabul were unarmed. Even the Afghan regime's account of the incident makes no mention of a Schmeisser, much less an allegation that the murder weapon came from U.S. personnel. Yet Bakhturin embroiders this part of his tale. "At the hotel, there was an American named Charlie. He was keenly interested, and asked us 'What are you doing here, what are you discussing?'" Bakhturin says it was Charlie—Chuck Boles—who planted the Schmeisser. "What the Americans wanted to prove with this is hard to say."

THROUGHOUT BAKHTURIN'S intelligence career, inventing information at odds with the facts was not only routine, it was a duty. Crafting disinformation was an ongoing mission he and his fellow KGB officers ignored at their peril. The Center in Moscow subjected all its officers to yearly reviews. Each operative had to demonstrate that fully one-fifth of their time was spent creating false stories, libels and other disinformation, all to confuse and weaken the Soviets' adversaries. In this context, it is only natural for Bakhturin to proffer lurid suspicions over the murder of Spike Dubs. Conjuring up conspiracies was his stock and trade.

And so, while sipping tea with Pyotr, he puts his tradecraft to work. "The fact is that the whole affair itself is dark. How and why was there such a conspiracy? The explanation could be the double game of Amin. Because with his blessing, by his order, the head of the Afghan security service, at that time Taroon, was there to hold some kind of measures against the Americans for not aligning with Amin. Therefore, it pushed Amin to do something that was necessary in some way, a way I don't completely understand. It may even be he was afraid that Dubs might reveal Amin's connections to the Americans. There was such a flirtation going on at that time. The Americans were betting on it."

The old spy says ample evidence exists to support this allegation. It's all spelled out in a book, published in Russia, about the Soviet war: "Virus 'A': How We Caught The Disease Of Intervening In Afghanistan." Bakhturin suggests Pyotr should read the book. It tells how Taroon took charge at the hotel. How he valiantly entered room 117, and personally finished off the two kidnappers. How Spike was really a CIA operative. That he was seen visiting the Hotel Kabul the day before the kidnapping, in the company of men resembling the kidnappers.

Why would Sergei Bakhturin recommend such a book? The footnotes hold the answer: he is credited as a source. The retired colonel was, and remains to this day, an active contributor to the false narrative that the Carter administration assassinated its own ambassador to Kabul, Afghanistan. Who, after all, was simply another expendable CIA asset.

Spike's foreign service officers scoff at the old spy's claims. "Taroon came nowhere near the hotel," says Mike Malinowski. "Jim Taylor doorstepped him in his office. Taroon didn't come out until after the attack." As for the ambassador's alleged links to the CIA, a look of disgust comes over Mike's face. "The Soviets knew damn well that Spike was a foreign service officer for the Department of State. It's inconceivable that if he had been at one point an officer of the CIA that that would have not come up in his confirmation hearings. He's a State employee, and you don't go around killing American diplomats."

Chuck responds with a wry grin to Bakhturin's claims about the Schmeisser and Spike's supposed visit to the hotel with the men who later took him hostage. "I guess at the age of 86, old Sergei's memory's is playing tricks on him. None of that stuff is true. If he and his people had any kind of real information at all they would have shoved it under our noses. But none of them would talk to me afterwards, Soviet or Afghan. They were too busy covering everything up."

IN PRESIDENT PUTIN'S RUSSIA, Sergei Bakhturin leads a charmed life in his twilight years. His storied history enabled him to become a founding member of an organization called Veterans of Foreign Intelligence. This is more than a club for retired Russian spies. Formed in 2002, the Veterans are tightly linked to Dignity and Honor, a nationalist group. From the start, the Dignity and Honor veterans have been passionate supporters of another former intelligence officer, Vladimir Vladimirovich Putin, who joined the KGB in 1976, one year before Bakhturin's arrival in Afghanistan. To Soviet-era Cold Warriors, Putin represents an enviable fusion of authoritarianism and state capitalism. The Soviet system was doomed to bankruptcy, both economic and doctrinal. By contrast, Putinism is a form of dictatorship that pays huge dividends, particularly for regime insiders.

Putin and his acolytes are known as *siloviki*—"people of force"—zealous nationalists who are serving or former members of the security or military services. The *silovki* are a cult, but not one languishing on the fringes of society. Instead, this is a network of political activists, thriving at the center of power. Putin relies on aging *siloviki* like Bakhturin to not only champion his regime's excesses, but to advocate the expansion of Russian influence around the world. Since Bakhturin's specialty was the detection and punishment of traitors within the Soviet intelligence and diplomatic services, he dismisses talk of Putin's alleged involvement in crimes on foreign soil. From the murder of Alexander Litvinenko, the defector killed in London by radioactive poisoning in 2006, to the Novichok nerve agent attacks on double agent Sergei Skripal in England and opposition leader Alexei Navalny in Siberia, Bakhturin insists treason is a crime the Russian state neither forgives nor forgets. Which is not to say Putin sanctioned the crimes, the old spy is quick to add. Such allegations are Western propaganda, nothing more.

Loyalty of this kind, unsurprisingly, is a two-way street.

While Putin's quest to be president for life is assisted by the *siloviki*'s devotion to him, the Russian leader repays veterans like Bakhturin by polishing the tarnished red stars of the Communist past. No subject demonstrates this more extravagantly than the KGB's campaign in Afghanistan. Putin never tires of celebrating the nation's *Afghantsy* veterans. He and his political allies have recast the conflict as a great patriotic duty. Historical justice, they insist, demands the denunciation of the Gorbachev government's condemnation of the war. The invasion only took place at the Afghans' invitation (a lie), and the sole purpose of the occupation was to help the Afghan people (an even larger lie).

For Sergei Bakhturin, the current Russian leader's revisionism is deeply personal and heartfelt. He was there. He not only knew Gen. Yuri Drozdov, whose men murdered Amin in cold blood, he was Drozdov's comrade in arms; at times, his fixer. Bakhturin provided crucial groundwork for Operation Storm-333, which is now perversely celebrated as a bold and heroic sacrifice by the KGB and Red Army. These days, he speaks wistfully of Drozdov, who died in 2017. "I often saw him in the Center, since his illegal intelligence unit helped in our search for traitors. We had such a warm relationship. 'Where are we going next time?' Drozdov would ask. And I answer: 'I don't know. We will go where we're ordered to go.' He was such a comrade! He was 91 when he died. I, too, have already turned 86."

At this, Bakhturin extends his hands. "Here are the remnants—now my fingers are bent with age. Time is passing."

It may be passing, but enough time has been granted to Sergei Bakhturin to indulge in his sentimental memories of past glories. In the realm of old warriors, he is among the luckiest. Despite his good fortune, he is not one to spare a thought for the men's lives he helped bring to a premature end. Perhaps it is too much to expect of an adversary, of a secret intelligence officer who took part in the murder at the Hotel Kabul. Still, it is striking that Bakhturin displays no appreciation whatsoever for the life stolen from Spike Dubs on Valentine's Day 1979. There can be little doubt this would offend the old spy's obligation to his duty, namely to continue lying about what really took place and his role in it. And, most of all, to pass on those refrains of disinformation to the current Russian regime. Where the lies can be repeated, embellished and made to last forever.

Chapter 16

Under a 21st Century Microscope

Unsolved cases have a way of gnawing at an investigator. A criminal inquiry gone cold can haunt the mind. Memories persist of having come up short, of failing to bring the guilty party or parties to justice. These phantoms don't fade over time; they prowl and multiply, especially in the mind of a professional with personal bonds to the victim. A professional who is convinced the facts were amply verified for the case never to have gone cold in the first place.

This was Chuck Boles' quandary in the years after the murder of Spike Dubs. He knew what happened. He and his team had established the truth. So why, he wondered, had his report on the investigation sunk without a trace? Why had State and the administration taken no action on his findings?

Eventually, Chuck could stand it no longer. One morning in 1999 at his home on the California coast, he climbed the stairs to his study and sat down at the family computer. He opened a new file and began writing a second report. Chuck's plan was to resubmit his original findings to State in DC, to convince them to reopen the investigation and share the results with the American public. To that end, he led off his account with basic, declarative statements regarding the fate of Ambassador Spike Dubs on February 14, 1979:

> The Afghan government, with the active support and

> material assistance of several Soviet KGB officers, murdered him. He was kidnapped by the Afghan Government and executed with a Soviet weapon supplied by the KGB.

Chuck wrote that if this was not the first incident of State sponsored terrorism, it was certainly one of the earliest. He realized the restatement of his findings might be greeted with skepticism in Washington.

> These are bold statements, to be sure. Many of my former colleagues may strongly disagree but I believe that a convincing case can be made that Ambassador Dubs' kidnapping and death did, in fact, occur as stated. It is the intent of this writing to present evidence to substantiate that claim.
>
> I am well aware that my judgement may be drawn into question because I was deeply involved as the Embassy Security Officer in Kabul at the time of Dubs' demise and also part of the investigative team searching for answers in the immediate aftermath. On the other hand, those experiences, now far removed from the emotions of the time, may provide insight not readily available to others.

Chuck explained why he was back at the keyboard, tapping out another recitation of the events some 20 years after they took place. Previously, he had been bound by his oath of secrecy as an employee of the Department of State. "Now, however, enough declassified and unclassified information has been made public to make the effort worthwhile." He cited testimony and documents that had surfaced during the Congressional review of the killing, and State Department records that had recently been declassified. And although Vasili Mitrokhin's complete analysis of the KGB in Afghanistan had not yet been made public, Chuck's review of the salient facts all but anticipated the revelations to come.

He zeroed in on the point in the standoff when "the KGB advisors began taking a more visual role." The point when Col. Bakhturin and his men went beyond merely advising the Afghan regime riflemen—and most particularly, when the mystery plainclothes policeman was armed by the KGB:

> One, in clear view of the Americans, loaded a small automatic pistol, which he then gave to a member of the Afghan security force. This weapon would play a major role in the investigation conducted after Dubs was killed.

In the years following his initial investigation, Chuck's research led him to believe he could identify the murder weapon. This was a slim, but very powerful, Soviet-made officer's pistol, the Pistolet Samozaryadnyy Malogabaritnyy, or PSM; in English, "Self-loading Pistol, Small-sized." In 1979, the PSM was virtually unknown to Western military and civilian firearms specialists. It had only been in production in the Soviet Union since 1973. Due to its small size and power, it became a favorite of the KGB and top level Communist Party officials.

Chuck's memory of the pistol passed by Klushnikov to the Afghan secret policeman remains clear: it was either a PSM or a weapon identical to it. As well, the PSM's 5.45 mm specifications could be a match for the .22-caliber bullets fired into Spike's head. Trouble was, the FBI firearms specialists who took part in Spike's autopsy in February 1979 would never have heard of the PSM, much less have had any experience analyzing bullets fired from the handgun.

As to who fired the headshots found to be the cause of death, Chuck recounted:

> Upon learning of the autopsy's findings, members of the American security team immediately recalled the incident in the hotel when a KGB advisor first loaded, and then gave a small automatic handgun to a member of the Afghan police. They also recalled the single shots being fired inside of the room after the automatic rifle fire from the hallway and across the street ended.

The Kalashnikovs went silent just as they had opened fire: on the hand signals of Col. Sergei Bakhturin. Similarly, the automatic weapons falling silent must have been the signal for the secret policeman to make his move inside room 117. He was able to discharge the five fatal gunshots, then retrace his steps as far as the bathroom by the time Chuck stepped through the doorway.

Summing up his report, Chuck wrote that the decision to murder Spike Dubs may have originated solely within the Afghan Communist regime, but it was ultimately embraced by the Soviets. No KGB officer would dare assume that authority on his own. Rather, Moscow Center directed the Kabul residency to facilitate the murder once the Soviet leadership realized the U.S. ambassador was a hostage. Spike, they realized, was now a prisoner held not only out of the Americans' reach, but also out of their sight. This was a target, a vulnerable adversary, the Soviets could not resist striking. In the aftermath, the killing could be disguised as a rescue mission, a creditable attempt to secure Ambassador Dubs' freedom—exactly the subterfuge resorted to by Moscow and its client regime.

To the contrary, Chuck wrote, the killing of the U.S. ambassador was an act of cold blooded murder, no less so than the KGB Center's order to execute both the third gang member and the random inmate substituted for the fourth man. Beyond this, Chuck believes the case was something more than murder. "This was an act of war. I thought so at the time and I'm still not convinced otherwise. They killed the American ambassador in broad daylight. It went beyond the man who pulled the trigger on that pistol. States did it—the governments of the Afghan Communists and the Soviet Union."

Chuck's second report came in at 36 pages. He copied and bound it and sent it via the U.S. Postal Service to the State Department in Washington. All he could do was hope someone would read it and pass it along to a senior officer. By rights, it should eventually be considered by someone with the authority to revisit the crime; to seek the resolution the Dubs case had always deserved—and which the country owed to its fallen envoy.

FIFTY YEARS to the day before the murder in room 117 of the Hotel Kabul, seven men gathered in a garage at 2122 North Clark Street in Chicago's Lincoln Park neighborhood. The fate awaiting those members of the notorious North Side Gang—or rather, the science of determining how they met that fate—is likely the only avenue left to explore in resolving one of the Cold War's most bedeviling cold cases. Because the St. Valentine's Day Massacre is more than just a legend of the underworld exploits of the North Side Gang's enemy, Al Capone. The analysis of that infamous crime scene in Chicago was a landmark event in forensic ballistics, the science of guns and the projectiles they fire. Like the bullets and bullet fragments brought home to Washington, DC with the victim of the 1979 St. Valentine's Day murder in Kabul.

Calvin Goddard was the forensics pioneer who supervised the scientific analysis of the Chicago massacre. At Northwestern University in 1929, Goddard and his associates were in the process of setting up the world's first crime lab focused on forensic ballistics. Goddard's lab is regarded as much more than a museum by his present-day disciples, scientists like Lucien "Luke" Haag. "It's almost hallowed ground for me. I taught there a number of summers as a guest lecturer and went to the actual room where Goddard used to fire guns into a wastebasket full of cotton."

Haag still marvels at Goddard's reconstruction of the garage massacre, determining the number and type of guns used, even the sequence in which each victim was hit. "Are the craters on the wall, the brick wall, the consequence of direct strikes, or are they bullets that have gone through someone, but destabilize and make much lesser marks? Because if we know that, we know where someone was standing when they got shot. But imagine if someone is down and executed. The bullet goes through them and makes a spall in the floor. Or we recover the bullet on the floor and we see that it's got bone particles in it, and we've only got one person for whom a wound has gone through bone. That's a reconstructive phenomenon. So the bone particles in the bullet that's now hit the floor; this person shows a head wound, and was down on the floor when shot."

From following in Goddard's investigative footsteps, Luke Haag went on to become one of the world's pre-eminent experts in forensic ballistics. He has authored hundreds of ground-breaking scientific papers. With his son Michael, he co-authored the bible on the science of recreating firearms-centric crime scenes, *Shooting Incident Reconstruction*. In a cold case such as the murder in room 117, specialists like Luke and Michael Haag represent the last, best chance of arriving at a clear and final determination of the question: Who killed Spike Dubs? The knowledge and technology they can apply was unavailable to examiners in the 1970s.

"It's the ultimate goal of forensic science. What can we exclude, what did not happen, what could have happened. And best of all: what did happen out of the possible choices, or theories as lawyers like to call them. I would call them accounts, or hypotheses. We can go back to these historical events where there's competing explanations and theories, and if we can find sufficient physical evidence, we can often rule out one explanation, and either confirm or support the other."

To Luke Haag, the Afghan regime's actions in the aftermath of the firestorm are revealing, and damningly so. The instant mopping up the crime scene; the zealous way all the weapons, bullet fragments and shell casings were made to disappear. All of this shouts out culpability: the knowledge that physical evidence would reveal the truth. Amin and Taroon realized the guns and munitions would demonstrate who should be held responsible for Spike's death by gunfire—themselves, and their KGB accomplices. This would explain the regime's bizarre attempt to seize the ambassador's body from the AID dispensary.

"I'm a lab guy. I look at the static aftermath of a shooting. The scene needs to be secured so nothing gets moved. First, what's the position of the victim's body? Photograph that. Then the obvious things, any ballistic evidence. Are there are apparent gunshot residues? A .22 rimfire cartridge, for example, is going to have one physical form of propellant in it. The propellant from an AK round, or in a Makarov, which is a common Soviet police pistol, is going to be physically and chemically distinguishable—especially physically, the physical shapes of those particles."

Luke sees little mystery in the objective of the tactical assault on room 117. "In the final analysis, it doesn't strike me as a true rescue attempt. It's just 'kill everybody there.' When the entry team gained access from the hallway, it had to be just chaotic. They're in kind of an 'oh shit' situation, because there's the potential for friendly fire. If the people breaching the door and the people across the street are working for the same entity, or under the same instructions, then they needed to work out a plan. Otherwise there's a chance, especially for the guys going through the door, to get struck. They're in harm's way as soon as they get down the hallway far enough that bullets can reach them from across the street, or even ricocheted bullets coming off walls, coming in at an oblique angle."

The outcome of the assault suggests a coordinated plan of attack. The breach team made it in and out again with no casualties, apart from the emotional breakdown suffered by one of the commandos. Immediately after the fusillade of automatic weapons ceased, the air of confusion provided enough cover for the fatal pistol rounds to be fired, and for the assailant to make good his escape, unseen but for Chuck's sighting of him in the bathroom doorway. For the Americans, getting Spike out of the hotel as soon as possible precluded the recovery of physical evidence. "Upon entering that room, it's just going to be smoke, haze, particles of rock, sheet rock, broken glass everywhere, cartridge cases from the entry team everywhere."

From a forensic ballistics standpoint, the regime's culpability looms still larger in the context of the bodies being put on show for the Embassy Kabul officers and the *Kabul Times* photographer, but then being removed before they could be examined. "There's so much physical evidence in them. The nature of the wounds, any ballistic evidence, traces on their clothing. From the viewpoint of a lab person, I want the bullets from the dead guy at the morgue. I want the bullets from the ambassador and the bullets from the two men on the floor. What if the same gun was used to kill the man who wasn't in the room at the time? That tells you a story right there. That somebody has offed the ambassador with, let's say a Margolin, a classic Soviet .22 target pistol, .22 rimfire. This has certain rifling characteristics. What if the dead guy has been killed with the same Margolin? It doesn't sound like something that an Afghan cop would be carrying, does it?"

However, Luke Haag believes a very different Soviet-made pistol deserves investigative analysis in the Dubs case: the PSM—the weapon Chuck believes he saw handed to the Afghan plainclothesman by the KGB's Alexi Klushnikov. Luke is a leading authority on the PSM, or compact self-loading pistol. In the late 1980s, the twilight years of Soviet Communism, Luke travelled to the USSR as a visiting scientist. His Russian counterparts already knew him to be one of America's foremost forensic ballistics experts. As fellow professionals, they welcomed him into their crime labs. There, Luke test fired PSMs, dismantled and studied them, and documented the weapon's unique 5.45 x 18 mm bottlenecked cartridges. What he discovered was a palm-sized, super-slim handgun that slips easily into a jacket pocket, but packs tremendous firepower.

The weapon's jacketed rounds—bullets encased in metal jackets—are able to penetrate two layers of the standard issue Kevlar bulletproof vests used by American law enforcement officers. As a result, the PSM is known as a "cop killer" and is banned from importation into the United States. It is this penetrative might that poses a conundrum in determining whether a PSM pistol was the murder weapon in the case of Spike Dubs. Because although its size and effectiveness make it an ideal close-quarters assassination tool, the post-mortem analysis by the Federal Bureau of Investigation casts a degree of doubt in the matter.

The FBI's findings were summarized in a cable from Cyrus Vance to Embassy Kabul on March 7, 1979. The FBI investigators listed the bullets and bullet fragments taken from the ambassador's body as specimens Q1 to Q9. Five of these were .22-caliber projectiles found in the head. Three of the five were .22 long rifle bullets, made of lead with a copper coating, and bearing six groove rifling impressions with a right twist. The fourth and fifth specimens were the nose and base portions of the same kind of copper-coated .22 long rifle bullets.

For Luke Haag, there lies the inconsistency. Because although the .22-caliber could be consistent with rounds fired by the PSM, the pistol's standard Soviet-made ammunition features a full-metal jacketed bullet with a steel-tip penetrator. The complete jacketing of the lead core of a bullet enables a greater muzzle velocity than simple copper plating. This is what gives the PSM its punch, combined with the cartridge's propellant. As well, the copper plating of .22 bullets is virtually unknown in Russia and Europe as a whole.

Most particularly, Spike's head wounds are inconsistent with the likely result of jacketed bullets fired at close range from a PSM, namely through-and-through wound paths. Almost certainly there would be five exit wounds accompanying the evidence of gunshots to the head, rather than the discovery by X-ray that all the bullets and bullet fragments remained lodged within Spike's skull.

But could there be another possibility, in light of Col. Bakhturin's boast that he and his men provided the ammunition for the assault on room 117? Might the PSM have been intentionally loaded with non-standard ammunition to deliver more contained discharges at close range? Determining that requires a thorough reinvestigation of the evidence—a reopening of the case file and all related materials. This consists of a cache of documents, photographs and physical evidence that should, by rights, remain in safekeeping in the vaults of the Department of State and the FBI.

LUKE HAAG believes a reexamination is entirely justified. Not only might the murder weapon finally be identified, but many of the questions left hanging in the State Department's public report could be answered. The language of the document cries out for reassessment. "The report says 'the ambassador died as the result of at least 10 wounds inflicted by small caliber weapons.' Well, define small. I have a sense of what small means to me. But I don't know what this writer, or this pathologist meant, if that's coming from a pathologist. And then I think of the heart of the matter: .22-caliber. Well, there are .22-caliber rifles that are very energetic, and then there are .22s that are often the choice of assassins, because they're not noisy, they're concealable. But the good news from a forensic standpoint is, because of that, the bullets usually stay in the body."

To a scientist's ear, the report's terminology lands with a thud. "There's mention of 'powder burns.' This is jargon. They really aren't burns, so that worries me when I see that term. I suspect a forensic pathologist will not call them burns, but powder deposits, or sooty deposits. Or even what's called powder stippling, where the powder particles make little punctate injuries in living skin. Then 'fired from point blank.' Again, this is jargon. Point blank is a shooter's term, not a pathologist's term. It means you don't have to aim high or low. So point blank can be across the room. What this should say is 'contact to three inches.' Well, that's not from across the street, that's not from someone entering the door. That's someone that's right there with the ambassador who's put the gun to, or near his head, and fired it."

What the State Department report did accurately cite were the stark discrepancies between the Afghan regime's account of the kidnappers' firearms and the ballistics evidence found by the FBI's forensics team. According to the regime, only four weapons were found in room 117: a submachine gun; a Star "mouse-killer" pistol with 10 projectiles; a 7.65 mm pistol with six projectiles; and an unexploded hand grenade, supposedly a British-made Mark 36 "Mills Bomb." In the autopsy at Walter Reed, none of Spike's wounds were found to have been made by munitions from a submachine gun, a 7.65 mm pistol or a hand grenade. The State report said U.S. experts had concluded the two .25-caliber bullets found in Spike's chest were consistent with having been fired from the Star pistol. But there is no information as to how that determination was made, especially since the examiners had no access to the pistol itself. None of the American eye-witnesses could positively identify any of the weapons. Gul Mohammed could not describe the type or make of handguns used in the kidnapping, and none of the Americans who entered room 117 after the assault noted any firearms—apart from Chuck's belief the KGB-supplied pistol was the spitting image of a PSM.

Luke views the .25-caliber bullets worthy of further investigation. "The outstanding thing about those two .25-caliber auto bullets is the FBI stating that one was steel-jacketed and the other copper-jacketed. In 50-plus years in forensic science, I have never seen a steel-jacketed .25-caliber auto bullet. American .25-caliber automatic ammunition is copper-jacketed with lead cores." One of Luke's German counterparts at Munich's crime lab provided him with a list of sources for steel-jacketed .25 automatic bullets. All are European countries. The Czech entry seems the most likely source, but here as well, further analysis of the bullets could lead to important new discoveries.

Overall, the bullet and bullet fragments found in Spike's body comprise a ragged array of munitions. "I must say that shooting mixed brands of ammunition does not sound very professional. This practice is more in keeping with so-called 'gang-bangers.' They can't legally buy ammunition so they trade and scrounge it among their thug buddies."

By contrast, the two rifle rounds recovered from the hotel floor by Bruce Flatin were found to be standard Soviet Bloc military issue. Vance's cable to Embassy Kabul states: "(The) FBI has identified the two bullets, one fired and one unfired, found at the scene of (the) shooting by Mr. Flatin as being AK-47 type or equivalent. Probably Soviet made." Along with amateur wording—the items should be described as one live round and one spent cartridge—the analysis is maddeningly inadequate. For instance, there's no mention of the color of the lacquer, or absence of it, around the bullet in the live round.

This would identify it as being of Czech, Bulgarian or Russian manufacture. More importantly, the spent cartridge would bear marks that would reveal not only where it was manufactured, but likely the exact make and model of Kalashnikov from which it was fired. Not a word is devoted to that evidence, either in Vance's cable or the State report.

Then there is the unanswered question central to the fatal headshots: from what range were those bullets fired? Vance's cable states: "(An) estimate of distance (is) dependent upon existence of gunpower/firearms residue on clothing. Extensive examination underway by FBI. Results may be available in one or two days." Unfortunately, the trail ends there. The only further information to go by is the "point blank to three inches" wording in the State Department's public report—which also begs another look at the autopsy photographs and the ambassador's clothing.

Indeed, multiple factors warrant a thorough reexamination of the physical evidence in the Dubs case, aided by the countless advances made in forensic sciences since 1979. For instance, Luke says, "The FBI report makes no mention of the presence, appearance and number of cannelures on these bullets." Cannelures are the grooves arrayed around the base of the bullets. "One of the functions of cannelures is for product identification. The remnants of cannelures can reveal the identity of even a heavily damaged bullet. Cannelures visible in the bullets and bullet fragments examined by the FBI will be in their autopsy bench notes and photographs." Bench notes are the records created during the process of the post-mortem.

There is also no indication in the Vance cable and State report that sufficient analysis was made of rifling characteristics. Rifling refers to the spiral grooves in the bore of a firearm that cause the projectile to spin, stabilizing its flight. "The FBI examiner points out the 6-right rifling characteristics in the .22 bullets. That's very, very common in the vast majority of .22-caliber firearms. But when the same ammunition is fired in a revolver, there can be a phenomenon known to firearms examiners as "skid marks." These occur when these soft lead bullets transition from the unrifled chambers into the forcing cone and then rifling of the barrel. If those marks are present, once again they will be in the examiner's bench notes or photographs or both. It's also unclear from the report if the FBI examiner measured the widths of the land impressions created by this 6-right firearm. If so, these measurements can reduce the long list of possible firearms from which the bullets were fired."

CHAPTER 17

RESOLUTIONS THEN AND NOW

CHUCK BOLES received no response from Washington to his second investigation report. But neither did the envelope come back to him stamped "*Return To Sender.*" Apparently, the Dubs case was held by the Department of State to be not only unsolved, but unsolvable. And there was every indication it would stay that way. Yet this much is certain. Under the microscope of a 21st century forensic ballistics examiner, even the very limited physical evidence recovered from the crime scene at the Hotel Kabul could still provide conclusive results today. In fact, the Dubs affair checks off all the boxes that justify the reopening of a cold case file.

First, new information has emerged from multiple witnesses such as Vasili Mitrokhin and Chuck Boles, not to mention from one of the responsible parties, Sergei G. Bakhturin. Second, newly unearthed or declassified records in the three subject nations, the United States, Russia and Afghanistan, continue to yield new facts deserving of reconsideration. And third, significant physical evidence, almost certainly retained in the U.S. government's custody and control, could be reexamined with the aid of science and technology undreamed of in 1979.

More than four decades later, the evidence Spike Dubs brought home to Washington, DC can once again come to the service of the country, and the citizens, for whom he sacrificed his life. One issue that could finally be laid to rest: why did the Carter administration appear to give up on the investigation? President Carter and Secretary Vance spoke of a tireless dedication to combatting terrorism, leaving unspoken the need to identify Spike's killers and exact just retribution. Yet Vance's cable exchanges with Embassy Kabul speak to an urgent need to know what really happened. The administration was acutely aware that CBS News anchor Walter Cronkite wasn't the only American who felt the murder fueled the perception the United States was a "helpless giant, kicked around and insulted at will."

Carter and his closest advisers appear to have concluded there was something missing. There was no smoking gun, much less the fingerprints of the culprits who pulled the trigger. The facts available, at that time, were judged insufficient to justify a more robust showdown with the Soviet Union. Which is precisely why the Dubs file should be reopened; why the new U.S. administration should accept this as an *obligation*—particularly in view of continuing Russian efforts to hide the truth. Because establishing that truth today is wholly consistent with the objectives of the original investigation four decades ago: preserving the integrity of America's historic role in global diplomacy.

The only surviving member of Spike's immediate family fully supports a reinvestigation. To Lindsay Dubs McLaughlin, there is literally a world of reasons why the United States should try once again to conclusively prove who killed her father, and why. "I feel it would lead to more insight about what is occurring in Afghanistan and that part of the world today. Anything that can shed some kind of light, or bring some sort of understanding of these events, might go some of the way towards seeing our way out of these troubles. So it would be great if the American government wanted to pursue the case and figure out exactly what happened, but not just for the sake of it.

More for seeking wisdom about what were the factors, what was really at play."

Predictably, this opportunity presents itself when the United States is once again grappling with the question: what is to be done with the American presence in Afghanistan? The most sensible way to begin looking for answers to this question is to fully comprehend the conflict's origins—and to debunk misconceptions. For instance, Americans have become conditioned to hearing that the Afghan war is their country's longest because U.S. involvement dates all the way back to the months following the 9/11 attacks in 2001. Well, the class of '79 at the American International School in Kabul can set us straight on that score. "I was there as a high school senior when the war started," says Mark Flatin. "Now I'm 59 years old with grandchildren. That's how long it's been going on."

Then there are the larger misconceptions, such as the dysfunctional covert support program to the anti-Communist resistance. Successive U.S. administrations failed to grasp that responding haphazardly to terrorism only fans its flames. Case in point, the Afghan mujahideen leader who benefited more than any other from the CIA's largesse: Gulbuddin Hekmatyar. Many of us who have reported on this ruthless, anti-Western extremist over the years need to use the fingers of both hands to count the friends, colleagues and acquaintances, Afghan and non-Afghan, whose murders trace back to Hekmatyar and his *Hizbi Islami* organization. During the civil war that preceded the Taliban's rise to power, Hekmatyar was Prime Minister of the mujahideen provisional government. As such, he was the only leader in the world who routinely leveled rocket barrages on his own capital city. After the Taliban were sent packing from Kabul, Hekmatyar's men preyed on U.S. and coalition troops. Yet, ever the survivor, in 2016 he signed a peace deal with the U.S. backed Afghan government. After his return to Kabul, he ran in last year's presidential election—unsuccessfully, given the voting public's memory of the atrocities he unleashed against them.

Other warlords came back to haunt the Langley brain trust in even bloodier ways. Jalaluddin Haqqani was described as "goodness personified" by Charlie Wilson, the Congressman from Texas who shifted the CIA's Operation Cyclone into high gear. Having spent the frigid New Year of 1988 with Haqqani's "freedom fighters" in action in his native Zadran Valley, I can confirm the man was adept at killing Soviet troops. But he was also a zealot backed by fundamentalist Islamist elements in Saudi Arabia and Pakistan. It was no surprise he joined the Taliban, serving as the Islamic Emirate's Minister of Borders and Tribal Affairs. Still less surprising: he aided Osama bin Laden's escape from U.S. forces in 2001. Haqqani later formed his own terrorist front to assist the Taliban's war on American forces and their allies. With good reason, the Haqqani Network is held responsible for the most appalling and gruesome attacks on Afghan civilians, government employees and international forces.

Finally, there are more recent misjudgments. Money is not really the root of all evil, but it has definitely been the root of most failures in Afghanistan. Since 2001, the United States has spent $132 billion in reconstruction efforts, with the Pentagon's warfighting costing some $800 billion more. Adjusted for inflation, the U.S. has spent more on Afghanistan's reconstruction than on the Marshall Plan to rebuild Western Europe after World War II, according to John Sopko, the Special Inspector General for the American government's Afghan program, or SIGAR.

As early as 2007, I was among the growing number of foreign correspondents reporting on the systematic looting of Western aid projects. This ran the gamut from simple misappropriation of funds to more elaborate frauds. One of most corrosive scams was the use of "ghost" or non-existent police officers, in some cases entire outposts, to syphon off money intended to foster responsible law enforcement. Thus not only was justice impeded, criminality was rewarded.

In 2019, the *Washington Post* published a definitive investigative review on SIGAR's findings, known as the Afghanistan Papers. The series reported the testimony of a three-star Army general who helped manage the war for the Bush and Obama administrations. "We were devoid of a fundamental understanding of Afghanistan—we didn't know what we were doing," Douglas Lute told investigators in 2015. "What are we trying to do here? We didn't have the foggiest notion of what we were undertaking."

Spike Dubs came from a different school of global endeavor: the school of knowing what you are doing before committing a lot of generals, guns and money to the task. Yes, hindsight is 20/20. And it would be oversimplifying this most byzantine of quandaries by suggesting all of the answers lie in the reinvestigation of the murder of America's first wartime ambassador to Afghanistan. But there can be no denying Spike's recommended course of action has never been pursued to any practical degree. He advocated getting aid to the Afghan people, not to warlords or carpetbaggers or political leaders subject to corruption.

There lies the only solution. Peace must be secured for the civilian population. Without this, there can be no withdrawal of international forces from Afghanistan. Abandoning the Afghan people would once again turn their land into a haven for terrorists. This is a lesson we should not need to learn again. The facts are before us, ready for reconsideration. Just like the evidence from the murder in room 117 of the Hotel Kabul.

Epilogue

THE MEMORIES of that tragic Valentine's Day followed Embassy Kabul's foreign service officers, and their loved ones, to every corner of the world. Some say they were strengthened by the trauma and sadness, by the lasting imprint Spike's loss made upon them, both personally and as career diplomats. All of them remember the ambassador's warmth and humor and professionalism. Over the years, they carried those values and standards to one overseas mission after another.

Mike Malinowski was sworn in as U.S. Ambassador to Nepal in 2001. Three times he earned the State Department's Superior Honor Awards for his work: as principle officer at the U.S. Consulate in Peshawar during the final years of the Soviet occupation of Afghanistan; for his work during the Gulf War; and finally, in Kathmandu, Nepal.

Doug Wankel spent 26 years with the Drug Enforcement Administration, retiring in 1996 as Chief of Operations. Time and again he returned to Afghanistan. In 2003, he rejoined the DEA as Chief of Intelligence in the country, as well as Director of the Kabul Counter-Narcotics Task Force, based in the reopened Embassy Kabul.

After Chuck Boles delivered his investigation report to State in DC, he went on to postings in Colombia and Israel. He returned to the security division at Foggy Bottom in 1985, and served as the State Department's deputy director of counter intelligence from 1988 until his retirement in 1990.

After moving on from Embassy Kabul, Jeannene Cramer served at U.S. missions in Dakar, Cairo, Paris, Jakarta and London, as well as State's Bureau of Medical Services in DC. She retired in 2000 after 22 distinguished years in the foreign service.

David Litt served 34 years as a career U.S. diplomat, including his term as Ambassador to the United Arab Emirates from 1995 to 1998.

After postings to Jordan and Lebanon, Bernie Woerz served in Washington as chief of the Post Management Office, then as a special aide to the Assistant Secretary of State for Administration. He was Consul General in Curaçao from 1992 to 1995. Recalled from retirement for a dozen temporary assignments, Bernie journeyed to capitals like Caracas, London and Moscow–and, in 2005, made a bittersweet return to Embassy Kabul.

Technically, Tom Gouttierre retired in 2015 after 41 years as the director of the Center for Afghanistan Studies at the University of Nebraska at Omaha. In reality, he has never stopped sharing his knowledge of Afghanistan and the Afghan people with students and journalists, diplomats and government officials.

Lloyd Rotz and his family were among the last staffers and dependents to leave Embassy Kabul in August 1979. Following one more posting to Colombia, Lloyd left State and returned to private practice. His son Steve earned an engineering degree, then pursued a career in business development and marketing in the technology sector. His classmate Mark Flatin was drawn to finance and carved out a successful career in investment banking. The boys' teacher, Jim Gurnett, returned home to Alberta, Canada. He has served as a member of the province's legislative assembly and remains active in politics and community service.

Following Kabul, Jim Taylor served in State's Bureau of

Political and Military Affairs. His work focused on Egyptian-Israeli relations after the signing of the Camp David Accords. He then served in Tel Aviv before returning to State in DC in 1988, monitoring the Soviet withdrawal from Afghanistan.

Louise Taylor also returned to Washington. In 1983, she was named chief of the Afghan and Persian language branch of the Voice of America. She later served in Tel Aviv and Rabat, Morocco before returning to DC. She retired in 2000.

Bruce Flatin left Kabul for Washington in November 1979, becoming an office director for State's INM division, International Narcotics Matters. He went on to serve as the worldwide director of the Office of Refugee Resettlement, and in 1989 was named to State's Board of Examiners.

Several of the foreign service nationals who served under Spike found new homes in the United States, including Doug Wankel's driver, Ewaz Ali, and Chuck Boles' security assistant, Abdul Ghafari.

After losing Spike, Mary Ann Dubs left the Congressional Record to pursue a career in foreign service for the State Department. Mexico City was her first posting. In 1985, aged 40, she lost her life to leukemia.

Spike's first wife, Jane Wilson, won a significant victory for the ex-spouses of former diplomats. Her alimony payments stopped after Spike was killed, and benefits went only to the surviving wife. Jane took her case to Congress, compelling State to amend its policies and recognize the contribution made by spouses during their partners' overseas postings.

After college, Lindsay Dubs went into teaching. She and her husband Billy McLaughlin started a family, later settling in a tranquil, forested retreat in the Shenandoah Valley north-west of Washington, DC. Surrounded by nature and guided by faith, they enjoy a growing family and look to a better future for their community, their country and the world.

Afterword

IN THE YEARS following the U.S.-led expulsion of the Taliban regime in 2001, the Hotel Kabul was rebuilt and extended by the Agha Khan Foundation. Renamed the Kabul Serena Hotel, the lavish new complex bears little resemblance to the original structure. Tragically, its walls have echoed with the same savage violence that rocked its predecessor.

In January 2008, four Taliban militants attacked the Serena with rifles, grenades and explosive vests. Two Afghan guards were killed by the terrorists, as well as a Filipino female employee, a Norwegian journalist and an American. Three of the attackers were killed, one was captured. Six years later in 2014, the Serena was attacked again by four teenage gunmen. Before the young Talibs could be cornered and killed, they murdered nine guests in the hotel restaurant: two Afghan children and their parents; two Bangladeshis; and one person each from Canada, New Zealand and Paraguay.

At the time of these attacks, the Taliban leadership enjoyed safe haven in Pakistan—as they do to this day.

Sources And References

This book is based on original source material drawn from interviews with participants and witnesses recorded from April 2017 to December 2020. Several individuals cannot be named due to their connections with sensitive current matters in international affairs. Others are presently chronicling the abuses of authoritarian governments and remain unnamed in the interests of personal safety.

This account relies in part on three histories recorded and published by The Association for Diplomatic Studies and Training, the world's largest collection of oral accounts on the history of U.S. diplomacy. Bruce Flatin was interviewed for the association's Oral History Project on January 27, 1993. Jim Taylor was interviewed for the project on December 5, 1995, with Louise Taylor's interview recorded on January 19, 2001. By capturing and preserving the experiences of U.S. foreign service officers in their own words, the association not only renders an invaluable service to students and researchers, but to the American public. As evidenced by Spike's story, the practice of international relations needs constantly to be refined and improved. The association's archive also stands as a bulwark against corrupt political influences, both from abroad and, as recent history has shown, from certain domestic quarters as well.

Commendably, the Department of State has declassified

portions of its archives relevant to these events, including a good number of cable exchanges of the time. However, other records, such as those disclosed by WikiLeaks, indicate there remains a significant quantity of documentation that has yet to benefit from the light of public access. Particularly in view of ongoing efforts by malign foreign entities and individuals to conceal the true circumstances of this crime, the release of the remainder of the Dubs file appears to be decidedly in the public interest.

REFERENCES

Introduction

8 **the U.S. "distracted by one geopolitical crisis heaped upon another":** China's actions in Vietnam, the crisis in Iran and troubled arms talks with the Soviets are recounted in Jimmy Carter's *Keeping Faith,* Zbigniew Brzezinski's *Power and Principle* and *Hard Choices* by Cyrus Vance. See Related Bibliography.

Chapter 2

20 **Spike Dubs "a positivist":** *Washington Post,* February 15, 1979, "Ambassador Dubs: Eager, Knew Post Was Tough."

21 Tom Gouttierre's success with Afghan basketball: *Sports Illustrated,* "The Wizard Of Kabul," July 22, 2013.

Chapter 3

26 **arrests of Embassy Kabul's Afghan Foreign Service Nationals:** cable from Chuck Boles to State Department's Security Office on March 27, 1979, "Afghan Harassment of Embassy FSNs."

30 **12,000 Afghans murdered by PDPA regime:** this estimate for those killed at Pul-e-Charkhi prison alone. Many more civilians lost their lives in rural areas. See Human Rights Watch, *Afghanistan: The Forgotten War: Human Rights Abuses and Violations of the Laws of War Since the Soviet Withdrawal,* 1 February 1991.

31 **Americans' discomfort with doctors' plot:** Spike Dubs agreed with Washington's decision not to back the counter-coup. He wrote that it might "raise unwarranted expectations among the coup leaders about (the U.S.) ability to influence events decisively..." *Foreign Relations of the United States, 1977-1980,* Volume XII, Afghanistan, p. 60, citing cable 6128 from Kabul. Department of State Office of the Historian.

Chapter 4

39 **Spike's skill at ping-pong and his good humor:** *Washington Post,* February 15, 1979, *op. cit.*

40 **the complexities of Afghan society and culture:** in Part II of his definitive work, *Afghanistan,* Professor Louis Dupree explores the ethnicity, language and religion of the Afghan people, as well as the country's folk lore and music. See Related Bibliography.

49 **the PDPA leaders' Marxist pronouncements:** Taraki's and Amin's statements are quoted from the Journal of Ambassador A.M. Puzanov, July 11, 1978.

49-50 **Ponomarev's warning to Taraki:** *The Diary of Anatoly Chernyaev,* published by The National Security Archive at https://nsarchive.gwu.edu/briefing-book/russia-programs/2018-05-25/anatoly-s-chernyaev-diary-1978.

51 **the administration's focus not on Afghanistan:** *Keeping*

Faith, Carter; SALT II, p. 217; the growing storm in Iran, 438-442. Also, *Power and Principle,* Brzezinski; SALT II, p. 182; 278; China and Vietnam, p. 411-413; Iran, p. 279, 354-355.

52 **tensions between Brzezinski and Vance:** *Power and Principle,* Brzezinski; p. 11, 37, 42-43, 63, 143. On p. 40, Brzezinski complains Vance's staff "caricatured me personally as well as my views," and Vance failed to "put a stop to that sniping." Also p. 37 of *Hard Choices,* Vance; claims that Brzezinski's memos would misstate Vance's positions, forcing Vance to clarify his views with Carter.

53 ***Oklahoma!*:** Lyrics by Oscar Hammerstein II and Richard Rodgers.

Chapter 5

55-56 **Khomeini's return from exile to Iran:** *Power and Principle,* Brzezinski p. 362-389; *Keeping Faith,* Carter p. 438-442.

61-64 **Gul Mohammed's account of the kidnapping:** cable from RSS Ron Kelly to State, February 17, 1979, "Interrogation of Ambassador Dubs' Chauffeur."

Chapter 7

81 **response to the crisis by the State Operations Center:** Department of State Newsletter, March 1979, No. 210.

82 **concurrent crises at Embassy Tehran:** *Power and Principle,* Brzezinski p. 389-392; *Keeping Faith,* Carter p. 443-453.

Chapter 8

97 **Col. Bakhturin's operational role at the Hotel Kabul:** cited in *Washington Post,* "Soviet Role Alleged In Dubs' Death," February 22, 1979.

107 **tourists Sandy and Mayer Stiebel at the Hotel Kabul:** *Associated Press,* "As Police Attempt Rescue Kidnappers Shoot Dubs," February 15, 1979.

109-110 **summary of cables from Kabul to State:** Department of State Newsletter, "St. Valentine's morning in the Operations Center," March 1979, No. 210.

Chapter 10

123 **"tough" and "calculating" Anatoly Dobrynin:** *Power and Principle,* Brzezinski p. 152.

131-132 **interview of Commandant Taroon:** February 19, 1979 cable from RSO Boles to State, "Kidnapping and Killing of Ambassador Dubs–Interview with Taroon"

Chapter 11

142 **regime's order to "eliminate" witnesses including Spike:** Jim Taylor in *Embassies Under Siege: Personal Accounts by Diplomats on the Front Line,* p. 66. See Related Bibliography.

Chapter 12

151 **Gul Mohammed cleared by polygraph:** March 6, 1979 cable from RSO Ron Kelly to State, "Kidnapping and Killing of Ambassador Dubs."

154-156 **CIA memo on covert options for Afghanistan:** *Foreign Relations of the United States,* Department of State, *op. cit.,* p. 106.

Chapter 13

161 **Chuck Boles "unquestionably one of the best":** April 2, 1979 cable from Bruce Amstutz to State, "Transfer of RSO Boles."

162-164 **White House meeting chaired by Walter Mondale:**

Foreign Relations of the United States, op. cit., p. 139, Minutes of the April 6, 1979 meeting of the Special Coordination Committee.

166 **Embassy Kabul stresses Spike's beliefs on Afghan policy:** June 2, 1979 cable from Bruce Amstutz to State, "Senate Amendment on Aid to Afghanistan."

167-168 **NSC meeting of Soviet and Afghan specialists:** July 19, 1979 memo to Zbigniew Brzezinski, *Foreign Relations of the United States, op. cit.*, p. 160.

168 **Soviets likely to "unseat" Amin:** *Power and Principle,* Brzezinski, p. 427. On July 23, 1979, Brzezinski advised Carter that Amin's "Communist terror tactics were proving counterproductive."

170-171 **August 1979 CIA report on aiding Afghan resistance:** *Foreign Relations of the United States, op. cit.*, p. 172.

173 **Soviets "stunned" by Taraki's murder by Amin:** The Kremlin's animus against Amin is obvious in an October 29, 1979 memo signed by the KGB's Andropov, Defence Minister Dimitri Ustinov, Andrei Gromyko and Boris Ponomarev. The memo stressed "the necessity of doing everything possible not to allow the victory of counter-revolution in Afghanistan or the political reorientation of H. Amin towards the West."

177 **the Soviet invasion "an extremely grave challenge":** December 26, 1979. *Foreign Relations of the United States, Department of State, op. cit.*, p. 265.

Chapter 14

181 **the declassified State report on Spike's murder:** *Department of State,* M/CT—Office for Combatting Terrorism, Country and Functional Files, 1980–1982, and Terrorist Incident Files, 1973–1976, 1976, 1980–1981,

Lot 83D135, Box 12, *Dubs, Adolph Amb—Afgh, Kidnapping Death—Feb 14, 1979–1980.*

184 **Spike's murder "Soviet ineptitude or collusion":** *Power and Principle,* Brzezinski, p. 413.

185 **excerpts from the archive of Vasili Mitrokhin:** *The KGB in Afghanistan,* Woodrow Wilson International Center, Washington, 2002.

Chapter 15

197 **Bakhturin's intelligence career:** his autobiographical account appears in a book about Soviet forces in Afghanistan: *Afgan, snova Afgan* (*Afghanistan, again Afghanistan*), A. Andogskii, Yuri Drozdov, V. Kurilov, and S. Bakhturin. Moscow, 2002. Bakhturin omits any mention of Spike's murder, much less his role in the assault on room 117.

198 **Russian book about the Soviet war:** *Virus A: How We Got Infected by the Invasion of Afghanistan,* by Vladimir Snegirev and Valery Samunin. The book credits Bakhturin as one of the authors' sources.

Chapter 16

201 **Excerpts from Chuck Boles' second Investigation Report:** Published here for the first time.

210 **FBI's ballistics findings "summarized in a cable":** Cyrus Vance to Embassy Kabul, March 7, 1979, "Kidnapping and Killing of Ambassador Dubs."

219 **Charlie Wilson says Haqqani is "goodness personified":** *Charlie Wilson's War,* George Crile, p. 473. See Related Bibliography.

Acknowledgments

Completing this book would not have been possible without the openness and patience of the former foreign service officers who consented to be interviewed. These veterans endured repeated rounds of questioning and follow up queries, often focusing on painful memories. From the earliest stages of my research, it was clear they remain tightly bonded by a dedication to professional duty and honor. This became an avenue allowing the most pointed of inquiries, which in turn I have strived to respect by relaying their words accurately and in good faith.

Given the period of time this crime has been framed as a mystery destined to remain unsolved forever, I realized that Lindsay Dubs McLaughlin might turn down my request to revisit the loss of her father. Instead, she took note of my idea and raised the stakes. Rather than simply retelling the story, why not try—sincerely try—to find out what really happened? It was a challenge that could not go unanswered. Thanks to Lindsay's candor and faith, work continues on the reinvestigation.

Penetrating the remnants of the Iron Curtain in Vladimir Putin's Russia is a difficult undertaking, and not without peril. For now, I must express my gratitude only by way of assumed names. To Alexi, Ekaterina and Pyotr, your fearless journalism will one day contribute to a thaw in Russia's current deep freeze of democratic freedoms. And you will be right there, telling the story.

Many colleagues and friends have buoyed this project along and deserve special thanks. Greg Banning immersed himself in the story, bringing its pivotal moments to life. Brian Brennan, Vicki Barnett and Bob Blakey applied their keen editorial eyes to the text. Special assistance was graciously provided by Kevin Bishop, Kit Johnson, Franco Fragomeni, Peter Jouvenal, Brian Kent, Sen. Mike Duffy, Dan Donovan, Richard Leibner and the late Stu Witt. Stu's special gift was to keep his clients laughing, however tough the going might become. Committing these materials to hard drives relied on the talents of Duane Empy, George Stover and Joe Egan, while Karl Schadow excelled in archives research. Michael Wynn and Roxann Corpuz at Full Blast Creative were responsible for rendering the digital content into a format our printer Darrell Martindale could run with. All of them helped transform this story into something that can be held in both hands and perused at will.

For her patience and support, year after year, Michelle Comtois is a most wonderful ally. Incalculable thanks go to her and to my late sister, Susan. In life, Susan Kent Davidson brought inspirational force to her writing and editing. In the words she left behind, she continues to teach the importance of craft—the meticulous, liberating pursuit of excellence.

Finally, the people of Afghanistan. Still now our attention is drawn to their country by way of suicide bombings, battlefield atrocities—and histories such as this. The Afghans have endured a grisly succession of civil wars and proxy wars; wars of superpower aggression or retribution; turf wars and ethnic wars and wars the cause of which is hard to recall and still harder to explain.

We foreigners will keep going back. We will continue telling our stories. But there is one message above all we must always bring home. Only by restoring the Afghans' security can we ever hope to ensure our own.

Related Bibliography

Andrew, Christopher, and Vasili Mitrokhin. *The Mitrokhin Archive: The KGB in Europe and the West*. London, 1999.

Brzezinski, Zbigniew. *Power and Principle: Memoirs of the National Security Adviser*, 1977-1981.

Carter, Jimmy. *Keeping Faith: Memoirs of a President*. 1982.

Crile, George. *Charlie Wilson's War: The Extraordinary Story of the Largest Covert Operation in History*. New York, 2003.

Dupree, Louis. *Afghanistan*. Princeton. 1973.

Girardet, Edward. *Killing the Cranes: A Reporter's Journey Through Three Decades of War in Afghanistan*. Chelsea Green Publishing, 2011.

Gordievsky, Oleg. *Next Stop Execution: The Autobiography of Oleg Gordievevsky*. London, 1995.

Haag, Michael G. and Lucien C. *Shooting Incident Reconstruction*. Academic Press, July 13, 2011.

Kalugin, Oleg. Spymaster: *My Thrity-Two Years in Intelligence and Espionage Against the West*. New York, 2009.

Kent, Arthur. *Risk and Redemption: Surviving the Network News Wars*. Interstellar Inc., 1997; Chapter 3, *Reporting the War on the Roof of the World*; and Chapter 5, *Cold War to Old War: Return to Afghanistan*.

Macintyre, Ben. *The Spy and the Traitor: The Greatest Espionage Story of the Cold War*. London, 2018.

Mitrokhin, Vasili. *The KGB in Afghanistan*. Washington, DC, 2002; https://www.wilsoncenter.org/publication/the-kgb-afghanistan

Taylor, *James E. The Murder of Ambassador Dubs, Kabul, 1979*; Chapter 4 in *Embassies Under Siege: Personal Accounts by Diplomats on the Front Line*, Sullivan, Joseph G. (ed.). Brassey's, Washington, 1995.

Vance, Cyrus. *Hard Choices: Four Critical Years in Managing America's Foreign Policy*. 1983.

Photo Credits

First Photo Section

Page 1: (top) Elmore Rigamer collection, (bottom) Jeannene Cramer collection; ***Page 2***: (main) Lindsay Dubs McLaughlin collection, (insets) National Archives and Records Administration (NARA); ***Page 3***: NARA; ***Page 4:*** (main) David Litt collection, (bottom) Jeannene Cramer collection. ***Page 5:*** (main) Lindsay Dubs McLaughlin collection, (bottom) David Litt collection, (top right) Jim Gurnett collection; ***Page 6:*** (main and insets) Jeannene Cramer collection, (tank) Elmore Rigamer collection. ***Page 7***: (top, bottom) Elmore Rigamer collection, (ball team) Steven Rotz collection. ***Page 8***: Steven Rotz collection; ***Page 9***: Thomas Gouttierre collection. ***Page 10***: Mike Malinowski collection; ***Page 11***: NARA; ***Page 12***: public domain, (soldier) Arthur Kent photo.

Second Photo Section

Page 1: public domain; ***Page 2***: public domain; ***Page 3***: (top) public domain, (bottom) personal collection; ***Page 4***: (top, bottom right) personal collection, (bottom left) public domain, (background right) Arthur Kent photo; ***Page 5:*** (top) public domain, (background) NARA, (bottom) personal collection; ***Pages 6-11***: Skywriter Inc.; ***Page 12***: NARA.

Third Photo Section

Page 1: (main) State Department; (headlines) Times-Post service, UPI, AP; ***Page 2***: Public domain; ***Page 3***: Chuck Boles collection; ***Page 4***: (main) State Department, (bottom) public domain; ***Page 5:*** (background) NARA, (main) Skywriter Inc.; ***Page 6***: Skywriter Inc.; ***Page 7***: Skywriter Inc.; ***Page 8***: (top) public domain, (insets) NARA; ***Page 9***: (Main) Skywriter Inc., (right) personal collection; ***Page 10***: Lucien Haag collection. ***Page 11***: Arthur Kent photos; ***Page 12***: Arthur Kent photo.

Index

Afghanistan 9, 13, 14, 21, 33-36, 56, 59, 67, 87, 114
allure of 10-12, 15, 22, 39-42, 60
Afghan army 14, 18, 26, 28-29, 73-74, 79, 92, 95, 118, 130, 138, 151, 160, 172, 177-179
CIA involvement in 162-165, 36-37, 134, 154-156, 159-160, 162-168, 170-171, 175, 177, 179, 185, 187, 189-190, 198, 218-219
Communist coup, PDPA regime 11, 17, 23, 27-30, 32-34, 36, 45-50, 53-54, 56-57, 64, 70, 74, 76, 81, 96-97, 109, 119, 121-124, 126-127, 133, 136-137, 146, 152-153, 159-162, 164, 167-168, 170-180, 185, 188, 205-206
history of 40-41
Pakistani involvement in 50, 154-156, 159-160, 162-165,
secret police (Ministry of Interior) 25-26, 29, 36, 48, 68, 74, 76, 83, 93, 99, 102-103, 146, 153, 170-171, 190, 204-205
sightseeing and fishing 35, 41-42, 52-53, 77
Soviet involvement in 33-38, 130, 134, 147, 149, 159-160, 162-165, 167-168, 172-180
U.S. involvement in 25, 27, 50-54, 57, 81, 110, 140-145, 147-148, 154-156, 159-161, 162-172, 173-180
Agha Khan Foundation 224
Ahmad, Sher 146
AID (see USAID)
Ajar Valley 41
Alexander the Great 11
Ali, Ewaz 26,
American International School in Kabul (AISK) 11, 14, 61, 77, 158, 168-169, 178, 218
Amin, Hafizullah 24, 27-31, 44-49, 56-57, 62, 68, 71, 76, 85-86, 91, 97, 117, 121, 123-124, 127-128, 132-136, 138, 142, 146, 153, 157, 159, 167, 171-175, 178, 182, 185, 188-190, 195, 197, 200, 208
Andar, Mohammed 78
Ashrat, Ghulam Jailani 53
Associated Press (AP) 133-134
autopsies 112-115, 126, 130-131, 141, 143, 148, 161-162, 181-184, 202-206, 212, 214
Azizi (officer) 89-90, 106

Badakhshan 121, 135
Bakhturin, Sergei G.
appears at kidnap scene 7-8, 84-87
conduct at kidnap scene 24, 89-92, 97-100, 104
contacts with U.S. counterpart 84, 157
dress and countenance 7-8, 84

duties as embassy security officer 35
history and training as KGB officer 33-34
interviewed in 2019 192-201, 216
relationship with his ambassador 35-36, 38
revealed in defector's archive 191
role in Soviet invasion 176-177
searches for moles, traitors 38
subverts Afghan leadership 173-174
ballistics 130, 141, 161, 183, 206-210, 212, 217
Bamiyan Province 41
Bangladesh 224
BBC 120, 134
Bell, Griffin 163
Beloit College 17
Berlin 33
Bhutto, Zulfikar Ali 50
bliztkreig 17
Boles, Chuck 42-44, 59, 67-68, 70, 73-74, 76, 78-79, 84, 89, 92, 98, 101-105, 108, 117-119, 122-123, 125, 127-128, 131-132, 137, 145-146, 148-154, 156-157, 161-162, 176, 182-184, 197-198, 203-206, 209, 213, 216, 221
Brezhnev, Leonid 20, 173, 178
Brzezinski, Zbigniew 51, 52, 152, 162-165, 177, 184
Buczacki, Jeffrey 81
Butkus, Dick 36

Canada 14, 18, 222, 224
Capone, Alphonse G. "Al" 206
Carlucci, Frank 163,
Carter, Jimmy 20-21, 55, 97, 124, 128, 130, 140, 147, 154, 159, 166, 170, 177, 217
Carter administration
indecision and infighting 8-9, 51-52
kidnapping response 71-72, 81-83, 87-88, 96-97, 109-112
prioritizing Iran 56
priorities in Dubs investigation 122-123, 125, 127, 131, 141, 144-146, 148-153, 161-162, 176, 216
public report on Dubs case 183-184, 212, 214
Central Intelligence Agency (CIA) 61, 83, 151-152, 185, 187
covert actions in Afghanistan 154-156, 159-160, 162-168, 179, 218-219
misreading Soviets' Afghan
intentions 174-176
outnumbered in Kabul 36-37
prioritizing Iran and Pakistan 34, 50, 52
reliance on Pakistan's ISI 164-165, 170-171, 177, 179
Chicago 12, 17-18, 206
Chicago Bears 36
chargé d'affaires 19, 20, 127, 146, 166, 171, 173,
Chicken Street bazaar 11-12, 57
Chief of Station, Kabul 37, 61, 151-152, 175
Christopher, Warren 97, 123, 163
Cold War 8-9, 10, 16, 92, 116, 121, 124, 147, 158, 194, 199, 206
Columbia University 27
Congressional Record 21, 223
Cramer, Jeannene 13-14, 58-59, 61, 75, 93, 108, 112-114, 126, 129, 143, 148, 222
Cronkite, Walter 140, 217
Cuban Missile Crisis 18-19
curfews 12, 32, 118

Da Afghanistan Bank 63-64, 89, 91, 94-95, 99, 122, 138, 196
Daoud Khan, Mohammed 28
Dari (language) 12-13, 47, 60, 62, 75, 92, 132, 170
Detroit 11

diplomatic community in Kabul
American 11, 13, 14, 31, 36, 41, 48, 57, 61, 66-67, 77, 81, 92, 96-97, 109-110, 123, 125, 128, 130, 132, 136, 138, 142, 144, 158, 168-169, 178, 218. *See also* U.S. Embassy Kabul
Bulgarian 13, 35
Chinese 25, 59, 114
Czechoslovak 15, 35, 159
East German 167-168
French 25
Soviet 7-9, 15, 25, 33-34, 37, 41, 49, 75, 84-87, 173-180. *See also* Soviet Union
West German 25, 46,
disinformation 33, 162, 201
by regime, post-murder 126, 131-137, 183
by Soviets, post-murder 121, 136-137, 188-191, 195-201, 217
Dobrynin, Anatoly 123-124, 136
Drozdov, Yuri 177-178, 200
Drug Enforcement Administration (DEA) 11, 24, 26, 57, 83, 221
Dubs, Adolph "Spike" 8, 22, 31, 36, 52, 118, 120-121
appointment to Kabul 21
approach to diplomacy 20, 22-24, 44, 54
assessment of Afghan regime and contacts with leadership 22, 27-28, 32-33, 45-48, 54, 56
athleticism 39
correspondence with daughter Lindsay 20, 24, 26-27, 32, 4 1-42, 44, 45, 50, 52, 57, 88-89
education 17, 18
enjoying life in Kabul 43, 58, 59
his policy aims for Afghanistan 54
impressions of Afghanistan 39, 41-42
kidnapping, prelude to 55-60
kidnapping 61-64
as hostage at Hotel Kabul 64-66, 68-71, 75-76, 79-81, 83, 85, 89-90, 94,97, 100-105
lifesaving attempts 107-109
serves as Moscow chargé d'affaires 18
marriages 21
music and song 39, 53
nickname, origins 17
parents 18
post-mortems of 112-115, 126, 130-131, 141, 143, 148, 161-162, 182-183, 204-205, 212, 214
post-mortem investigation and findings 161-162, 181-184, 202-206
reasons for joining State 18
reasons justifying re-investigation 216-220
residence memorial, leaving Kabul 128-131
reputation 17, 25, 39
subject of Soviet and Afghan disinformation 120-124, 126-127, 131-137, 142-144, 194-198,200-201
surveilled and assessed by the KGB 20, 184-191
travels with wife Mary Ann and daughter Lindsay 52-53
wartime U.S. Navy service 17
Dubs, Alexander "Al" 111
Dubs, Jane Wilson 18, 21, 110-111, 140, 223
Dubs, Mary Ann Parsons 21-22, 24, 52-53, 88, 110-111, 125, 127-130, 140, 223
Dubs McLaughlin, Lindsay 18-20, 24, 26, 32, 41-42, 44, 45, 50, 52-53, 57, 88-89, 110-111, 123, 125, 128, 140, 147, 183, 217-218, 223, 229

East Bloc 7, 35, 159
East Germany 33, 167-168

Embassy Kabul (U.S. Afghan mission) 13, 14, 31, 36, 41, 48, 57, 61, 66-67, 81, 92, 96-97, 109-110, 123, 125, 128, 130, 132, 136, 138, 142, 144
  Afghan staff 26, 53-54, 171
  communications challenges 71-72, 87
  defence attachés 15, 66, 149
  mission reductions 146-148, 166-169, 171; 151, 160, 166, 167, 169, 174, 175, 181, 209, 222
  perceived security of 60
  report on human rights abuses 57, 70
  staffing numbers 25
  Vance's cables to 81, 160-161, 210, 213, 217

Farsi (Persian language) 13
Fighting Kachaloos, The (volleyball team) 12-13
Financial Times 133
Flatin, Bruce 67-68, 70, 73-75, 78-79, 85-86, 89-91, 97, 100-101, 106, 117-118, 148, 157, 213, 223, 227
Flatin, Mark 77, 117, 169, 218, 222
forensic sciences 113, 130, 141, 161-162, 182-183, 196, 206-207, 209-210, 212-214, 216

Genghis Khan 11
Georgetown University 18
German (language) 75, 89-90, 117
Germany 14, 18, 33, 167, 170, 213
Ghafari, Abdul 70, 73, 75, 123, 131-132, 148, 153-154, 170, 223
Girardet, Edward 40
Goddard, Calvin 206-207
Gorbachev, Mikhail 180, 194, 200
Gouttierre, Marylu 21,
Gouttierre, Thomas 21-22, 28, 46-48, 80, 184-185, 222
Gromyko, Andrei 49, 124, 172

Haag, Lucien "Luke" 206-215
Haag, Michael 207
Hammadi, Saadun 56
Haqqani, Jalaluddin 219
Harvard University 18
Hazara 40, 164
Highland Park, Illinois 107
Hizbi Islami 218
Hekmatyar, Gulbuddin 218
Herald Tribune 44, 60
Herat uprising 159-160
hot line (US-Soviet) 19
Housego, David 133
Hussein, Saddam 56

India 14, 31, 59, 158, 188,
Intercontinental, Kabul 12-13, 86, 134
investigation of Dubs case 122-123, 125, 127, 131, 141, 144-146, 148-153, 176, 216
  Chuck Boles' investigation report 161-162
  Chuck Boles' second report 202-206
  official State report on 183-184, 212, 214
Iran 8, 13, 34,
  Carter administration policy on 51-52, 55, 82, 87, 96, 97, 110, 152, 176, 179, 182, 185, 194
Islamabad 13, 34, 50, 59, 61, 88, 114, 122, 154, 158, 165
Ivanov, Boris S. 37

Jalalabad 14, 53

Kabul Police 69, 72-73, 78, 91
Kabul Radio 173
Kabul Serena Hotel 224
Kabul Times 44, 46, 56, 121, 126, 132, 136, 209
Kabul University 25
Kalashnikov assault rifle 14, 30, 74, 95, 98, 100, 105-107, 131, 148,

158, 191, 205, 213-214
kamikaze attack, casualties at Leyte 18
Kandahar 25, 52, 145
Kansas City, Missouri 11
Karmal, Babrak 178, 190
Kennedy, John F. 19, 142
KGB (Soviet Committee for State Security) 7-9
  Alpha group 174, 177, 196
  Cheka origins, nickname 20, 189
  culture of fear and repression 19, 20
  Directorate K 38
  deception, as espionage tradecraft 191
  declared officers 7, 33, 37, 78, 85
  disinformation, as tradecraft 33, 121, 190, 197
  First Chief Directorate 34
    illegals 36-37, 200
  Moscow Center (headquarters) 185, 188, 197, 200, 205
  Second Chief Directorate 20
  spying on Afghan regime 49
  Ninth Directorate 85
  undeclared officers 37
  Zenit group 174, 177
Khrushchev, Nikita 19-20
Khyber Pass 158
kidnap gang
  hijacking of limousine 62-64
  hostage standoff at Hotel Kabul 64-65, 67-70, 72, 79-80, 89-91, 92, 99-107
  morgue display by regime 117-119
  regime authorities' false claims about 132-136
  US conclusions about 161-162, 183-184
  weapons allegedly used by 212
Klushinkov, Alexander S. 78, 85, 106, 190, 195, 204, 209
Kremlin 19, 160, 172, 173-175, 178-179, 181, 184-185
Kuchi nomads 145
Kutepov, Yuri I. 85, 190, 195

Leyte, Battle of 17-18
Lippman, Tom 135
Litt, Beatrice 22, 125
Litt, David 22, 94-95, 125, 129, 158
Loynab, Adilah 54
Lubyanka building 19, 194

Malinowski, Mike 12-13, 26, 29-30, 58, 66-68, 70-71, 73-75, 78-79, 85, 90, 99-106, 115-119, 136, 138, 148-149, 168, 198, 221
Malinowski, Karen 12, 57-58, 115
Marik, Warren 36-37, 52, 83, 91-92, 101-106, 122, 138, 159, 168
Massoud, Soroya 154
Matson, Dick 82
McLaughlin, Billy 223
Mexico 9, 12, 223
Michigan 15-16, 61
Mills Bomb (Mark 36 grenade) 212
Ministry of Interior (Afghan secret police) 36, 68, 190
  arrests and intimidation by 25-26, 48, 53-54, 153, 170-171
  obstruction of Dubs investigation 131-132, 146
  role in kidnap response 74, 76, 83-84, 93, 99, 102-103, 204-205
  terror tactics against civilian population 29-30, 173
Mohammed, Gul
  ambassador's driver 42-43, 55, 58, 60-61, 66-68, 80, 115, 212
  cleared of suspicion by polygraph 150-152
  his account of kidnapping 62-64
Mohammed, Lal 73-74
Mondale, Walter 142, 162-163
Moscow Center (KGB headquarters) 185, 188, 197, 200, 205

mujahideen, anti-Communist
resistance 31, 50, 156, 159-160, 163-166, 171, 177, 179, 218
Munich 213

Najib, Mohammed 47
Navalny, Alexei 199
Nepal 59, 221
New Zealand 224
Nicaragua 51
North Side Gang 206
Northwestern University 206
Norway 224
Novichok nerve agent 199

Observer, The 133
Oklahoma! musical 157-158
Oldsmobile, ambassador's car 43-44, 55-56, 58, 60-64, 66, 70, 73, 150-151, 156
O'Keeffe, Charles 128
Operation Storm-333 177, 200
Operations Center (State Dept.) 72, 81-82, 88, 97, 110
Osadchy, Viliov
declares Bakhturin to regime 33
exchanges cables with Moscow about Spike Dubs 185, 187
KGB rezident in Kabul 38
role in murder cover-up 188
role in invasion preparations 174
Ottawa, Canada 18

Paghman 27
Pahlavi, Reza 51-52, 55
Paraguay 224
Pashtun 40, 164
Pashtunistan Square 67, 105
pathology 112, 130, 143, 148, 161, 211-212
Parwiz, Shuja 26
Peshawar, Pakistan 13, 48, 114, 158, 169, 170, 221
People's Democratic Party of Afghanistan (PDPA) 11, 17, 23, 32, 56-57, 64, 185, 205-206
Amin and Taraki leadership cult 27-30, 46-50, 170-180
arrests of U.S. employees 25-26, 48, 53-54, 153, 170-171
divisions and infighting 45-46, 170-180
faction Khalq (Masses) 27-30, 127, 167, 172, 178, 185
faction Parcham (Flag, Banner) 28, 30, 45, 47, 178, 185
post-murder cover-up 119, 121-124, 126-127, 133, 136-137, 146, 152-153, 188
reliance on Soviet aid 34, 36
response to kidnap crisis 74, 76, 81, 96-97, 109
Saur Revolution 11, 46, 49, 78, 134-135, 167
Soviets' decision to invade 167-168, 170-180
subject of U.S. human rights report 57, 70
subject of U.S. policy shifts 159-161, 163-164
Phillipines, Omroc Bay 18
PSM (*Pistolet Samozaryadnyy Malogabaritnyy*; Self-loading Pistol, Compact) 204, 209-211, 213
Putin, Vladimir V. 193, 199-200, 229
Puzanov, Alexander M.
as Soviet ambassador in Kabul 34-35
at Spike's memorial and airport departure 129-130
ordered to broker talks with regime leaders 172, 175
relationship with Col. Bakhturin 38
relationship with Afghan regime 49
role in cover-up 137

Qader, Abdul 45

Quainton, Anthony 88, 96, 109-110

Rabat, Morroco 122
Radio Moscow 120
Red Army (Soviet military) 33, 179, 181, 184, 189, 200
rezident (KGB) 33, 38, 174, 188
Rhodesia 51
Rigamer, Anna 59, 114
Rigamer, Elmore 58-59, 114, 125, 128
Rio de Janiero 10
Rotz, Christie 14, 60, 168
Rotz, Lloyd 14-16, 61, 75, 78-79, 90, 97-98, 101-105, 108, 112-114, 116, 129, 131, 137, 141-143, 222
Rotz, Marlene 14
Rotz, Steve 14-15, 20, 60-61, 77, 116-117, 120, 158, 168-169, 222
Russia 18, 45, 131, 180, 198-199, 211, 216. *See also* Soviet Union
Russian 23, 45, 78, 89. *See also* KGB, Soviet Union
  arms and armament 214
  cover-up of Dubs case 217
  defectors, double agents 187
  forensic scientists 210
  government officials 19-20, 28, 49, 123, 144, 163, 177, 178, 189-190, 194, 200-201
  hostility towards Spike Dubs 184-186
  journalists 192-193
  KGB operatives 7-9, 19, 23, 35-38, 48, 74-75, 78, 85-87, 92-93, 97-99, 104-106, 134, 138, 145-146, 157, 170, 191, 199
  language 19, 89, 100, 104-105, 168
  military officers 175, 178
  mission in Kabul 11-12, 15, 35, 84, 86-87, 158

Saifuddin (Maj.) 74-75, 90-91
Sahar, Yousuf 78
Salang Pass 41
SALT II arms negotiations 51
Sandrock, John 65
Sandrock, Nancy 65, 150
Saur Revolution (April 1978 Communist coup) 11, 46, 49, 78, 134-135, 167
Schilling, Jessie 145-146
Schlacter, Barry 133-134
Secretary's Award 140
Shenandoah Valley 223
Sherdil, Sohila 26
Shulman, Marshall 21
siloviki 199
Schmeisser submachine gun, or MP40 196-198
Smith, Ian 51
Somoza, Anastasio 51
Sopko, John 219
Soviet Union (Union of Soviet Socialist Republics; U.S.S.R.) 7, 9, 12-13, 15, 24-26, 131, 144, 149, 213, 217, 219, 222-223
  arms talks with U.S. 8, 51, 140, 177
  Institute of Oriental Studies 184-185
  intelligence aims and practices 34-38
  KGB officers during kidnap crisis 78, 84-86, 89, 92, 95, 97-106
  KGB revelations in Mitrokhin archive 181-191
  post-incident strategy and intrigues 121, 123-124, 129, 133-138,
  prelude to and invasion of Afghanistan 172-180
  Spike Dubs posted to 18-21
  support for Afghan Communist regime 28-33, 45-51, 54, 73, 154-155, 159-160, 162-168
  responsibility for ambassador's murder probed 146-147, 157-158, 192-200, 203-206

weapons and actions in forensic review 208-210
Soviet Bloc 13, 20, 167, 213
Special Inspector General for Afghanistan Reconstruction 219
Star pistol 212
Stiebel, Mayer 73, 107, 133
Stiebel, Sandy 73, 107, 133
St. Valentine's Day 9, 57-58, 89, 116, 149-150, 157, 188, 194, 200, 221
St. Valentine's Day Massacre 206-207
sub-Saharan Africa 51
Sullivan, William 51-52, 82, 83

Tajbeg Palace 178
Tajik 40, 164
Taliban 156, 184, 218-219, 224
Tamerlane (Timur) 11
Taraki, Nur Mohammed 28-30, 44-51, 56, 85, 123-124,153, 159-160, 172-173, 175, 178
Taroon, Sayed Daoud 58
affectations as secret police chief 29
conduct during kidnap crisis 68, 74, 76, 78, 83-85, 93, 96, 98, 105, 134
interviewed after murder 131-132
intimidates Afghan employees of U.S. embassy 54, 153-154
killed in inter-faction gunfight 172-173
obstructs U.S. investigation 146
relationship with Soviets 48
role in post-murder cover-up 189-190, 195, 197-198, 208
seeks to arrest Tom Gouttierre 48
terrorizes Afghan civilians 30-32, 122-123, 150-151
Taylor, Louise 14, 25, 59, 157-158, 168, 223, 227
Taylor, Jim 13-14, 31, 59, 71, 75-76, 83-84, 93, 105, 130, 134, 142, 158, 168, 175-176, 198, 222-223, 227
Tokyo 10
Toon, Malcolm 124
Toyota 58, 61, 91
Tully, Mark 134
Turkey 14,
Turkmen 40
Turner, Stansfield 162-165

USAID (U.S. Agency for International Development; also "AID") 25, 53-54, 75, 94, 147
dispensary in Kabul 13-16, 58, 61, 75, 93, 105, 108-109, 112-114, 117, 121, 126, 129-130, 208
U.S. Department of State 7-8, 10, 11, 13, 15, 20-22, 51-52, 56-57, 79, 84, 86-88, 115, 133, 136, 138, 140-141, 162-163, 166-168, 170, 171, 175, 198, 202, 203, 206, 216, 221-223, 227
communications during kidnap crisis 71-72, 81-83, 87-88, 96-97, 109-112
department's regard for Spike Dubs 17-18
embassies in Kabul region 59
Foggy Bottom (headquarters metonym) 22, 72, 142, 161, 222
official report on Dubs case 181-184, 195, 211-215
threat assessment 9, 59-60, 161, 167-168
treatment of Dubs investigation and report 122-123, 125, 127, 131, 141, 144-146, 148-153, 161-162, 176, 216
U.S. Embassy Islamabad 59, 122, 154
U.S. Embassy Kabul 13, 14, 31, 36, 41, 48, 57, 61, 66-67, 81, 92, 96-97, 109-110, 123, 125, 128, 130, 132, 136, 138, 142, 144

Afghan staff 26, 53-54, 171
communications challenges 71-72, 87
defence attachés 15, 66, 149
mission reductions 146-148, 166-169, 171; 151, 160, 166, 167, 169, 174, 175, 181, 209, 222
perceived security of 60
report on human rights abuses 57, 70
snubbed over assessing Soviet intentions in Afghanistan 175-176
staffing numbers 25
Vance's cables to 81, 160-161, 210, 213, 217
U.S. Embassy Tehran 51, 56
under attack 82, 87, 97, 109-110
hostage taking 176
U.S. Embassy Moscow
Cuban Missile Crisis 18-19
turf war over assessing Soviet intentions in Afghanistan 175-176
United Nations 13, 25
University of Nebraska Omaha 22, 47, 222
University of Wisconsin 27
U.S. Marines
at Embassy Kabul 43-44, 59, 66, 77, 109, 129-130, 158
at Embassy Tehran 82, 110
USS Caldwell 17-18
U.S.S.R. (see Soviet Union)
Uzbek 40, 164

Vance, Cyrus 21, 51, 52, 81, 85, 86, 91, 96, 97, 110, 124, 140, 142, 148, 161-163, 210, 213, 214, 217
Vietnam 8, 51
Vietnam War 37, 58, 177, 180
Voice of America 44, 55, 120, 223
Volga German community 18
Volkswagen (VW, Beetle, Bug) 13-14, 61, 126

Wallemborg, Leo 81
Wankel, Doug 11-13, 24, 26, 31, 57-58, 83, 91-92, 98-107, 115-116, 122, 137, 147, 168, 221
Wankel, Marilyn 57, 116
Washington, DC 8,
Washington Post 44, 60, 135, 220
Washington University in St. Louis 18
Wilkins, Dennis 149
Woerz, Bernie 10, 57, 71, 75-76, 130, 222

Yugoslavia 18, 42

Zahir Shah, Mohammed 27, 41
Zia-ul-Haq, Muhammed 50, 160, 164, 177